ENCYCLOPAEDIA OF
INDIAN GOVERNMENT:
PROGRAMMES AND POLICIES

ENCYCLOPAEDIA
OF
INDIAN GOVERNMENT:
PROGRAMMES AND POLICIES

Vol. 24

Textile Industry

Edited by

Satish Tiwari

ANMOL PUBLICATIONS PVT. LTD.

NEW DELHI - 110 002 (INDIA)

ANMOL PUBLICATIONS PVT. LTD.
4374/4B, Ansari Road, Daryaganj
New Delhi - 110 002

Encyclopaedia of Indian Government: Programmes and Policies

First Edition, 2000

ISBN 81-261-0515-1 (Set)

[Responsibility for the facts stated, opinions expressed, conclusions reached and plagiarism, if any, in these volumes is entirely that of the Editor. The Publisher bears no responsibility for them whatsoever.]

PRINTED IN INDIA

Published by J.L. Kumar for Anmol Publications Pvt. Ltd., New Delhi - 110 002 and Printed at Mehra Offset Press, Delhi.

Contents

Preface

Encyclopaedia of Indian Government: Programmes and Policies contains authoritative information on about fifty departmental policies and their future developmental programmes.

Organised to be completed in 40 volumes, this gigantic work covers Agriculture; Atomic Energy; Chemicals and Fertilizers; Coal; Commerce; Communication; Culture; Defence; Education; Environment and Forests; External Affairs; Finance; Food & Consumer Affairs; Food Processing Industries; Health and Family Welfare; Home Affairs and Internal Security; Human Resources; Industry; Information and Broadcasting; Labour; Law, Justice and Company Affairs; Non-conventional Energy Sources; Ocean Development; Parliamentary Affairs; Personnel, Public Grievances and Pensions; Petroleum and Natural Gas; Planning and Programme Implementation; Planning and Statistics; Posts and Telegraphs; Power; Rural Development; Science and Technology; Social Justice and Empowerment; Space; States Affairs; Steel; Steel and Mines; Sugar and Edible Oils; Surface Transport; Textiles; Tourism; Urban Development; Water Resources; Women and Child development etc.

Based on the information derived from authoritative sources, this work contains authentic facts and figures. I am deeply beholden to all the scholars whose writings are cited or substantially made use of in the present work. I am also thankful to Anmol Publications Pvt. Ltd. for undertaking publication of this encyclopaedia. I am solely responsible for shortcomings in presentation of matter.

Encyclopaedic in nature, this will prove a dependable reference work for scholars and academics besides those appearing for different competitive examinations.

—Satish Tiwari

Preface

1

Textile Management

Management must be concerned with human needs, whether in the supply of good or services to human beings, for which purpose an undertaking comes into being, or in the production of goods and the procurement of services that are provided by human beings.

Management is essentially a living thing conducted by living beings, and to be effective it must create the conditions in which human beings can succeed, and, for this reason, although systems are necessary, management must not rely exclusively on sterile, impersonal methods'. Furthermore, it must be tightly knit and have unity of purpose and, in its approach to its functions, it must be systematic and analytical. It should, therefore, rely on a logical sequence of thought built upon diagnosis of the problem, followed by fact-finding and an interpretation of the facts. This, in turn, leads to the formulation of decisions, followed by instructions, and finally to a checking of the results. The criterion of success, which is the achievement of the purpose, is the effectiveness of the operation measured in terms of profit and the well-being and contentment of all connected with the undertaking.

To state the principles formally, therefore, there must be planning in relation to purchasing, production, marketing and sales, finance, and personnel; there must be control to ensure that the objectives are being effectively pursued; there must be co-ordination of the activities and effective communication to achieve, by administration, the optimum results and, finally, motivation to ensure that all the human beings engaged in an undertaking are interested in the success of the enterprise. Each stratum of management in the larger organization has its special responsibilities, whereas in the smaller organization these must be arranged as groups of responsibilities for the limited nucleus of executives employed. In the larger organization, the duties of the top management are to formulate a policy that will ensure both profit and good working relations, to create the conditions in which employees can be expected to succeed and to delegate power to those who can act and through whom it can expect to control operations and measure performance.

The duties of the intermediate management are to disseminate policy information to junior management, to fulfil all control functions in relation to production, selling, and design, and to ensure and measure the effectiveness of all operations, whether in human or machine terms. Junior management is mainly concerned either with the operation itself, particularly in the case of administration, or with the issuing of direct instructions to the workers or junior staff and the supervision and immediate control of the operation. Each part of an organization has its own special problems, and for each the approach to its functions is somewhat different. For practical purposes the major functions can be divided into: *a.* purchasing, *b.* production, *c.* marketing and sales, *d.* finance, and *e.* personnel.

Purchasing: In purchasing, the objective must be to ensure the supply of the correct raw materials or manufactured products in the appropriate quantities and qualities for conversion or use at the right time,, commensurate with minimum stockholding. Such a function requires experience and special skills and a wide knowledge of the product and customer requirements. Such expertise can only be acquired from a broad knowledge of the sources of supply, combined with the ability to specialize over the narrower front of the individual undertaking. It involves an intimate knowledge of the raw materials to be purchased coupled with a continual study of the markets and market conditions. A comparison of the results obtained from the purchases, both technically and financially, is implicit in the function.

Production: Production management should be aimed at producing planned goods to an economical and acceptable design at the level of quality commercially required and at the minimum cost consistent with satisfactory working conditions and the maintenance of plant and buildings in a good state of repair. The fulfilment of such functions requires technical expertise, the appreciation of statistics and costs, and the exercise of control over productive, administrative, and inspection functions, coupled with the ability to plan and organize production, to manage personnel, and to draft reports.

Marketing and sales: The management aims grouped broadly under marketing and sales are basically to plan the product type, the volume of production, and the customer outlets. The functions undertaken must ensure that the product is marketed in an acceptable form and manner, that sales areas and markets are organized, that distribution passes through satisfactory channels to the final outlets, that payment is made for the goods, and that the service given is satisfactory. It is essential to ensure that there should be adequate awareness of the product on the part of the consumer, whether by promotion in any of its forms, such as advertising, display, or technical information, or by personal contacts. The satisfactory fulfilment of the functions of marketing and sales requires special managerial aptitudes, including not only the ability to organize and to understand human psychology but also a temperament conducive to good human relations.

Finance: The management aim must be to secure an adequate supply of finance to purchase the physical means of production, whether buildings', machinery, or raw material, to pay 'wages and salaries, and to cover expenditure for repairs and the maintenance of buildings and plant. Stocks of process goods, finished goods, and goods in transit must be financed, as also must debtors. Adequate reserves, must be built up to provide, for the renewal of capital equipment or to bridge periods of difficult trading conditions. Unlike the other functions of management, financial responsibilities do not in the main require a deep psychological understanding of human beings or the ability to manage personnel.

Personnel: In this field, management must have as its aim the recruitment of staff and productive labour in the right volume and of the right calibre. It must arrange for the training of recruits and for satisfactory working hours and conditions. There must be an understanding of the law relating to employment and safety and a knowledge of trade-union relations and wage-payment methods.

Management hierarchy

The analysis of management organizations has gradually resulted in a change of view as to the structures that may be regarded as usual or desirable. Whereas these were thought of at one time as falling into certain preconceived patterns, such as, 'line management', 'line and staff', or 'functional', it is now generally accepted that most organizations, we except for very small undertakings, are usually a combination of line and staff structure and, over industry as a whole, at best fall into only a very general pattern. Within the textile industry, however., although there are many and various organizational structures in detail, they do, in relation to the operation undertaken and the size of the enterprise, tend to fall into a broad pattern. Basically, to be effective, the delegation of authority and responsibility within an organization must conform to a declared and understood pattern, whether the authority is directly delegated to subordinates who are conversely responsible to their seniors, or is derived from a designated co-ordinating or specialist function designed to serve or assist those who fulfil directly delegated functions.

Each organization must furthermore, determine precisely what authority is delegated and define what responsibilities in each case arise from such delegation. Although in practice human beings in association rarely conform continuously to a planned pattern, a definition of duties and a deliberate determination to avoid or prevent short-circuiting an organization, no matter whether from above or below, is an essential criterion for the happy and successful operation of any undertaking.

Direct responsibilities

The simplest form of organization is one in which the owner, using his own capital, employs one or more operatives to fulfil a single operation or function, e.g., a small wool-cloth commission mender employing a few menders. In this case, the seeking-out and organization of the work, the control of the labour, invoicing and book-keeping, receipt and despatch of the goods, wages and other payments, etc., would probably all be undertaken or supervised by the owner. Thus there is no delegation, but, if such a business expanded, then a not unusual step might well be the employment of a working forewoman to supervise the work while the owner concentrated on expanding his connexion with manufacturers.

This organization, which is the simplest form of line management, with responsibilities delegated directly to one subordinate, is only a short distance from a management hierarchy with a lengthening of the line of authority from executive director to manager to foreman.

Specialist responsibilities

It has been pointed out that most organizations conform to a 'line-and-staff' structure, and it is not difficult to see that the simple structure outlined above requires only the addition of a general clerk, with delegated responsibilities for wages payment, for its shape to change.

As businesses become more complicated, simple structures cease to be fully effective, and delegated direct functions, existing side by side with specialist or advisory functions, parallel in importance to those directly delegated, are needed to assist the chief and other senior executives. In such cases, actions taken by certain subordinates fulfilling different specialist delegated functions, whether the subordinates are responsible to the same or to other superiors, need to be acceptable to other subordinates on the same level in order to ensure the effective running of the enterprise.

Consultation or exchange of views on matters of mutual interest are therefore usual and create a lateral relationship, e.g., a weaving-shed manager who is not a designer-manager needs to consult the designer or head of the cloth-construction department to ensure correct interpretation of a design; conversely, the designer must consult on the practicability and weaving efficiency of his proposed cloth constructions. The integration of lateral and specialist responsibilities within an organization in a manner likely to ensure effective and harmonious relationships is vital to the health of the whole organization.

Co-ordination

In large organizations, because of the breadth of the operation and the highly specialized nature of some of the functions, it is essential to co-ordinate formally all specialist functions and responsibilities as well as to ensure a line of delegated authority. In one very large textile organization, the chief authority lies with three executives, one of whom is the chairman, who divide responsibility between them for operations, administration, and finance.

Thus three quite separate vertical controls are imposed on all sections of the undertaking, and these must be co-ordinated at all levels. Additionally, a large organization may have specialized sections, such as an economics department, a marketing division, and a legal department, which, although they do not exercise control, must be brought effectively within the orbit of the whole. Co-ordination of management at different levels may take the form of delegated lateral functions, e.g., personnel and accounting functions tied in with productive and commercial functions at each level of management; or delegated specialized functions, such as medical and first aid duties organized as a separate responsibility by a single company doctor for all branches; or committee procedures involving the interested parties where co-ordination is not the responsibility of a nominated executive. In all cases, to be effective, decisions must be precise and suitable authority established to ensure the implementation of the appropriate decisions.

Organisations

When men come together as a group, whether for the purpose of acquiring a livelihood or for social reasons, a determination of the relationships between them by custom or by rules is essential in order to facilitate the attainment of the objective and to minimize friction and misunderstanding. In a business enterprise, organization is rightly regarded as 'the framework of management' and it is within this framework that interrelationships and the pattern of responsibilities must be determined and, activities delineated in order to prevent duplication or unnecessary overlapping.

An organization must be so framed as to take into account the objectives to be pursued, the policy in relation to the objectives, and the methods by which the objectives are to be achieved. Thus a clear exposition of an organization must determine not only the responsibilities of those engaged but also the means to be employed for planning at all levels, and in so doing it must pave the way to ensuring satisfactory lateral relations with a minimum of imposed co-ordination.

The definition of responsibilities in relation to the objectives, although the most essential, is also the most difficult undertaking in framing an organization. Looked at from the apex of the plan, 'the design must seek to provide effective delegation of authority-plus-responsibility and so create the framework for the full and effective exercise of the management initiative of the persons appointed to the positions, while preserving their over-all co-ordination in common practice and purpose'.

The view has often been expressed that it is the magnitude of modem companies alone that has necessitated the practice of creating formal organization structures. This, however, is not so, for as soon as an undertaking progresses beyond a single head and one step of delegated responsibility, the problem of orderly human relationships arises. Even under today's circumstances, arguments are often advanced for making the organization fit the individuals rather than the converse of this. In practice, where this happens, a company may flourish for a time under the domination of one or more strong characters, but, where an organization is personalized, when circumstance or age brings about a change, such companies often encounter serious difficulties. Whereas it is inevitable that strong personalities will give rise to modified organizational structures, sometimes to the advantage of the enterprise, inbuilt safeguards, usually in the form of boards of directors, should ensure that the framework neither is ruptured nor falls into decay through lack of appreciation of this problem. In laying down the principles on which an organization should be framed, many writers have insisted on the need to limit the number of subordinates answerable to one executive and have often specified four to six as being the effective maximum.

Much, depends, however, on the nature of the functions performed, the quality of the personnel, and the degree of over-all integration necessary to the effective running of the enterprise. It is, for example, not impossible to conceive, in a medium-sized vertically integrated woollen-textile business, of a managing director who delegates his responsibilities directly to managers or heads of department, makes himself responsible for co-ordination in relation to eight departments, namely, wool-buying, spinning, weaving, dyeing and finishing, design, commercial administration and production control, sales (home and export), and secretarial and accounting functions, and possibly also retains in his hands the ultimate executive responsibility for an overseas company.

This does not imply, however, that another form of organization would not be workable under the same general set of conditions if, for example, the chief executive of the company were a man of smaller stature or had less efficient executives or the company were somewhat larger. An equally feasible organization would be, for example, one in which the managing director, although he retained wool-buying, delegated the production functions to one subordinate, the commercial and selling to another, and the secretarial and accounting to a third, and created an engineering department to serve the whole. Indeed, other equally effective organizations could be framed to meet the same set of circumstances.

Although specific limitation of delegation, in terms of the numbers of directly responsible subordinates, cannot be regarded as a principle, and an organization must not be regarded as other than a living, thing that is capable of being modified to meet circumstance, it is important in each given set of circumstances to guard against either inadequate or excessive delegation and to be constantly alive to new needs that arise from a change of individual executives or the effects of increasing age.

Organizations are often regarded as one of two kinds, namely, 'centralized' or 'decentralized'. In fact, however, these terms are somewhat meaningless, since the shape of any effective organization must depend, first, on the type of enterprise being organized, secondly on the geographical relationship of each part of the company to the others, and, finally, on the size of the undertaking.

Many textile companies are now, to some degree, vertically integrated, since they cover many textile operations and form, in effect, a combination of undertakings operating in what would previously have been regarded as separate industries. In such cases, not only may the undertakings differ widely technically, e.g., spinning, weaving, and dyeing, but they may also be separated geographically and be unbalanced in terms of sectional volume of output if considered as wholly vertical undertakings. In the latter case, this would further give rise to the need to organize sales from each major section within the company producing in excess of the company's requirements. In general terms, therefore, two major principles should be borne in mind that might at first sight appear to be contradictory, first, to apply the maximum degree of decentralization where specialization of function is possible and, secondly, to maintain the maximum centralization in terms of essential control and responsibility for major decisions, particularly in terms of policy.

Thus, in a small organization, it would be reasonable to expect a high degree of centralization, tapering to complete centralization in a one-man enterprise, whereas in a very large undertaking the converse would apply, not only because of the need to ensure the co-ordination of major functions at all levels, but also to overcome the probable administrative problems of technically separate and geographically separated undertakings within a company.

The primary purpose of an organization chart is to show management relationships within a company in such a manner as to define responsibilities and authority. There is a second and equally important purpose, namely, to compel clarity of thought on the part of the chief executive and his subordinates and thereby prevent overlapping, doubt, and irritation.

In practice, it is not normally necessary to publish highly complicated and sophisticated graphical representations, as long as everyone within the organization understands his or her function and relationship with those normally in the same orbit. When, however, charts are drawn up it is advisable to employ the accepted method of showing relationships and to show direct relations with a vertical continuous line, lateral relations with a horizontal continuous line and functional or specialist relations with a broken or dotted line. It is usually adequate for internal purposes to display complete copies of an organization chart only at the highest executive level and to circulate appropriate parts of the whole chart to subordinates in each section of the organization.

Without a definition of the functions and responsibilities depicte, an organization chart is a meaningless and empty framework. It is therefore essential, first, to give each of the functions included a descriptive title that has a direct reference to the responsibility to be undertaken, and secondly, to give a clear resume of the duties and relationships involved. It is necessary to indicate to each executive to whom his responsibility lies, who is directly subordinate, with whom and for what purpose he must co-operate or maintain a functional relation, and, finally, what is expected of him in order to fulfil his duties in harmony with the company's policy. The method by which these desiderata are achieved is to draw up 'schedules of responsibilities' for all senior executives, including the managing director, showing, first, the occupation, secondly, to whom the executive is responsible, and, thirdly, for what he is responsible.

The last point is sometimes dealt with in considerable detail, depending on the size of the company and the complexity of the organization, but usually only the major responsibilities are stated and from these flow those less important. If, however, there is inadequate definition, it is frequently necessary to resort to a higher authority for a ruling in cases of a difference of view between two executives. In this manner, a kind of case-law is built up in many companies. At the same time, however, codification is desirable in order to ensure continuity over a period of years or, conversely, in order to have information to hand to help in reassessing a group of duties if circumstances bring about a substantial change in the company's structure. Where responsibilities below those of senior executives are concerned, it may again be desirable to have some codification of duties if there are several functional relationships with a consequential risk of overlapping, but often the function itself determines the duties to be fulfilled.

The research approach to development, quality control, and management was only in its infancy, the first co-operative research associations (the present Wool Industries Research Association and the Cotton Silk and Man-made Fibres Research Association) not having come into being until the end of the first world war. Most companies, by today's standards, were relatively small and therefore administratively fairly uncomplicated; the production and variety of man-made fibres were limited, whereas 'giants', as they were then regarded, such as the Lancashire Cotton Corporation, were a relatively new departure.

Today, new sections of the textile industry been developed and new filaments and fibres, involving new techniques, been introduced into most branches of the textile trade, not only are there entire new ranges of hitherto unknown end-products, but, additionally, there has been a vast increase in the size of some of the companies engaged. Perhaps the best illustrations of this arc that Imperial Chemical Industries, which before the Second World War had no direct-involvement in the production of textile fibres' is now estimated to have over £300M invested, and that in 1964 Courtaulds Ltd had sufficient power to acquire on a single occasion the above-mentioned Lancashire Cotton Corporation and the almost equally significant Fine Spinners and Doublers Ltd. It is apparent that such major changes in the structure of the industry involve a lengthening of the chain in the management hierarchy and, in larger firms, call for new management techniques.

A considerably wider range of responsibilities placed in fewer hands demands expert and specialist assistance over a wide range of subjects in order to ensure that quick and correct decisions are made. Direct management control, in terms of a chief executive moving continually in each part of his company, enquiring at first hand, and thereby forming judgements at first hand also, is no longer always possible and, in substitution for it, good communications and the supply of internal information and statistics are vital.

The point must be made at the outset that many of the management aids described are not necessarily essential in smaller companies, nor need they be an integral part of an organization as long as access to them externally is possible and the management is fully aware of the aids available to it. In general, there are eight major groups of management aids, and, although many more individual aids could no doubt be listed, each would, by and large, fall into one of the main groups. The eight are as follows:

a. Statistical and cost control

b. Laboratory control

c. Operational research

d. Work study and method study

e. Scientific research and development

f. Specialized professional services

g. Official and semi-official information services

h. Communications.

Statistical and cost control

Statistics are an obvious concomitant of all management functions, even if they comprise, in the first stage, only a report at the end of the week of total production, wages paid, sales effected, etc. The step from this to the use of statistics as a cost-control aid is a very small one, since, for example, production figures related to wages cost for that production and compared each week produce a control figure.

To move from this point to comparing and thereby forecasting and controlling the whole of a company's activities in terms of sales and production planning, costing and standard costs, budgetary control for purchases and stocks, financial planning in the form of cash budgets, comparative statistics of performance, etc., is a natural sequence.

There are a wide range of functions, which include not only, for example, the vital control of the physical and chemical condition of a fabric during processing in a dyehouse, but also, in all aspects, the physical and chemical testing of the product and of the materials used in the manufacture of the product, both as a check on the quality of the product and for the purpose of comparison with a competitor's product.

Operational research

This more recently developed and important aspect of research is concerned with the application of scientific methods in helping to make decisions in complex situations. It is a somewhat separate branch of scientific research, although it is undertaken as a special project by some of the larger co-operative research associations. To a great extent, research into decision-making, whether in terms of production, commerce, or administration, is undertaken either by specialists within a company or by professional consultants with the requisite specialized experience.

Work study and method study

Larger companies employ full-time organization and

methods officers, several work-study officers, and sometimes specialists who concentrate on wage-payment methods. Even where officers are employed by a company, and generally there is a work-study officer, it is by no means unusual to engage professional consultants for highly specialized investigations when the internal staff is either not sufficiently competent or fully occupied with routine duties.

Scientific research and development

The term 'research' is perhaps one of the most over-used and often abused words in the management language. It is too often forgotten that the earliest industrialists achieved miracles in machinery design, cloth design, internal organization, and commercial and, financial structures without using the word 'research'.

At all times, it must be borne in mind that research is an attitude of mind and an approach, and in this sense all intelligent and progressive men in industrial and commercial management or design departments are research workers to a greater or less degree. Scientific research and development on an organized scale as a separate management aid are, however, a vital tool of management that can be ignored only at the risk of ultimate industrial extinction.

This management aid covers a wide range of responsibilities from fundamental scientific investigations to ad hoc investigations of urgent scientific and technological problems. It implies not only investigations into things but also enquiries into human behaviour, whether in the actual operation undertaken or the wider sphere of human and group relations.

Specialized professional services

The number of specialized professional services has increased sharply over the last quarter of a century, and it is to be expected that the process will continue. The extent to which professional services are used and whether the services are jointly or singly rendered by members of the staff, by a department within a company, or by external organizations and individuals depends on the knowledge, background, and ability of the managerial executives and the size of the company.

There is an increasing tendency for senior executives in larger companies not to involve themselves deeply in specialized problems or to apply themselves to time- and energy-consuming investigations but to introduce, or seek advice from, consultants, who are many in kind and number and cover an extremely varied field.

This practice is not without its dangers, for not only does it result in an ever-narrowing horizon for top executives, who should take a broad view, but it also adds a heavy and increasing burden to the overhead costs of a company.

The work of the outside specialists in some fields is empirical and based on a comparative analysis of operations in other companies and industries, but, in a majority of cases where their services are employed, the services rendered fall into well-defined professional categories, such as the legal or accounting profession. In listing several professional aids, available, either within a company, if large, or on a fee-paying basis, it is not intended to resort to any description of the services$ since, they are to a great extent self-defined. The most important professional services available are as follows:

i. business consultants, including:

   a. production engineers (including time and motion engineers)
   b. business-organization advisers
   c. commercial advisers

d. marketing consultants

e. technical advisers

f. personnel advisers

ii. civil, mechanical, and electrical engineers

iii. architects

iv. economists

v. chartered accountants and cost consultants

vi. taxation consultants

vii. insurance brokers and consultants

viii. investment and financial advisers

ix. legal advisers

x. estate agents and surveyors

xi. advertising specialists

xii. public-relations advisers

xiii. travel services.

Official and semi-official information services

A considerable amount of information is disseminated to industry, or is available to industrialists, from various official and semi-official sources, The information covers a wide range of subjects, such as industrial statistics.$ export services, overseas information, industrial legislation, trade news, commercial abstracts, etc.

The information comes from five main sources, namely, (i) government departments, (ii) the Textile Council, (iii) trade associations and trade unions, (iv) commercial libraries, and (v) suppliers. The government departments mainly concerned are the Board of Trade and the Ministry of Labour, which, through their official organs, disseminate both statistics and relevant news matter. Additionally, the Civil Service staff makes itself available for assistance in many directions. The Textile Council covers, in particular, the widest range of official statistical and administrative needs of the cotton and man-made-fibres section of the industry, and, although it operates independently, its members are appointed by the government.

Trade associations, guided in policy, by representatives of the trade and usually supported by a permanent staff, are involved in all matters of policy connected with their particular branch of the industry and usually both circularize their members and give personal assistance.

Communication

Quick and easy communications within an organization, internally and externally and up and down the line, are as essential an aid in running a business effectively as they are to the successful conduct of a military campaign. Although the techniques differ according to whether a company is very large, large, medium, or small, the objectives are the same. These are, on the one hand, to ensure the presentation by a company of a good face externally in order to assist recruitment of staff and labour, explain policies, or enhance prestige., and, on the other hand, internally, to achieve the policies laid down through suitable operating instructions and to ensure the maintenance of good working relationships by means of the widest exchange of views and opinions by all concerned in the workings of the company.

The larger the business, the more difficult it is for executives to ensure good communications and large companies must resort increasingly to formal devices and organizational methods. A large company would, for example, employ both a public-relations department and a government-relations department to ensure that the appropriate image is projected externally. Internally, the executives may resort to staff associations, works councils, periodic conferences, news letters, house magazines, suggestions schemes, and formal channels for complaints in order to enhance morale and to provide a Substitute for direct personal relations between the top echelons of executives and operatives generally. The more naturally communications flow, both upwards and downwards, by personal contact, and the more information is shared, even to the extent of information concerning strategic policies and financial results, the better, as a rule, are relations between employer and employees.

When any company expands beyond a certain size, usually determined by the numbers employed, an organization co-ordinated through divisions or subsidiary companies or both is usually the only satisfactory means of ensuring a good corporate spirit.

The physical means of communication, which are many and varied, may be divided broadly into: (i) written communications, (ii) verbal communications, and (iii) visual communications. In (i) and (ii), the type of communication differs to some degree according to whether the use is for internal or external purposes.

Written communications or internal use may take the form of memoranda or letters, if a Permanent record is desirable, and may be single or duplicated if the information is required by several executives whose responsibilities must be co-ordinated. As far as the physical handling of internal written communications is concerned, these may be circulated by a junior member of the office staff or resort may be made to such systems as pneumatic tubes, where there is a constant exchange of information. External communi-cations, which are normally a two-way traffic, are usually by letter mail, telegram, or teleprinter, but they can also take the form of the postage of electrically recorded tapes and voice belts for transcription on receipt.

Internal verbal communications are of two main types, by telephone or by the telephone supported by a short-wave central calling system or a public-address system, with loud-speakers at appropriate points. Internal telephones are of two kinds, an extension of the G.P.O. system and private systems operated by key-callers or by the more usual dialling method. External verbal communications are generally effected by G.P.O. telephone, either public or direct private lines being used. Tape and other recorders may, however, be employed and messages played back by the recipient.

Visual communications, which are only used internally, range from systems using codes of coloured lights for calling personnel to closed-circuit television. These systems are almost invariably personalized to meet the differing needs of each organization. The methods of communication outlined above are by no means the only ways in which executives can keep in touch or information and statistics vital to the running of a company be exchanged. Nor must it be assumed that even more varied and advanced methods will not be introduced.

The means of communication used by each organization differ widely and are dearly dependent on the size of the company and the geographical distribution of its assets. Personal preference also plays a part, and some senior executives, where highly confidential matters are concerned, sometimes still prefer to transmit their view through informal gatherings or a third party.

Management organization

It has been pointed out earlier that management

organizations are living entities and as such must also be capable of growing or contracting or taking on new forms as change and circumstances require. In the textile industry, there are, however, five main factors that influence the kind of management organization likely to be suitable in a given set of circumstances. These are:

a. Size

b. Type of undertaking

c. Geographical factors

d. Human factors

e. Growth and decline.

Size

Little stress need be placed on the effect of size, since it is well known that in the textile industry companies range in size from those with one man and a few staff to giants controlling innumerable companies. Such wide variation calls for an elastic approach to, and a considerable variety in, the form of organization.

Type of undertaking

Apart from the modifying influence of the part of the industry in which a company operates, account must be taken of the basic structure of the textile industry, which consists of horizontal and vertical undertakings operating side by side. It is apparent that the management organization in a horizontal undertaking, that is to say, one which, although having attached to it the necessary ancillary operations, performs broadly one major function only, e.g., spinning or weaving, is substantially less complicated than a vertically organized undertaking.

In the former case, not only is the organization of production relatively simple, but there is also only one general type of end-product to sell. In the latter case, however, there are several units producing what in a horizontal organization are different end-products and, although these may build up through each process to one main end-product, it is probable that sales of surplus production at each stage will be necessary to maintain efficient operation.

Geographical factors

Location and local practice exercise some influence on the kind of organization built up, but more important is the obvious effect on a company of having branches located in different parts of the country or even abroad. In these cases, the degree of central control is inevitably modified by physical separation and extended communications.

Human factors

Although organizations that are effective over long periods of time are not consciously built around individuals, variations in human ability, temperament, age, and opportunity profoundly influence and, modify almost every organization. Where, as is sometimes the case in very large companies, an attempt is made to impose a standard pattern on its various branches, there are generally instances of unsatisfactory human relations., sometimes accompanied by a loss of efficiency. The influence of the human factor on management organization is particularly marked in private companies or those companies which have just emerged as public companies.

Growth and decline

Businesses are capable of growing and declining, not only as a result of human effort or inertia ' but also because of fundamental changes in fashion and in human needs. In a growing or declining company, therefore, there is a conscious need constantly to readjust to changing circumstance. Success in these cases can only be achieved by planning reorganization as far ahead of events as possible and preparing managerially for a situation before it arises. An example of rapid growth is the increase in the capacity of the warp-knitting section of the industry, in which several weavers, as well as knitters and garment-makers, have organized warp-knitting sheds.

Decline is exemplified by the domestic flannel section, which has been virtually extinguished by fashion change and the introduction of central heating on a major scale. Where a section of the industry is in decline, decisions by individual companies are necessary to determine what field of enterprise, if any, should be entered as an alternative, or whether the decline should be accelerated or resisted. On these vital decisions rest not only the redeployment of labour, the increase or decrease of staff in a modified organization but also decisions relating to commercial policy or even liquidation.

Comparative organization

To some degree, small management organizations are a microcosm of the larger and, like living cells, may be duplicated and reduplicated according to the size of the company.

A vertical organization is broadly a grouping of horizontal organizations, each of which undertakes the production of a part of the whole product, and a giant undertaking is a complex combination of both. In each case, it is the methods of co-ordinating the whole in order to achieve efficiency and economy that call for analysis, intuition, and organizing ability.

Horizontal organizations of varying size

It has been pointed out previously that vertical organizations are in some respects groupings of basic horizontal structures, and it is therefore proposed to give a wider range of examples of horizontal organizations from various branches of the textile industry. The organizational schemes set out below, namely, one example each of a cotton spinner, a worsted spinner, a cotton weaver, a man-made-fibres dyehouse, a hosiery manufacturer, a lace manufacturer (leavers), and a warp-knitter, demonstrate both the similarities and the differences of structures in the industry.

This organization is typical of a more highly organized spinning mill that has been substantially re-equipped. Output weekly is approximately 100,000 lb. of average 20s counts, delivered on cone and beam. Heads of production departments (carders, etc.) are responsible for production and maintenance of quality. Assistants under their direction undertake the mechanical maintenance of machinery and work on a three-shift basis.

This example is of a small partnership that is traditional in both its attitudes and organization. General management, sales, and secretarial functions are all undertaken by the partners, the direct productive management functions being left to a mill manager. The trainee son undertakes several unspecified duties as a means of learning the business.

Organization of senior management

In considering the organization of the senior management and administrative responsibilities and in touching on the general functions and duties, it is important to bear in mind the many factors that may modify each individual organization. In general, however, and irrespective of the size of the company, it is necessary to provide for the following senior responsibilities. There must be provision for a. policy-making; there must be b. a chief executive or chief executives to set the policy in motion and to ensure that it is fulfilled; there must be provision for fulfilling the usual duties of c. functional officers; and, finally, d. the services to ensure efficient fulfilment of the policy must be available.

Policy-making

According to the size and type of company, policy-making may be the function of one man or of boards of directors of up to 20 or more members (each again with or without other duties). No matter what the composition of the policy-making body is, the functions are the same, namely, to create the conditions in which the company's objectives can be achieved in the simplest and most efficient manner through the appointed chief executive or executives.

In the case of the large textile companies, the board is usually composed of a blend of non-executive directors with broad qualifications of experience or accomplishment and several executive directors with specialized divisional, sectional, or departmental knowledge.

Medium-sized companies normally have a board composed of from five to ten members, of whom a majority would probably be executive directors, whereas small companies might have a board of only from two to four directors, each of these probably being an executive director.

Much thought has been given to the ideal composition of policy-making bodies. In general, for independent companies of rather larger size, there is considerable value in having a board composed of a non-executive chairman, assisted by one or more external directors with specialized or general business qualifications, and a larger number of executive directors, representing the most important sectional interests within the company. Such a composition enables the chairman in his senior position not only to be impartial.

Chief executive

The duty of the chief executive, or chief executives if the responsibility is divided, is to translate, initiate, and carry into effect either directly or through other executives, whether these are fulfilling line or staff functions, the policy laid down by the board. The chief executive may be the chairman of the board or the managing director, or the latter may share the responsibility with one or more joint managing director. In each case, however, the appointed person or persons are responsible to the board for the conduct and success of the enterprise. The working relationships between the senior executives are extremely important to the harmonious conduct of affairs. Where a chairman retrains executive authority in his own hands, he will usually delegate some of his powers immediately to a managing director and/or other executive directors.

The relationship between these executives is usually only successful where the chairman has executive responsibility over a wide field, has confidence in his immediate subordinates, and allows them to use the maximum of personal initiative. In cases where a managing director is chief executive, he would usually direct all operations of a day-to-day nature either personally or by delegation, and he would refer back to his chairman only when exceptional problems arose. In a textile company, an organization relying on joint managing directors not responsible to an executive chairman is not usually satisfactory unless one of the partners is dominant by temperament or seniority. Only in such circumstances is there a reasonable expectation of avoiding the risk that a company will be divided into two or more inadequately co-ordinated parts. In some large companies, it is not unusual to resort to formal management committees where there is no obvious candidate as chief executive, or the chairman or managing director is over-busy, or where problems of co-ordination arise owing to conflicting personalities. Such committees are a negation of the management function and when formed should be regarded only as an unsatisfactory temporary expedient.

Functional officers

Functional officers fulfilling staff functions are many in number and kind and may be added to, given modified functions, or transferred to other duties if the situation changes. The main and more usual executives, however, are the company secretary, the company accountant, the personnel manager, the organization and methods officer, and the designer. The professional services that a company needs from time to time are ever-increasing, and the kinds of service available are self-explanatory. Some description of the responsibilities of the five listed above is, however, desirable.

A company secretary may be a whole- or part-time executive. He may undertake only the minimum formal functions required of him by law and custom or he may be required to fulfil innumerable duties, including, in a small company, some management or even selling functions, in order to make the fullest use of his time and services. It is not unusual for a medium-sized company to employ a secretary-accountant or a secretary-cost accountant, supported by a small group of clerical accounting staff or perhaps one or two additional senior staff. As companies become larger and legal and administrative problems more involved '.the function of the secretary as chief servant of the board and recorder of its policy decisions is increasing in importance.

Sometimes the secretary becomes, or is, a member of the board.

This, however, is not usually an ideal arrangement in view of the special relationship of such an officer to the chairman and the chairman's special relationship to the managing director, to whom the secretary must, in most respects, be subordinate. Although an accountant cannot work in a vacuum, in a large company this particular function can be detached to some degree from the day-to-day management duties, provided that management accountants and cost accountants undertake the routine duties connected, for example, with the invoicing, cashier's and accounts departments, etc.

The accountant's chief value to a company lies not in the preparation of the profit-and-loss accounts and the balance sheet but in the interpretation of the host of analysed statistics and figures that are a by-product of his main function. With the broad knowledge made available in this manner, a good accountant is of great value to the chief executive, and it is not unusual for this officer to have a seat on the board of directors.

Personnel officers are not regarded as being necessary under all sets of conditions, particularly in medium-sized and smaller companies. Many efficient managers prefer to deal with their own recruitment, staff, labour, and wage problems, and, where this is possible, the personal contacts throughout a mill are sometimes more satisfactory. In the larger company, however, it is essential to ensure equality of conditions and remuneration in all branches, and for this reason alone a personnel officer is necessary unless the chief executive or production director is very active and supervises this aspect of management personally. Where no personnel officer is employed, it is not unusual to have a welfare officer with more restricted authority to supervise the first-aid, sanitary, canteen, and similar facilities. An organization and methods officer is generally employed only in the larger companies, since many of his responsibilities are normally included among those of the mill or departmental manager. In a large organization, however, a specialist fully engaged in reviewing every part of the company and seeking out new approaches to a problem, either personally or through assistants, such as those engaged in work study, can have a dynamic as well as a unifying influence on the organization and administrative and management practices of a company.

The policy of employing such an officer, an arrangement that is becoming more usual, stems partly from the successful results achieved from operational research in the co-operative research stations. The designer has a very special and sometimes extremely important function in the textile industry. Within his purview must come not only design but also cloth construction, costing, and fabric development. Good design is an essential part, not only of exclusive and expensive textile apparel fabrics that would be unsalable without special design qualities, but also of almost all types of fabric, including carpets, produced by the industry.

Although the designer must have artistic and creative ability, he cannot work in a vacuum and certainly not without the fullest regard for his medium. His expertise must be basically that of a craftsman, and a close relationship with the production, commercial, and technical sections of his company as well as with external fashion and technical influences throughout the world can alone bring a full measure of success. In a large company engaged in the production of clothing fabrics, several designers would be employed, each concentrating on a group of fabrics having special characteristics or a special end-purpose, and even in a small company, mainly engaged in a fashion trade, it would be unusual to find only one designer. In those branches of the apparel-fabric trade supplying fabrics to the *haute-couture* garment manufacturer, it is not unusual for the chief executive to assume the function of head designer in addition to his other more general responsibilities.

Service departments

Separate service departments are usually only organized individually in large and, to a lower degree, medium-sized companies. In small companies, it is customary for these functions to be dealt with by individuals or to be integrated within other departments. Services that may be required from time to time and are available to management are numerous and varied and can usually be supplied professionally on a fee-paying basis. It is not unusual, however, for a large company to have services available through the following departments: maintenance and engineering, transport, central purchasing, economics, marketing, research, estates, legal, and public relations.

Organization of productive functions

The relationship of the functional officers both to the chief executive and to the divisional and mill directors or managers is clearly shown in the organization charts, and it is therefore not intended to confuse the issue in describing the organization of the productive functions by making other than passing reference to this relationship whenever necessary. Although throughout the textile industry the management hierarchy in relation to production is broadly similar in each branch, the attitudes of mind that are necessary to determine the approach to management problems are dissimilar. The main processes of production that have to be -undergone, either in whole or in part, in all branches of textiles except non-woven and some bonded-fibre fabrics, are first the production of a yarn, secondly the processing of the yarn into a fabric, and thirdly, except for carpets and spun-dyed loomstate fabrics, the treatment of the grey fabric to render it attractive or suitable for its appropriate end-use, or to achieve both purposes.

Yarn production requires either a chemical engineering approach if the yarns are of the continuous-filament type or a physico-engineering approach if they are spun by any of the usual processes. The production of the fabric, irrespective of whether the process involves weaving, circular-knitting, warp-knitting, or lace-making machinery, etc., is a mechanical-assembly operation, whereas the dyeing and finishing of fabrics are a physico-chemical operation.

In the fulfilment of his duties, a production manager (or director), has three major problems. The first is to control the productive units by effective delegation of responsibility and authority, the second to inform himself of the progress of operations within the units, and the third to ensure that the units are serviced efficiently in order to operate successfully. A production director's or mill manager's main responsibilities will include some, or all of the following: a. buying and selling, b.. production planning, c. control of production, d. maintenance of plant and buildings, e. labour and welfare, f. administration g. capital-equipment policy, and h. external liaison.

Buying and selling

These functions include the purchase of raw materials or materials for further processing and the buying of spare parts, machine accessories, and general stores and minor equipment essential to the production operations. Selling as a function involves the handling of by-products, wastes., scrap, and any other unwanted materials.

Production planning

Programming, which is the key to customer satisfaction, quality, and machine efficiency, should be controlled by the manager from the point of the order's being placed with his mill to the completion of the product.

Control of production

This responsibility, which outstrips the others in importance, involves the direct supervision of all subordinate managers or foremen in the fulfilment of their duties, policy in relation to running hours to achieve the required output, machine efficiency, material yields, quality control, cost control, discipline, and a host of other smaller matters.

Maintenance of plant and buildings

This responsibility would be dealt with by the mill manager directly or, in a larger organization, through a maintenance foreman or an assistant maintenance or engineering manager. The duties involved, in addition to ensuring that the machinery and buildings are kept in good state of repair, include supervision of the efficiency of the services, such as electricity, gas, water, compressed air, etc., and sometimes the supervision of new installations or modifications of machinery and the construction of new buildings.

Labour and welfare

In addition to the importance of ensuring an adequate and contented labour force and staff, many problems connected with wage-payment methods, recruitment and training, safety and compliance with the Factory Acts, satisfactory canteen and welfare services, satisfactory working conditions, etc., fall, directly or indirectly, within the sphere of the manager's duties. These responsibilities in a large company would be sub-contracted in part to functional officers, but the ultimate responsibility in the mill would still be that of the manager. In smaller companies, these responsibilities are partly dealt with directly by the manager, e.g., wage-payment methods, or sub-contracted to subordinates who have other responsibilities, e.g., recruiting and training undertaken by an assistant manager or foremen.

Administration

In taking responsibility for administration, a manager would normally have three types of staff, namely, general clerical staff, technical clerical staff, and a wages staff headed by an accountant. In a mill of average size, this staff, apart from the technical clerical staff, would be normally responsible to the accountant, but the technical clerical staff often would be directly responsible to the manager.

Capital-equipment policy

Planning for the future of a production unit is an important duty of the manager. An able manager would normally be clear in his own mind as to the policy in relation to capital renewal that he would like to pursue up to 10-15 years ahead. His capital budget would in any case cover at least three years forward.

External liaison

External contacts with trade associations, research organizations, machinery makers, etc., directly and, with new ideas, indirectly through journals, conferences, mill visits, symposia, etc., are an essential part Of a manager's duties. As much as any other factor, these are valuable, not only in enabling him to keep abreast of events, but also in stimulating fresh enthusiasm by comparison and example.

Organization of vertically integrated commercial

The various sections of the textile industry have had their

own methods of organization, ranging from examples in the wool section of the industry, where verticality has obtained almost from the sheep's back to the retail over-the-counter piece-goods trade, to what used to be the normal practice in the cotton section, where sales of grey fabric might pass through two or even more hands before reaching the final consumer in the finished state. Under modern conditions, however, the impact of large retail distributors such as Marks and Spencer, the effect of the vast increase in the cost of capital equipment for production, and the decrease in volume of simple bulk trade capable of being manufactured profitably and competitively in this country have been responsible for much rethinking.

This has led to merger and rationalization on a major scale, whereby the burden of fixed assets and the power of the consumer may be counterbalanced by organizationally strong groups, aiming commercially at production on a massive scale of economic cloths capable of bringing an over-all profit. The forms that merger and rationalization have taken have varied considerably in practice, but in every case integrated selling at a level as close to the final consumer as possible has been implicit in the accepted philosophy. In reviewing the organization of integrated commercial and sales functions, three factors must be considered: a. policy requirements, b. management requirements, and c. functions of personnel.

Policy requirements

An effective policy requires first, co-ordination of operations; secondly, determination of products and markets; and, thirdly, a decision as to which channels of trade to use.

Co-ordination of operations: The major value of the integration of commercial and sales functions with the functions of production lies in the possibility of an orderly and balanced flow of goods from raw material to final consumer.

It has become increasingly obvious that the major bugbear of the textile industry has been the continuing cycle of excess and shortage of supply depending on what is termed 'confidence' or what could perhaps more correctly be described as commercial over-sensitivity to current events in appreciating future needs. These recurrent waves of optimism and pessimism affecting several points along the productive and supply line have led to over-ordering in relation to demand, and, from this, to over-stocking, followed by under-ordering, price falls, and the clearance of accumulated stocks.

With the increase in the size of groups, it has been possible, by coordinating all sales of broadly similar products through one central commercial organization, to prevent overlap, to discourage weak selling, and to determine priority in terms of the type of sales to be made and deliveries to be promised.

Determination of products and markets: Almost every production organization has its more successful and its less successful fabric types and, equally, each sales organization tends to become entrenched in conducting certain types of business with a higher degree of success. If prosperity is to be maintained, change is frequently needed in the type of fabric produced in relation to demand and in sales attitudes to possible, as opposed to preferred, production. In an integrated organization, a central commercial control has the duty, as well as the opportunity, of viewing the production and selling functions dispassionately and of pursuing those policies that reasonably satisfy both productive and selling interests and those that maximize profit under existing market conditions.

Determination of channels of trade: Only a knowledge of the whole market, arising from operations in several of its sectors, can determine those fabrics that pass through the different trade channels. It is not unusual for integrated companies to pass different types of fabric through each of the main channels, namely wholesale, making-up, direct to the mail-order house or retailer, as well as to the merchant converter.

Management requirements

The organization of integrated commercial-management functions is complex and in practice takes the form of a continuing circle.

Commercial information: Information is the key to successful commercial management, whether in terms of markets, trade and economic trends, price movements, financial status of clients, or a host of other relevant factors. The necessary information is gleaned from salesmen, available companya nd trade statistics, market research, fashion- and financial-information services, bankers, trade journals, and other sources.

Fabric interpretation and design: When the general fabric requirements have been ascertained and decisions made as to the types to develop, hypothetical constructions must be costed in order to determine commercial viability before embarking on design and development.

Production planning: Once decisions have been made on the fabric ranges to be marketed, production planning must come into operation and production set in motion. Planning must be so organized as to determine the size of the range, the types of fabric to be presented, the volume to be produced and marketed, the rates at which to produce, the stock level to be aimed at, and over-all priorities.

Marketing: Responsibility in marketing lies primarily in finding markets and in creating and maintaining demand where new and established products, respectively, are concerned. The main weapons used in textiles are statistics, advertising, display, patterning, packaging, and presentation. The extent and degree to which each is used are determined by the product itself and the market in which it is sold.

Sales: Selling may be conducted in several ways, i.e., by direct human representation, by written word, or by telephone. Operations maybe conducted through sales representatives direct from the mill, through selling offices strategically placed at home and overseas, by mail order, through export warehousemen and confirming houses, and through agents at home and overseas.

Functions of personnel

The range of personnel employed in an integrated organization, and the titles given in the different sections of the textile industry to the various functions, differ considerably from company to company. The main functions are the same, however, even though, in some sections of the industry and in the smaller organizations, the same executive may undertake two or even a group of functions.

Commercial director or manager: The commercial director or manager is often the most important executive in a company, responsibility in practice frequently being undertaken by the managing director himself or by a joint managing director. It is, however, not unusual for a managing director to be supported by a commercial director and a production director, each having equal status. In a medium-to-large company, the commercial director may be supported by as many as six people exercising different executive functions and even more executives.

His duties are, first, to use his judgement on the basis of available information, secondly, to set in motion and co-ordinate all operations that collectively result in the production and selling of the company's fabrics, and, finally, to control those operations that are not otherwise managed by the appropriate line or staff executives in such a manner as to ensure a satisfactory over-all profit to the company.

Accountants: Although accountants undertake several duties that are only indirectly connected with commercial functions, many of their functions are a necessary link in the chain, not only in supplying production, sales, delivery, and other statistics, but also in preparing analyses of turnover, costs, profits, and sales forecasts and in maintaining control of finance and credit.

Designer: The function of the designer in a vertically integrated organization varies in the textile industry from section to section. In all sections, however, he works closely with the commercial director or manager. The part played depends to some degree on the extent of fashion involvement, the nature of the textiles produced, and the size of the company. In the woollen- and worsted-manufacturing sections, for example, it is not unusual, because of the high degree of craftsmanship required, for the designer to manage the production unit also.

On the other hand, in the preparation of ranges of printed fabrics, the designer often has no connection with the textile industry except that lie produces and sells designs suitable for a particular end-use. This is also true of printed-fabric colourist. Where the production of plain types of fabric is concerned such as simple continuous filament or cotton fabrics, the designer is often no more than a cloth-construction specialist having technical but not fashion skills. In large design offices, the head designer may have a staff capable between them of a wide range of skills, which the head designer co-ordinates, and in some very large companies there may be several designers working in parallel and not always on different classes of fabric.

Converters: The employment of converters would usually apply only to large integrated organizations, some of which might have as many as four or five, each responsible for a different type of fabric, such as, prints, piece-dyed dress goods, furnishings, etc. The employment of converters would only be appropriate in those sections of the textile industry, primarily the cotton, silk, and similar sections, in which horizontal organization has been customary. Their responsibilities would usually be considerably narrower than those of the merchant converter, the purely commercial functions being undertaken by marketing managers.

Production planner: The production planner has the primary duty of giving service to the customer by ensuring that orders placed are delivered by the mill in relation to the priorities determined by the commercial manager. Although he plans from the centre, he should have a full knowledge of the machinery available, rates of production, machine limitations, yarn availability, and all factors likely to influence the decisions of the commercial manager. He would normally be supported by a machine programming clerk resident in each mill or major department.

Marketing managers: In a large organization, the commercial director or manager would be supported by either an assistant commercial manager or an appropriate number of marketing managers, whose duty is for each to take responsibility for the success of his section, e.g., grey-fabric sales or converted-dress-goods sections, by controlling the commercial aspects of range-making, sales, production, stockholding, despatch, pricing and profit margins, credit control, etc.

Sales managers: Whereas in a small organization a sales manager might undertake all the duties described above, except those of the management accountant and the designer, and work from the mill through one or two sales representatives, or through an appropriate number of agents, or even alone, such an arrangement would be inadequate in the larger company. Sales managers supported by sales representatives would, in the latter case, take responsibility for effecting all sales within a defined area or all sales over a larger area for a given type of product.

Organization of merchant-converter functions

Although the function of the merchant converter has declined in importance with the rise of the large and giant integrated companies, particularly in the cotton and man-made-fibres sections, merchant converters still have an important part to play, especially in fashion textiles and in serving the small wholesaler and maker-up who requires only limited quantities of a wide range of fabrics.

Unburdened by the pressures of fixed assets in the form of machinery and industrial buildings, he is able to move quickly in the face of continual changes of demand and is in a strong position to import novelties or to meet sudden changes in fashion by importation.

The function of the merchant converter (a function appropriate only in those sections of the textile industry in which a grey cloth can, by being dyed and printed or subjected to other processes and finishes, be modified to fulfil several end-uses or afford variety to a given end-use) is to procure cloth in the grey state, whether a standard product or the result of his own requirements, use his expertise in choosing the manner in which to dye, finish, or print it to satisfy the market in which he intends to sell, fulfil all the commercial functions described in C (i), (iv), (v), and (vi) (and also, for small merchant converters, (vii)), and, finally, fulfil for small and- modestly financed wholesalers and makers-up the functions of banker.

Merchant converters operate in widely differing markets and include in their sphere of operations dyed and printed dress fabrics, suitings, shirtings, furnishings, and household and industrial textiles. In most cases, the merchant converter is influenced in his operations by seasonal conditions, and in negotiating his purchases he endeavours to balance these with an off-take covering more than one season. In all cases, however, the organization he adopts to conduct his business is basically similar.

Thus the merchant converter buys at home or imports grey fabric; organizes to his own specification, and at an appropriate rate of output, the dyeing, finishing, or printing of the grey fabric with his selected dyers and printers; finances stocks; fixes his selling prices; arranges credit terms; organizes his selling outlets through sales representatives or agents; and delivers the fabric in suitable quantities to his customers. Thus, in the course of undertaking his responsibilities, the merchant converter fulfills directly or indirectly a wide range of functions. The strength of his position is in the high degree of co-ordination in his operations, and the weakness is the inability of any but an exceptional man to be expert in so many different spheres.

Departmental management organization

Although there may be a greater or less degree of complexity, the principles or organization employed in buying raw materials are similar, irrespective of the sector of the industry being served. Where, however, raw material is purchased both at home and overseas, departmental organization is obviously more complicated and a wider range of control statistics necessary. Given a policy in relation to the raw-material types to be standardized, the proportion to be purchased at home and overseas, purchase prices, stock policy, method of financing, preferred merchants, continuity of supply, etc., the buyer still has specific a. professional, b. clerical, and c. technical responsibilities to organize or to fulfil.

Professional responsibilities

The home buyer may or may not be a member of the board, and may operate separately from the spinning division or as a senior executive within it. Close co-ordination of policy must, however, be arranged, in relation to both the managing director and the spinning manager. Although an overseas buyer, located, for example, in Australia, would be responsible to the home buyer, he would operate independently once his instructions had been received.

The home buyer would, however, appraise his wools on receipt as a check on the overseas buyer's quality standards and purchase prices, and he would also appraise and buy wools at auction sales or from local wool merchants on his own account. Instructions to an overseas buyer would normally be transmitted by cable in code giving the types required, relative priorities, maximum quantity to purchase, price limits, and indication as to whether to buy only at public auction or privately from merchants or scourers.

Although the home buyer would be responsible for determining financial arrangements with the overseas wool broker from time to time, once the season was under way., all matters appertaining to bidding by the broker in a sale room, arranging for scouring before shipment, internal transport and shipping, payment of expenses and supply of clerical assistance to the buyer, and any extra assistance needed for appraisal would be arranged by the overseas buyer in conjuction with the broker.

Clerical responsibilities

A buying office would normally have a relatively small staff. The main clerical duties entail the entry of the purchase ledger and, arising from the purchase ledger, the payment of accounts due, the claiming of discounts and other business matters, the stock ledger sub-divided to show wool type and bale movement from point to point, and finally the entry of suitable records of raw materials sent into mill and by-products returned to warehouse. Correspondence, the sending and decoding of cables, the interpretation of statistical analyses, and other normal day-to-day office duties would also be part of the function.

Technical responsibilities

Technical responsibility cannot be dissociated from the duties of a professional buyer. Once purchases have been made, it is essential that appropriate standard blends at a standard humidity should be made from the varying deliveries, and cost and performance during processing evaluated against expectation during appraisal. Performance would usually be determined, first, by costing the blended raw material in relation to the original bale weights and values and checking against standard cost; secondly, by ascertaining yields and from them cost at various stages of processing up to the point of the spun yarn; thirdly, by assessing behaviour during processing and the physical characteristics of the yarn produced; and, finally, by ascertaining the weight and value of the by-products. The routine work, other than clerical work, necessary to fulfil these functions would not normally be done by the buyer or his staff, but would be regarded as part of the technical-control functions within the mill, for which the buyer and the mill manager would have a joint responsibility.

Production departments

In order to organize his mill effectively, a production manager, irrespective of the sector of the textile industry in which he is engaged, usually conforms to a certain general pattern of organization for his production departments to ensure effective control. Primarily, his need is to organize his production flow, staff, labour force, and machines to obtain long and unbroken runs of output, with as high a degree of specialization as possible, and thereby to increase efficiency and output, reduce costs, and ensure the highest standard of quality. In order to achieve this, all departments must be supported by efficient production-planning techniques, technical control, work and method study, and mechanical, electrical, and other types of maintenance. A mill manager would also have such personal assistants as the size of mill allowed and a clerical staff involved to some degree in the operation of production departments and specialized functions.

Although all these functions must be fulfilled, whether or not they are undertaken by individual staff or departments or grouped together with other functions and undertaken by one or other members of the staff depends largely on the size and type of the undertaking, managerial preference, and available personnel. The key to the efficient organization of production is the determination of the optimum size of units within the mill or factory in terms of managerships, foremanships, or charge-hand and operative sections. These can only be arrived at by a knowledge of the operations and of all aspects of working conditions, coupled with a scientific study of each operation viewed in relation to the type and quality of product, the machinery installed, and the staff and operatives available.

Although, in many sections of the industry, unit sizes have crystallized either as a result of machine-group-outputs, e.g., a worsted-drawing plant laid down for a narrow range of counts, or custom of the trade, or in agreement with trade unions, the constant impact of new machinery and methods and the pressures of competition demand a continuing review of the size, shape, and staffing of each production unit. One may consider as an example that, although the manager of a large orthodox woollen-spinning plant supported by an assistant manager might break down the organization into six foremanships, the foremen being supported by four overlookers, on the basis of a wool-warehouse department, a teazing department, and four carding and spinning units, consisting of twelve 60-in. carding engines and 8000 mule spindles, the position would, change remarkably if modern machinery were installed. Carding sets about 100 in. wide, large-package ringframes, or high-speed roller-bearing spindle mules would give vastly increased production per unit and this, combined with the accuracy of machinery of modem construction, would lead to a complete reshaping of the organization of the staff and labour force.

The same situation would apply where Lancashire looms, often organized on the basis of 8-14 looms per weaver and 4 or 5 weavers' sections per overlooker, were replaced by orthodox automatic looms, with or without Unifil or box-loader attachments, or pirnless or unconventional weaving machines, such as the Sulzer or Kovo types.

Similarly, in a dyehouse, the introduction of beam-pressure dyeing machines with electronic automated controls for synthetic-fibre fabrics would not only alter production methods and substantially increase output per machine compared with a jigger dyehouse, but would also call for a completely reshaped scheme of organization and staffing. Similar examples could be instanced from almost every part of the textile industry.

There is thus no continuing perfect shape or organization for any department or unit of production in any textile company, but only a permanent need with all the aids available to seek out and introduce effective organizations of optimum size that are capable of giving the most efficient and economical results. Two important aids that a manager uses in organizing his production departments are technical control and work and method study. Each of these functions may be undertaken by a trained individual or a department, or, in a small organization, it may be the part-time responsibility of an assistant manager or even a production foreman.

Technical control is exercised in several ways and differs according to the operations controlled. In a spinning mill, for example, the control exercised would be mainly that of the physical testing of yarns and a check on the machines to ensure that they were operating efficiently and at the maximum potential rate of output. In a dyehouse, physical and chemical controls would be established to ensure correct processing and satisfactory quality. Work and method study falls under two main heads, and, where a large organization is concerned, the staff would include an organization and methods officer and a work-study officer.

Each might have one or more assistants and both positions might be organized as part of the same department. In practice, the expertise of each officer is essential in finding the most economical and the most acceptable way of organizing or reorganizing each productive department. As the titles suggest, the functions involved consist in measuring and analysing data, drawing conclusions, and recommending ways of achieving the best conditions and most productive results.

The functions of clerical staff within a production organization vary widely according to the degree of centralization. Broadly, however, such staff is involved in the procurement of supplies and spare parts requested by the storekeeper and checked by the manager, the preparation of wages sheets and data, technical correspondence, and statistical analysis of production-control figures, where these are not supplied by a central organization.

Commercial departments

The detailed shape and organization of commercial departments and the extent to which they tie in with the selling organization vary in relation to the section of the textile industry under consideration. There is, however, a relationship between their complexity or simplicity and the type of product sold.

In order to give a wider picture, a complex commercial organization dealing with a wide range of cloths will be broken down into its components and the responsibilities of each section described. Once the commercial director or manager, together with his marketing managers and his sales managers, has decided on the range of fabrics to be produced and sold, a sequence of operations is set in motion, each of which is the responsibility of a different department. With one exception, all six departments concerned are under the commercial manager's direct control and each department fulfils several functions. The six departments are: a. design department, b. converting department,

c. marketing department, d. production department, e. financial department, and f. advertising department.

Design department

Design departments vary in size according to the degree of fashion involved or complexity of the fabrics marketed, or both. The number of designers employed does not necessarily bear a relation to the volume of a firm's output. A head designer would normally be responsible for six functions, and the extent to which he would delegate would -depend on the demands made on his department. The six responsibilities are (i) to develop ranges of cloth of the type and design required by the commercial manager and converters, (ii) to construct, theoretically, the required cloths before production, (iii) to cost the cloths theoretically constructed in order to ascertain price suitability, (iv) to produce the chosen fabrics in pattern looms or machines; to arrange for dyeing and finishing or other processes, and to develop the selected fabrics until they are commercially acceptable, (v) to establish standards of fabric performance, and (vi) to retain and catalogue the construction and technical data of accepted standard fabrics and retain lengths of fabric for comparison with bulk production as required.

In undertaking these responsibilities in a larger design room, the head designer would delegate responsibility to assistant designers for different categories of cloth, each being assisted, when necessary, by a cloth" construction expert, who would usually indent for or purchase the necessary yarns. Costing would be undertaken by a cost clerk and his staff, working in close conjunction with the company cost accountant and receiving his technical instructions from the designers.

The pattern production room would be under the

control of a foreman, who would usually be responsible for setting and maintaining the machinery and supervising the operatives. Each designer would normally undertake responsibility for ensuring that his patterns were dyed and finished satisfactorily. The holding and distribution of standard cloth patterns and the filing of design data, etc., would be undertaken by a warehouseman and a clerical assistant.

Converting department

Although a converting department, in view of its commercial involvement in selling, functions more effectively if separated from the design department, it nevertheless needs to have the closest possible relationship with it. The various converters employed in such a department have four functions to fulfil. The first function is that they must act as the eyes and ears of the commercial director; secondly, they must interpret market needs in terms of fabric and design; thirdly, they should help to sell their ranges when launched; and, finally, they must bear joint responsibility with the marketing manager for placing stock orders and for the stock levels of their ranges of fabric.

Marketing department

Marketing managers are the functional link between the commercial director and the sales managers and in this capacity interpret the former's policy in the smooth transfer to the customer of the fabric produced. A marketing manager is involved in six main functions, his primary function in most cases being to co-ordinate activities.

These functions are as follows: (i) joint responsibility with the converters for the preparation of ranges and the physical despatch of these ranges to the sales managers and the sales representatives; (ii) the responsibility for pricing fabrics for the sales managers in accordance with the policy laid down by the commercial director and for notifying the sales offices of any withdrawals or changes in the ranges or repricing; (iii) the acceptance of orders submitted by the sales offices, the placing of 'make orders' with the production manager, the confirmation of delivery promises given by the production manager and the servicing of customer's requirements and complaints through the medium of the sales offices; (iv) the control of the warehouse and warehouse staff through a manager or foreman, this control including packing and despatch, transport, and shipping; (v) control of stocks, in both volume and value, and the clearance of repudiated contracts, dead stocks, seconds, etc.; and (vi) credit control.

Production department

The key to the smooth organization of both production in the mills and effective sales service lies in the policy pursued by the commercial manager through the production manager. It is not, in fact, unusual for this section to be directly controlled by the commercial manager, with a production planner as a right-hand man. The responsibilities of the planner, in the case of a manufacturer, are: (i) to budget output for a few months in advance; (ii) to organize, where appropriate, the purchase of yarn; (iii) to organize machinery in relation to stocks and the orders placed; (iv) to control production during manufacture in relation to priorities and further processing and despatch; and (v) to control, in conjunction with the marketing manager, over-all stocks in relation to budget policy.

Provided that an efficient statistical service is maintained by the management accountant, a small staff with a sound technical background is capable of controlling a large productive organization. Where several production units are being programmed and the units are geographically separated, the production budget is generally discussed in conference at regular intervals between those primarily concerned, namely, the commercial manager, the production manager, the mill managers and their machine programmers, and sometimes the marketing managers.

Financial department

A separate department for the handling of financial matters connected with the commercial departments, such as credit control, accounting, invoicing, etc., is unusual, a centralized department, under the control of the management accountant, being more customary. It is proposed to deal with these matters in the next section of this chapter.

Advertising department

Whether or not advertising is undertaken on any but a minor scale depends on the section of the textile industry to which a company belongs and the channels employed for the sale of its products. Only larger companies have advertising departments, the responsibility in other cases being undertaken by the marketing managers or commercial manager.

A certain amount of publicity of a simple nature is undertaken direct through the chosen medium, either alone or jointly with a maker-up or retailer, but campaigns are usually only conducted with the help of professional agents, who are aware, through experience and statistical records, of the means of producing the greatest impact in relation to expenditure. In addition to advertisements in journals, magazines, and newspapers, other forms of advertising are relevant and take the form of show cards, special displays, and other visual means, including television.

Financial and secretarial departments

During the last two decades, circumstances, in addition to the increase in the size of companies, have demanded much rethinking of the methods of organizing the financial and secretarial departments of a company. Many of the duties, which in an average-size company would have been dealt with by the manager or secretary or by the two in co-operation, must now be dealt with by professional officers and specialists. Although, in a small public company, a qualified secretary-accountant, with a suitable department in support, may still undertake the necessary work, the functions involved are, in fact, fourfold and in a large company would require four basic but co-ordinated departments for satisfactory fulfilment. The functions are those of a. company accountancy, b. management accountancy, c. cost accountancy, and d. secretarial duties. In describing these functions, it is most important to bear in mind that they should be regarded as a group and that almost any one may be linked up with another and even all four undertaken as a single group of responsibilities.

Company accountancy

In a large independent company, or where a large company is part of a group, it is usual to employ a chief accountant, who, in the latter case, also provides the financial link with the group headquarters. Such an official would be responsible for the preparation of budgets of expected performance and have the duty of reporting back, after detailed analysis, actual results to his board or to headquarters each month. The budget would usually include forecasts of turnover, profit, capital employed, profit ratios, cash requirements, cash flow, capital expenditure, etc., for the coming year, and in some cases for three years ahead. The chief accountant would normally have few staff if any, since the whole of the data required for his function would be prepared as a by-product of the management accountant's department, and secretarial assistance would often be provided from a pool.

Management accountancy

The responsibilities of the management accountant, are becoming increasingly complex as mechanization and the introduction of electronic equipment change the nature of his approach to his functions. The management accountant is generally responsible for certain internal controls and has five main departments to assist him, namely, (i) statistics, (ii) wages, (iii) invoicing, (iv) accounting., and (v) credit control

Statistics: Most statistical departments are to a greater or less degree mechanized, even modest organizations having machines with some of the characteristics of small computers. The statistical department would produce, in addition to the statistics required for-the chief accountant, analyses of sales and turnover., broken down by sales office, customer, and fabric, Of stocks by fabric numbers and yarns by type for the commercial manager, of cost and costing data for the cost accountant, of plant records, and much other essential information.

Wages: The payment of wages is a specialized function, especially where piece rates or bonus rates are employed in production. From the entry of the wage sheet by the employee to the actual payment of the wage, there are at least ten stages of entry, calculation, and checking. The wages department normally has a head wages clerk and a few clerks. Most wages offices are mechanized to some degree.

Invoicing: The invoicing department works very closely with the service section of the marketing departments, the warehouse, and the packing and despatch departments. In most organizations, the preparation of the invoice, advice, and delivery notes is not as yet a highly mechanized operation. Where shipping and export orders are involved, complicated documents in considerable volume are called for. The department is usually organized by a departmental head supported by several invoicing typists. It may be expected that much of the work in larger companies will be undertaken by electronic machines in the near future.

Accounting: The preparation of sales ledgers and purchase ledgers and the handling of monetary transactions are highly specialized and, even in small companies, substantially mechanized. According to the size of the department, this work may be controlled either by a cashier or by two heads of departments, one of whom would be the cashier. The key staff is often composed of male clerks in order to- ensure continuity of operation.

Credit control: Although in a smaller company this is usually undertaken by the cashier, in the larger company, which may have substantially more than 3000 live accounts at home and overseas, a credit-control clerk with a small staff may be required to maintain effective control of credit., including overdue and risk situations, payment promise, and the assessment of new risks. A credit-control clerk usually works to a formula where overdue accounts are concerned, the principle being determined by the commercial director.

Cost accountancy

The main function of the cost accountant is to ascertain from data supplied by a statistical department and by the factories and mills and after analysis of overhead and wages costs, revenue expenditure., etc., the production cost per unit of each different product at all the appropriate points of processing. The department is usually relatively small since costs, once ascertained, are often expressed as standard costs for the purposes of comparison of estimated with actual performance and need only be reassessed when there is a substantial change in either wages and other costs or in the method of production. The cost data arrived at form the basis of the statistics used by the costing section of the design department.

Secretarial duties

Every company is compelled by statute to have someone legally responsible for the return of specific company information to certain government departments. This function, combined with several other reasonably compatible duties, provides enough responsibility in any but small or subsidiary companies for the employment of a company secretary. The secretary's office is a convenient centre for drawing together responsibilities that have no natural place elsewhere within the organization. Thus, in addition to performing statutory duties and doing secretarial work in relation to the board and other committees, banking formalities, share transfers, inter-company relationships, etc., it is not unusual for the secretary to deal with all legal, insurance, and property matters, as well as with staff salaries, pensions, charitable appeals, and various other not dissimilar matters. In many smaller organizations, he is also responsible for the receipt and despatch of mail, stationery stores, and such printing and duplicating as are undertaken internally. A company secretary is usually supported by a confidential secretary, although assistance may be drawn from other sources.

Sales departments

Sales departments may be organized in various ways, but, irrespective of the method of organization, the most vital factor is the ensurance of rapid and accurate communications in both directions and of exemplary customer-service in terms of quick delivery of a satisfactory product. The most effective means of communication include direct private telephone lines, telex, and teleprinter. In determining the method of organization, regard must be paid to the types of customer to be supplied. These may include one or several of the following: wholesalers, makers-up, department stores, mail-order houses, retailers, and other industries.

In each case, although the strategic plan may be broadly similar, the tactical approach must be appropriate to the particular type of outlet. Not only is there likely to be a wide variation in the size and type of order, but buying seasons open on different dates, business terms vary, the required degree of personal representation differs, and even commercial standards of quality are not always comparable. Sales organizations may therefore be built up on the basis of one of three forms or on a combination of each. An organization of one kind would be required where the sub-division of sales effort was by product, of another kind where sales generally were organized by areas, and of a third kind where a particular type of customer, for example, a department store, a large mail-order house, or an industrial company, was concerned.

In a small company, not only may the commercial control be exercised from the mill, but sales may also be organized and directed from the same location. In these cases, much of the selling may be undertaken by the managing director or the sales director, and, where custom makes it possible, through one city in the vicinity, such as Manchester in relation to manufacturing units in Lancashire.

In the larger company, however, more complex methods of selling are inevitable owing to the variety of both product and outlet, and normally sales offices or agents would be located at strategic points in the country, in order to serve particular areas. Apart from Manchester and London, where confirming houses operate, export sales would nevertheless usually be conducted from the commercial headquarters through agents or representatives located overseas.

Area sales offices, irrespective of location, undertake similar responsibilities. Once the ranges of fabric have been received and the sales manager or agent has been informed of the appropriate prices for each class of customer and his discretionary negotiating price limits, the ranges would be shown to customers approved by the sales manager through sales representatives, with a view to securing initial customer reaction and sample or bulk orders. Orders received by representatives would be telephoned and confirmed in writing, or reported personally to the sales manager in appropriate cases, or to the service clerk for transmission on suitable order forms to the counterpart service section at headquarters. After confirmation or amendment by headquarters, the order would be recorded in both the sales office and the headquarters sales section and the necessary production or release from stock set in motion.

2

Functions and Organisational Set-up

The Ministry of Textiles is responsible for policy formulation, regulation, development and export promotion in respect of the textile sector including cotton, wool, silk, jute and other fibres, and handicrafts. However, it does not deal with noncellulosic synthetic fibres such as nylon and polyester acrylic.

The developmental activities of the Ministry are oriented towards making adequate quantities of raw material available to all sectors of the textile industry and augmenting the production of fabrics at reasonable prices from the organised and decentralised sectors of the industry. Towards this objective the Ministry lays down guidelines for a planned and harmonious growth of various sectors of the industry. Special emphasis is given to the development of handlooms in view of its large employment potential.

The Ministry monitors the techno-economic status of the industry and provides requisite policy frame work for modernisation and rehabilitation. The Ministry coordinates the activities of Textiles Research Associations and lends financial support to them for undertaking research and development.

The Ministry of Textiles is headed by a Secretary who is assisted in discharge of his duties by 4 officers of joint secretary status and the Development Commissioners for Handlooms and Handicrafts, Textile Commissioner and the jute Commissioner.

The principal functions of the Ministry are:-

— Textile Policy & Coordination

— Man-made Fibre

— Cotton Textile Industry jute Silk

— Wool & Woollen Industry

— Powerloom Industry

— Export Promotion

— Planning & Economic Analysis

— Integrated Finance Matters

— Computerisation

Boards

All India handicrafts board

The All India Handicrafts Board has been constituted under the chairmanship of Minister of Textiles with the Development Commissioner (Handicrafts) as Member Secretary. The Board advises the Government in matters pertaining to the development of the handicraft sector.

All India powerloom board

The All India Powerloom Board was constituted as an Advisory Body under the chairmanship of the Minister of Textiles. It has representatives of Central and -State Governments, Powerloom Federations/Associations of Powerloom Industry as its members. The functions of the Board are to advise the Government on matters concerning growth and development of the Powerloom sector. The Board was reconstituted vide resolution dated 28.10.98. It has 29 members.

Central wool development board

The Board has been constituted with a view to promote growth and overall development of the wool and woollen industry. Various development schemes are implemented through the State Governments concerned. Facilities for testing are also provided. The Board has its headquarters at Jodhpur. It has 19 members.

All India handloom board

The All India Handloom Board has been constituted under the chairmanship of Minister of Textiles. The Board advises the Government on various aspects of handloom development.

Cotton advisory board

The Cotton Advisory Board is a representative body of Government/Growers/ Industries/Traders. It advises the Government generally on matters pertaining to production, consumption and marketing of cotton, and also provides a forum for liaison among the cotton textile mill industry, the cotton growers, the cotton trade and the Government. It was reconstituted on 21.4.97 and has 30 members.

Central silk board

The Central Silk Board was constituted with the objective of promoting the growth and development of sericulture in the country. The programmes for development of the sericulture industry are primarily formulated and implemented by the State Sericulture Departments.

However, the Central Silk Board supplements the efforts of the states by providing necessary support for research and development and extension and training through its countrywide network of units. Besides, the Central Silk Board organises production and supply of quality silkworm seed, mulberry cuttings etc. and also undertakes directly as well as jointly with the State Sericulture Departments, the implementation of various sericulture projects.

Jute advisory board

The jute Advisory Board advises the Government generally on matters pertaining to jute falling within the purview of jute (Licensing & Control) Order, 1961 including production estimates of jute and mesta. The Jute Commissioner is the Chairman. The Board is constituted for a period of 2 years. The Board was reconstituted in December, 1997. It has 20 members.

Attached and subordinate offices

Attached offices

Office of the development commissioner for handlooms

This office is headed by the Development Commissioner for Handlooms. It implements various schemes for the promotion and development of the handloom sector and has been providing assistance to handloom weavers in a variety of ways. Its subordinate offices are-Weavers' Service Centres, Indian Institute of Handloom Technology and the Enforcement Machinery for Implementation of Handloom (Reservation of Articles for Production) Act, 1985.

Office of the development commissioner for handicrafts

The office of the Development Commissioner for Handicrafts functions under Ministry of Textiles for promotion and expert of handicrafts. It is headed by Development Commissioner for Handicrafts and assists the State Governments in planning and executing development schemes for handicrafts. It has 6 regional offices at Mumbai, Calcutta, Lucknow, Chennai, Guwahati and New Delhi.

Subordinate offices

Office of the textile commissioner

The office of the Textile Commissioner has its headquarters at Mumbai with 8 regional offices throughout the country. The office is headed by Textile Commissioner. The Textile Commissioner acts as the principal technical advisor to the Ministry. This office is entrusted with the responsibility of implementation of various control orders. Through the network of regional offices, the Textile Commissioner carries out techno-economic surveys and advises the Government about the general economic health of textile units.

The developmental activities of the Office of the Textile Commissioner centres around planning the growth and overall development of the textile sector. 13 Powerloom Service Centres are functioning under the administrative control of the Textile Commissioner.

Office of the jute commissioner

Located at Calcutta, this office is entrusted with the responsibility for implementation of the policies of the Government in the jute sector. Just as the Textile Commissioner acts as the principal technical adviser to the Ministry on the textile industry, the jute Commissioner gives technical advice to the Ministry on all matters relating to the jute industry including the jute machinery industry.

Development councils

Jute manufactures development council

The jute manufactures development council was constituted as a statutory body under the chairmanship of Secretary (Textiles) with effect from 1.5.84 with the objective of increasing efficiency and productivity in the jute industry, the financing of activity for such development and for matters connected therewith. JMDC has been delegated all functions relating to export promotion in the jute Sector and to perform other activities on the domestic market of jute Sector as are performed by a Commodity Board. The activities of the Council are funded from the grants made available by the Central Government from the proceeds of cess on the production of jute levied under the Jute Manufactures Cess Act 1983.

3

Organised Textile Mill Industry

Cotton/Man-made Fibre Textile Mill Industry is one of the largest organised industries in the country employing nearly 10 lakh workers. Besides this, there are a large number of ancillary industries depending on this sector such as those manufacturing various accessories, spares, ancillaries and chemicals. Even on the modest assumption that a worker's family comprises of five persons, the direct dependants on the textile industry itself work out to about 50 lakhs. Salient aspects of this industry are discussed in the succeeding paragraphs.

Capacity

The Cotton/Man-made Fibre Textile Mill Industry has witnessed phenomenal growth during the last four decades. The spindleage increased from 2782 million in 1992 to 33.93 million and rotors from 113 thousand in 1992 to 317 thousand as on December 1998. The loomage, however, has declined in the organised sector from 1,69,000 in March, 1992 to 1,24,000 in December, 1998. The growth in capacity in Spinning and Weaving Sectors of the Industry since 1992 is as given in the table below.

Out of the total 1788 cotton/man-made fibre textile mills, 192 mills are in the public sector, 152 in the co-operative sector and 1444 in the private sector.

Capacity utilisation

The capacity utilisation in the Spinning Sector of the

Organised Textile Mill Industry has increased from 78% in 1992-93 to 85% in 1997-98, while the capacity utilisation in the weaving sector of the Organised Textile Mill Industry has remained between 51 to 54 percent during the last six years. A statement giving the capacity utilisation in cotton/man-made fibre textile mills since 1992-93 is given below.

Growth capacity in the organised mill sector

Year ending	No. of mills			Installed No. of		
	Spinning	Composite	Total	Spindles (mn.)	Rotors ('(00)	Looms ('000)
31.3.1992	846	271	1117	27.82	113	169
31.3.1993	874	268	1142	28.09	127	158
31.3.1994	909	266	1175	28.60	139	150
31.3.1995	1148	268	1416	30.70	185	139
31.3.1996	1294	275	1569	31.75	226	132
31.3.1997	1438	281	1719	33.15	276	124
31.3.1998	1504	278	1782	33.88	313	124
31.12.1998	1510	278	1788	33.93	317	124

Capacity utilisation in the textile industry

Year	Spinning	Capacity	Weaving	Capacity
	Installed Spindles (mn.)	Utilisation (%)	Installed Looms ('000)	Utilisation (%)
1992-93	28.09	78	158	51
1993-94	28.60	84	150	54
1994-95	30.70	81	139	51
1995-96	31.75	86	132	53

1996-97	33.15	86	124	52
1997-98	33.88	85	124	52
1998-99	33.91			

Production of spun yarn

The production of spun yam has increased from 1941 mn. kg. during 1992-93 to 2973 mn. kg. during 1997-98. The production of spun yarn during 1998-99 is anticipated to be 2860 million kg. The above data includes the production of yam from SSI spinning sector as well. The contribution from SSI sector has been about 4% in the total spun yam production. A statement showing the production of spun yam (including SSI units) during the last six years along with anticipated figures for the current year is given below.

Production of spun yarn-including SSI

(In million kg.)

Year	Cotton Yarn	Blended Yarn	100% Non-Cotton Yarn	Total Yarn
1992-93	1569	247	125	1941
1993-94	1697	305	140	2142
1994-95	1696	346	158	2200
1995-96	1894	395	196	2485
1996-97	2148	484	162	2794
1997-98	2213	583	177	2973
1998-99	987	306	86	1379
1998-99 (A)	2045	630	185	2860

Sickness/closure of textile mills

As on 31.12.98, there were total 1788 mills out of which 1510 were spinning mills and 278 composite mills. Out of this 284 cotton/man-made fibre mills (184 spinning and 100 composite) with an installed capacity of 6.99 mn spindles, 21,686 rotors and 58,500 looms were reported to be closed as on 31.12.98. As on 31.03.98, 220 mills (127 spinning and 93 composite) with an installed capacity of 5.75 mn. spindles, 10,813 rotors and 55,300 looms were reported closed.

The incidence of sickness and closure in the organised textile industry has been a matter of concern. One main reason for sickness is structural transformation resulting in the composite units in the organised sector losing ground to powerlooms in the decentralised sector, on account of the latter's greater cost effectiveness. The other causes of sickness/closure of the industry include low productivity due to lack of modernisation, stagnation in demand and inability of some units to expand in the export market, increase in the cost of inputs, difficulties in getting timely and adequate working capital, etc.

Closure of cotton/man-made fibre textile

Year Month End	No. of Mills			Installed Capacity			Employees on roll
	Spinning	Com-posite	Total	Spindles (000)	Rotors (No.)	Looms (100)	('000)
1992-93	64	59	123	3520	1776	366	178
1993-94	75	57	132	3590	3232	362	173
1994-95	74	58	132	3652	3904	366	178
1995-96	100	71	171	4668	6589	450	228
1996-97	118	91	209	5469	9270	542	252
1997-98	127	93	220	5752	10813	553	260
December 1998	184	1oo	284	6994	21686	585	299

Measures taken by the Government to tackle the problem of sickness.

(i) Setting up of Board for Industrial and Financial Reconstruction (BIFR) for timely detection of sick and potentially sick companies and for taking preventive ameliorative remedial and other measures which need to be taken with respect to such companies.

(ii) Setting up of Textile Workers' Rehabilitation Fund Scheme (TWRFS) to protect the interests of the workers.

(iii) Financial Institutions and Banks are also required to monitor closely the incidence of growing sickness.

(iv) The Expert Committee on Textile Policy which has been constituted in 1998 would be addressing the problems of sickness in the textile sector.

As per the information obtained from the Board for Industrial and Financial Reconstruction (BIFR), there were 399 Textile Mills registered with BIFR as on 18.02.99.

Number of mills State-wise registered with BIFR is given below:-

Name of the State/U.T.	No. of mills
1. Andhra Pradesh	29
2. Assam	4
3. Bihar	3
4. Chandigarh	1
5. Dadra & Nagar Haveli	3
6. Gujarat	73
7 Haryana	22
8. Karnataka	18
9. Kerala	5
10. Madhya Pradesh	16

11.	Maharashtra	75
12.	New Delhi	3
13.	Orissa	5
14.	Punjab	8
15.	Rajasthan	20
16.	Tamil Nadu	62
17.	Uttar Pradesh	38
18.	West Bengal	13
19.	Himachal Pradesh	1
	Total	399

Status of textile mills registered with BIFR as on 18.02.99

	Total
Registered with BIFR	399
Dismissed as non-maintainable	63
Scheme sanctioned by AAIFR	10
Scheme sanctioned 18(4) & 17(2)	69
Recommended winding up 20 (1)	101
Draft scheme circulated	7
Winding up notice	12
Failed and Reopened	3
Remanded by AAIFR/Court	2
Stayed by AAIFR/Court	6
Under enquiry	92
Declared no longer sick, hence discharged	25
Net worth became +ve during enquiry	3
Others	6

Textile workers' rehabilitation fund scheme (TWRFS)

In pursuance of the Statement of Textile Policy, 1985, the

Government has set up TWRFS to protect the interest of workers rendered jobless due to permanent closure of textile mills. The objective of TWRFS is to give interim relief to workers. Relief to the workers is provided only for 3 years on a tapering basis - 75% of wage equivalent in the first year, 50% in the second year and 25% in the third year. The scheme, as amended, covers also the partially closed mills.

The total number of units which were found eligible for assistance so far (as on 30.9.98) is 36. A total of 53,043 workers of 33 mills out of the 36 units have been disbursed relief of an amount of Rs. 108.12 cr up to 01.02.99.

During the current financial year up to 25.02.99, the Ministry has released Rs. 14.85 crore under TWRF Scheme.

Technology upgradation fund scheme

A special scheme for Technology Upgradation in the textile and jute industries has been proposed by the Ministry of Textiles. The objective is to enable the Indian textile industry to take urgent steps to bridge technological gaps in order to upgrade the quality of our textiles and to enable the industry to become more competitive in the international and domestic markets.

It has been seen that over the years while the spinning sector has done comparatively better by keeping pace with technological changes, the processing and weaving sectors, in particular, are in urgent need of technological upgradation. This is exemplified by the lack of modem processing and finishing facilities and of inadequacy in the number of state-of-the-art looms in the country. The ginning and pressing sector also needs to upgrade its facilities. During the VII Five Year Plan a Textile Modernisation Fund was set up and Rs. 750 crore had been earmarked for being provided by all the All India Financial Institutions to textile units. A total of over Rs. 1280 crores was sanctioned by IDBI up to 1991 under the scheme. However, the scheme was not continued during the VIII Plan period.

Similarly, for the jute Industry, a jute Modernisation Fund Scheme was operated from 1986. This scheme has also since been discontinued. Meanwhile, the jute industry has also been suffering from obsolescence and there is need for fresh investment in the industry for modernisation and technological upgradation.

The Ministry of Textiles therefore, proposed that a Fund be created and that concessional finance under the Fund be made available to weaving and processing sectors on priority. The jute industry as well as the apparel manufacturing sector would also be covered under the Scheme.

Government has since approved launching of a Technological Upgradation Fund Scheme for Textile and jute Industries to provide for interest incentive on loans from nodal agencies (IDBI, IFCI, SIDBI) with a view to modernisation and technological and quality upgradation of these industries so as to enhance the productivity, quality and competitiveness. The scheme would be operative for 5 years commencing from 01.04.99.

Production of cloth and employment generation

The weaving capacity in the organised mill sector has been stagnant for a number of years. The situation has not changed even with the removal of the restrictions in the creation of capacity in the textile mill sector, as permitted by the Textile Policy of 1985.

The production of cloth in the mill sector in 1997-98 was 1948 mn. sq. mtrs. as compared to that of 1957 mn. sq. mtrs. in 1996-97 The production of cloth in the mill sector is projected at 1920 mn. sq. mtrs. in 1998-99. The data on production of cloth in the mill sector, handloom sector, hosiery sector and the powerloom sector during the past few years is given below. The employment generation in cotton/man-made fibre textile industry as on 30.9.98 was 10. 11 lakh.

4

Powerlooms

The decentralised powerlooms sector plays a pivotal role in meeting the clothing needs of the country. Production of cloth as well as generation of employment have been rapidly increasing in the powerloom sector. This Sector not only contributes significantly to the cloth production in the country but also provides employment to millions of people.

The powerloom industry produces a wide variety of cloth, both grey as well as processed with intricate design. The contribution of Powerloom Sector to the total cloth production of the country is to the extent of 55% excluding the cloth produced by non-SSI weaving and hosiery/knitting units.

Powerloom fabric also successfully competes in the global market and contributes significantly in the export earnings of the country. Therefore, to encourage new and incremental Powerloom exports, the Government has earmarked specific export quota of fabric and made-ups to quota countries covered by Multi-Fibre Arrangement (MFA) for powerloom manufacturers since the year 1992. Starting with 3%, it was enhanced to 5% in the year 1993 and further to 10% from the year 1997.

The estimated number of powerlooms in the decentralised sector and its production and employment is as given below.

Growth of powerlooms, employment and production of cloth

Year	No. of power-loom unit	No.Powerlooms (Revised)	Employment
1992	309064	1200111	3000278
1993	310590	1239268	3098170
1994	319728	1314003	3285008
1995	326286	1365284	3413210
1996	333017	1411903	3529758
1997	349380	1523336	3808340
1998	355791	1576977	3942443

Present policy relating to installation of powerlooms

In terms of the Textiles (Development & Regulation) Order, 1993, every person, on installing a powerloom unit in the SSI Sector, should submit an Information Memorandum in a prescribed form to an officer, notified in this behalf by the State Government within whose territory such a unit has been installed, with a copy thereof to the Textile Commissioner, Mumbai.

Every person on installing any powerloom unit in non-SSI Sector (other than units requiring Industrial Licences), should file an Information Memorandum to the Textile Commissioner, Mumbai, within 30 days of installation for obtaining an acknowledgement thereof.

Census of powerlooms

The Government of India has conducted a joint census of handlooms and powerlooms with the help of the National Council of Applied Economic Research (NCAER). The census has been completed and the final report is under preparation.

Production of cloth in the powerloom sector

(in million sq.mt.)

Year	Production by Powerloom Sector	Total Cloth Production	% Share of Powerloom Sector in total prod.	% Growth in P.L., fabric over previous year
1991-92	13262	22978	57.71	-
1992-93	14644	25475	57.48	10.42
1993-94	15994	27898	57.33	09.22
1994-95	15976	28606	55.84	(-) 00.001
1995-96	17201	31958	53.93	07.67
1996-97	19352	34839	55.58	12.51
1997-98	20951	37436	55.96	08.26
1998-99	15658	27420.9	57.10	-
1998-99	21320	37450	56.90	01.76

Powerloom service centres

There are 13 Powerloom Service Centres (PSCs) functioning under the Office of the Textile Commissioner and 31 Powerloom Service Centres under the Textile Research Associations (TRAs)/State Government Agencies.

Performance of powerloom service centres

During the year 1998-99 (April to December, 1998) the Powerloom Service Centres run by the Office of the Textile Commissioner trained 419 persons, developed 550 new designs, and tested 3,960 samples.

The Powerloom Service Centres of the Textile Commissioner had, in the past, been providing services to the weavers free of charge. A system of charging a reasonable fee for some of the services was introduced with effect from 1st March, 1995. The PSCs have collected Rs. 46,700 during the year 1998-99 (up to August, 1998).

Modernisation & strengthening of existing PSCs

The powerlooms in the PSCs are very old and outdated and cannot run for a long time continuously. The looms and equipments in the PSCs and the machinery existing in the industry in the area do not match. In such circumstances, it becomes very difficult to attract people from that area for training. Since in many places, powerloom weaving is a family tradition, from a very young age such weavers become acquainted with the operation of the looms and weaving activity.

Weavers attending the training require training on the modern looms so as to keep pace with the development needs of the sector. Taking into consideration, the expectations of the powerloom industry and the need for the thrust on technological upgradation in the industry, the Ministry of Textiles has approved a scheme for upgradation of 21 PSCs at a cost of Rs. 16 crores (approx.) to be implemented during the 9th Five Year Plan period. Steps have been initiated for implementing the scheme.

Upgradation of PSC laboratories

Ministry of Textiles had also decided to upgrade the existing laboratories in the PSCs so that the entrepreneurs will have these facilities at nearby places. During 1997-98, it was decided to upgrade the laboratories of PSCs at Malegaon, Burhanpur, Surat, Kishangarh, Belgaum and Amritsar. Similarly 4 PSCs laboratories were also upgraded at Panipat Bhilwara, Ichalkaranji and Erode during 1996-97 During 1998-99,3 PSCs at Bhiwandi, Meerut and Doddabbalapur will be taken up for upgradation.

Computer aided design centres

The Government of India had sanctioned 10 Computer Aided Design Centres (CADC) at Coimbatore (Tamil Nadu), Karur (Tamil Nadu), Surat (Gujarat), Sholapur and Bhiwandi (Maharashtra), Bhilwara (Rajasthan), Erode (Tamil Nadu), Amritsar (Punjab), Bangalore (Karnataka) and Burhanpur (Madhya Pradesh) from 1993-94 to 1995-96. During 1997-98 four centres have been sanctioned at Ghaziabad (UP), Doddabbalapur (Karnataka), Ichalkaranji (Maharashtra) and Ahmedabad (Gujarat). Out of 14 centres sanctioned, 12 centres are operative. Establishment of centres at Amritsar and Doddabbalapur is under way.

Powerloom development and export promotion council (PDEXCIL)

In order to give thrust to the development of powerloom sector and promotion of export of powerloom fabrics, the Government had set up a separate Powerloom Development & Export Promotion Council (PDEXCIL) at Mumbai. The Council has come into existence with effect from 08.09.95.

All India powerloom board

The All India Powerloom Board was first constituted as an Advisory Body in November, 1981. This Board was reconstituted on 28.10.98, for a period of two years. It has representatives of the Central and State Governments, Powerloom federations/associations of powerloom industry, as its members.

Powerloom workers' insurance scheme

The Government of India introduced a Group Insurance Scheme for Powerloom workers in association with the Life Insurance Corporation of India during the year 1992-93. All Powerloom workers of age between 18 and 60 years and those who work during the year are eligible for insurance under this Scheme. The Scheme was reviewed and now a weaver, who had earned at least a minimum average pay of Rs. 700 per month during a year, can join the Scheme. Every member-of a family who satisfies the minimum income condition along with all other conditions of eligibility for the Scheme is eligible to join the Scheme.

The Scheme envisages an annual premium to be shared equally by the Central Government, the State Government and the Powerloom worker. For an insurance cover of Rs. 10,000 the annual premium is Rs. 120 Funds contribution of the Government of India is channelised through the State Government on reimbursement basis.

Benefits

(1) On death of a member, the sum assured of Rs. 10,000/- under the policy shall become payable provided the member is a Powerloom worker as defined for the purpose. In addition to the basic sum assured, the amount accumulated in the running account would become payable with interest of 11% per annum.

(2) On reaching the terminal date or being disqualified as a Powerloom worker, the accumulation in the running account only would become payable with interest at 11 % per annum.

(3) In case of death due to accident, an amount of Rs. 20,000 will be paid to the family member in addition to the accumulated amount in the member's running account, payable with interest of 11% per annum.

5

Handloom Industry

The Handloom sector plays a very important role in the country's economy. It is the largest economic activity after agriculture providing direct and indirect employment to more than 30 lakh weavers. Due to effective State Government intervention through financial assistance and implementation of various developmental and welfare schemes, this sector has been able to withstand the competition from the powerloom and mill sectors. As a result of these measures the production of handloom fabrics registered more than tenfold increase from a level of 500 million sq. metres in the early fifties to 7862 million sq. metres in 1997-98. The anticipated production for 1998-99 is 7170 million square metres. This sector contributes nearly 22 per cent of the total cloth produced in the country and also contributes substantially to the export income of the country. Handlooms form a part of the heritage of India and exemplify the richness and diversity of our country and the artistry of the weavers.

The office of the Development Commissioner for Handlooms has been implementing, since its inception in the year 1976, various schemes for the promotion and development of the handloom sector and has been providing assistance to the handloom weavers in a variety of ways. Some of the major programmes formulated by this office relate to:

(a) Employment generation programmes
(b) Modernisation and upgradation of technology
(c) Input support
(d) Marketing Support
(e) Publicity
(f) Infrastructural Support
(g) Welfare measures
(h) Composite growth oriented packages

All these measures aim at meeting the objectives enshrined in the Directive Principles of State Policy for the growth of decentralised handloom sector. In all the schemes, emphasis has been laid on providing assistance directly to handloom weavers, including upgradation of their skills and creating production facilities at all levels with adequate infrastructure at the village level.

Enforcement of handloom reservation act

The Handloom (Reservation of Articles for Production) Act, 1985 aims to protect millions of poor handloom weavers from the encroachment made on their livelihood by the powerloom and textile mill operators by reserving certain textile articles for exclusive production by handlooms. Eleven textile articles are presently reserved for exclusive production by handlooms vide notification dated 26.07.1996.

To ensure effective implementation of the Act, releases under the scheme 'Central Assistance to the States/UTs for setting up of Enforcement Machinery' has been made to the various States, namely, Bihar, Rajasthan, Kerala, Tamil Nadu, West Bengal, etc. The Scheme to set up Offices of Enforcement Machinery shall be fully funded by the Centre during the Ninth Five Year Plan. During the Tenth Five Year Plan Central Assistance will be reduced in a tapering manner @ 20% per annum. The State Governments have been asked to send their commitment to this proposal. On the basis of such commitments, funds are being released to different states. A sum of Rs. 44.30 lakhs have already been released to five states during 1997-98 and a sum of Rs. 36.60 lakhs to 4 states up to December, 1998 during the current financial year 1998-99.

The progress of implementation of the aforesaid Act by various implementing agencies during 1997-98 and 1998-99 is as follows:-

	1997-98	1998-99 (up to Dec. 98)
1. No. of powerlooms inspected	63569	50185
2. No. of FIRs lodged	21	7
3. No. of convictions	2	1

Input support

Handloom sector is largely dependent on the organised mill sector for supply of its principal raw material, namely, yarn. This sector uses the bulk of its yarn in the form of hanks. The Central Government has been making efforts to ensure regular supply of yam to the handloom sector at reasonable prices through - (a) Hank Yarn Obligation Scheme; (b) Loan assistance to the National Cooperative Development Corporation (NCDC) for setting up of new/expansion/ modernisation of weavers' cooperative spinning mills; and (c) scheme for supply of yarn to handloom weavers at mill-gate prices.

Mill gate price scheme

The Scheme was introduced in the year 1992-93 with an objective to supply yarn at Mill Gate Price to the handloom weavers through National Handloom

Development Corporation (NHDC). Under the Scheme, till the year 1994-95 the rate of reimbursement to the NHDC was @ 2% of the value of yarn supplied which has been enhanced from 1995-96 @ 3.5% and from 1997-98 onwards @ 4%.

The agencies covered up to 1994-95 were limited to State Apex/ Regional/ Primary Weavers Cooperative Societies and Handloom Development Corporations which has been extended from 1995-96 onwards to the Handloom Development Centres and Primary Societies having a turnover of more than Rs. 50.00 lakhs. Since 1997-98, All India Handloom Organisations, Handloom Development Centres, approved Export Houses, NGOs fulfilling CAPART norms, etc. are eligible to avail the benefit under the Scheme.

In line with the Government of India's decision to promote production of high value items in the handloom sector as well as the increasing use of jute and jute Blended yarn for production of jute and blended fabrics, the Government of India from

1996-97 has decided to include supply of Silk and jute Yarn also under the Scheme.

During the last 4 years, the following releases were made to NHDC under this Scheme;

Year	Amount (Rs. in lakhs)
1994-95	75.00
1995-96	100.00
1996-97	117.24
1997-98	300.00
1998-99	100.00

Under the Scheme, supplies of yarn have increased from

49.42 lakh kg. in 1993-94 to 117.00 lakh kg. up to December 1998.

Assistance to NCDC

Since the inception of the Scheme and up to the period October 1998, a sum of Rs. 92.50 crores have been released to National Cooperative Development Corporation (NCDC) for assisting 57 Weavers' Cooperative Spinning Mills. The Scheme has~ been discontinued w.e.f. 01.04.1998 (1998-99).

Employment generation

During the year 1997-98, a total production of 7862 million square metres of cloth was achieved. The direct and indirect employment generation on this production has been estimated at 124 lakh persons (provisional) during the year 1997-98. The anticipated production for 1998-99 is 7170 million square metres. Till September, 1998, the production has been 3435 million square metres.

Training of handloom personnel

Training in modern management techniques of production, marketing, accounting cost analysis, etc. is an essential input in the handloom development programme. There is also a need for personnel to be trained in design development and market trends.

To accept the challenges and for overall development of handloom industry, the Office of the Development Commissioner (Handlooms) has been implementing various training programmes to increase the know how of handloom personnel at different levels through various institutions like National Council for Cooperative Training (NCCT), National Handloom Development Corporation (NHDQ and National Cooperative Union of India (NCUI) and Petrofil Cooperative Ltd. etc. In the year 1997-98 funds to the tune of Rs. 48.73 lakhs were released to NCUI, NCCT and other organisations for imparting cooperative training. During 1998-99 (up to December 1998) Rs. 11.18 lakhs has been released to NCCT, NCUI and NHDC.

The NCCT has been conducting training programmes since 1979-80 to train and develop a management cadre in Handloom Cooperatives. The training programmes are meant for senior, middle and lower level management personnel working in the State Handloom Corporations/ Cooperatives. This organisation has been conducting various courses including Diploma for 18 weeks duration at Nagpur and Kalyani.

Funds to the tune of Rs. 16.12 lakhs were released to NCCT during 1997-98 and during the current financial year 1998-99 (as on December, 1998), Rs. 9.98 lakhs has been released to NCCT with a coverage of 350 beneficiaries up to September, 1998.

NCUI is conducting Education-cum-Development Programme for Handloom Cooperatives with the financial support from the office of the Development Commissioner for Handlooms as a Central Sector Scheme. The main objective of the Scheme is to develop handloom Cooperatives in the area and improve productivity and the economic condition of the weaver members.

The scheme has been amended to adopt the Team & Area approach and is to be implemented by NCUI. This aims to integrate development of the society as well as the specific area. For the current year, specific locations i.e. jodhpur, Varanasi, Nadia, West Tripura, Imphal and Thiruvananthapuram have been identified for Integrated Development. A sum of Rs. 22.59 lakhs has been released during 1997-98 and Rs. 1.19 lakhs during the current financial year (as on December, 1998) has been released with a coverage of 4998 beneficiaries up to September, 1998.

Weavers' service centres/Indian institute of handloom technology (WSC/IIHT)

Weavers' Service Centres and Indian Institutes of Handloom Technology constitute Research and Development Wings of the office of the Development Commissioner for Handlooms. 24 Weavers' Service Centres and 4 Indian Institutes of Handloom Technology have considerably strengthened the handloom industry with development of new designs, improvement in weaving and processing techniques in handloom skill, etc. throughout the country.

The decentralised training programme was introduced in 1987 with an objective to generate gainful employment, to upgrade the skills and to enhance the production and income of weavers. Under this Programme, assistance is provided towards the cost of material, looms, accessories, equipments, stipend to the trainees and honorarium to the Master Trainer. The implementation of the Scheme is made through the Weavers' Service Centre and in coordination with the State Government. Up to the year 1997-98, an expenditure of Rs. 545.24 lakhs was incurred to cover 9650 weavers. During 1998-99, the target is to cover 3,000 weavers. Till 30.12.98, 1997 weavers have been covered under this Scheme.

Publicity and exhibition

To provide marketing support to handloom agencies and the individual weavers, the office of the Development Commissioner for Handlooms organises the National Handloom Expos, District Level Events, Craft Melas, etc. in different parts of the country. For this purpose, the financial support is provided to the implementing agency towards infrastructure, publicity, etc. These activities are supportive to the handloom agencies, weavers and also to the consumer as it provides them an opportunity to purchase the handloom products of various states under one roof During the year 1998-99, a budgetary provision of Rs. 5.20 crores has been made for publicising the development activities of the handloom sector. In order to keep pace with the momentum and the acceleration of publicity gained in the past years, programmes were drawn well in advance in consultation with the State Governments.

During the year 1998-99, 11 National Handloom Expos and 4 Special Expos are to be organised in the different parts of the country. Till mid December, 1998, 6 National Handloom Expos at Ahmedabad, Agra, Lucknow, Vijayawada, Agartala, Bhubaneswar and 3 Special Expos at Delhi, Bhopal and Calcutta with a theme of Home Furnishing and Silk items have been organised.

The Office of the Development Commissioner for Handlooms has also been participating in the Craft Melas at Shilpgram (Udaipur), Suraj Kund (Haryana), Craft Bazaar at Madepura (Hyderabad), Taj Mahotsav (Agra) and Dilli Haat by sponsoring weavers for live demonstration of their crafts together with sale of handloom products. In order to give impetus to the marketing of handloom products, assistance is also provided to handloom agencies/ organisations like State Handloom Apex Federation, State Handloom Corporations, etc. to organise District Level Fairs (Melas), Festival (Paravs) etc. in various parts of the country. Till December, 1998, 66 District Level Events have been sanctioned to the various implementing agencies.

Scheme for handloom export development

The importance of the handloom sector in the national economy can not be over emphasised. On account of having the advantage of flexibility of small production run, uniqueness, innovation and adaptability to the exports requirement this sector can contribute towards export earnings. Export of handloom has been therefore identified as "Thrust Area" for the overall development of the sector.

The Government is exploring the possibility of making optimal use of the resource. In order to give substantial impetus to the export of handloom fabric, made-ups and other handloom items from the country, Scheme for Development of Exportable Products and their marketing has been introduced during 1996-97 Under the Scheme, the assistance is available for developing exportable products, for building up of production capability for export and thereafter marketing it.

National and State Level Handloom Corporations, Apex Cooperative Societies, Primary Cooperative Societies and Handloom. Cooperative Societies affiliated to registered with and sponsored by Councils/Corporations like, Handloom Export Promotion Council, Association of Corporations and Apex Societies of Handlooms, Handicrafts and Handloom Export Corporation-, Indian Silk Export Promotion Council, National Handloom Development Corporation, etc. are eligible for assistance under this Scheme. Private handloom exporters can also be assisted through HEPC.

The project cost in respect of the agencies sponsored by the State Government is shared by the State Government itself or by the beneficiary agency. The agencies sponsored by Central Government like; HEPC, HHEC, NHDC, ACASH, etc. are entitled to 100% assistance from the Government of India under the Scheme.

Since the inception of the Scheme in October, 1996, as many as 12 States have availed assistance under the Scheme. While during the year 1996-97 a sum of Rs. 250 crores was released under the Scheme to various agencies, during the year 1997-98, a sum of Rs. 468.50

lakhs was released. There is a budgetary provision of Rs. 500 lakhs under the scheme for the year 1998-99.

Project package scheme

Project Package Scheme introduced in the year 1991-92 has been continued during the IX Plan period in its modified form by merging the scope of the Integrated Handloom Village Development and Margin Money for Destitute Weavers Scheme. The restructured and expanded Scheme aims to provide necessary support in a comprehensive manner and to mitigate the pre/on/post loom problems of the handloom weavers. Besides the weavers in general, those belonging to the Scheduled Castes/Scheduled Tribes/Minorities/Women/People below poverty line would get special attention under the Scheme.

The State Governments are required to prepare specific need based projects. Funding between the Central and the State Government/ Implementing Agencies is on cost sharing basis. While the commercial components of the project will have 50% loan and 50% subsidy component, the non-commercial components would be funded on 100% grant basis.

During 1997-98, 769 projects covering 64, 989 beneficiaries with an outlay of Rs. 39.43 crores were sanctioned to various State Governments. During the current financial year i.e. 1998-99, up to 30th November, 1998, 360 projects covering about 35,000 beneficiaries and central assistance to the tune of Rs. 12.35 crores have been sanctioned to various State Governments. Graphical representations of projects, beneficiaries covered and central assistance released since 1991-92 to 1998-99 are as given below:

Handloom development centre scheme/dyeing units scheme

The scheme of Handloom Development Centres (HDC)

and Quality Dyeing Units (QDU) is under implementation since the year 1993-94. It was envisaged to set up 3000 Handloom Development Centres and 500 Quality Dyeing Units under this Scheme.

The aim of setting up of HDCs and QDUs is to make necessary arrangements for procurement of hank yarn, preparing production plans keeping in view the market demand and set up marketing outlets. During the 8th Plan period, 1588 HDCs and 313 QDUs were sanctioned to various State Governments involving release of Central assistance to the tune of Rs. 80.92 crores.

During the year 1997-98, 260 HDCs and 78 QDUs were sanctioned to various State Governments involving central grant assistance to the tune of Rs. 9.69 crores. A proposal for continuation or otherwise of the Scheme during 9th Plan is under examination in consultation with Ministry of Finance (Department of Expenditure) and Planning Commission.

Workshed-cum-housing scheme

The Government of India has introduced a Central Sponsored Scheme called "Workshed-cum-Housing Scheme" for handloom' weavers since 1985-86. The Scheme is implemented primarily with a view to provide suitable work place to the weavers and in turn to achieve better productivity. The scheme is implemented by the respective State Handloom Development Corporations, Primary Societies or any other specialised agencies set up by the concerned State Government for execution of such projects.

During the year 1997-98, the Scheme has been modified as per the recommendation of the Meera Seth Committee Report and the central subsidy has been enhanced as per details given below:-

Name of the component.	From	To (Per Unit)
Rural Workshed	4000	7000
Rural Workshed-cum-Houses	14000	18000
Urban Workshed	4000	10000
Urban Workshed-cum-Houses	14000	20000

During the 8th Five Year Plan, a total sum of Rs. 4,745.93 lakhs was released to State Governments for construction of approx. 80,630 units of Workshed/ Workshed-cum-Houses.

During 1997-98, a sum of Rs. 1302.00 lakhs was released to the State Governments for construction of 20309 Worksheds and Workshed-cum-Houses.

For the current financial year 1998-99, a budget provision of Rs. 1160 lakh is kept under the Scheme and out of this a sum of Rs. 209.76 lakhs (as on December, 1998) has been released to the State Governments.

Welfare package schemes

Thrift fund scheme for handloom weavers

Thrift Fund Scheme for handloom weavers was introduced in the 8th Five Year Plan as one of the special welfare measures from Government. The Scheme envisaged creation of a fund in the nature of a provident fund. The fund was created by contribution from the members @ 6% of wages earned by him and the contribution of 6% of the wages by the Central and State Governments. The contribution of 3% from Central Government was subject to a ceiling of Rs. 90.

The Government of India has revised this Scheme from the year 1991-92 and made it more flexible. The weavers belonging to corporate sector have also been covered under the scheme. The present funding pattern is at the rate of 8% of the wages from the weavers, 4% each from the Central and State Governments. The earlier ceiling of Government of India contribution of Rs. 90 per weaver per annum has been removed. Withdrawals by weavers have been simplified under the new scheme and powers have been delegated to field level officials.

During the 8th Five Year Plan, a total sum of Rs. 1348.50 lakhs were released to the State Governments to cover 2,13,191 weavers under this Scheme.

For the current financial year 1998-99, a sum of Rs. 800.00 lakhs has been kept under the Welfare Scheme and out of this an amount of Rs. 300.00 lakhs has been earmarked for the Thrift Fund Scheme.

Group insurance scheme

The Government of India had introduced a Group Insurance Scheme for Handloom Weavers throughout the country from the year 1992-93 in order to meet the socioeconomic obligation of weaver towards his family and the uncertainty of his working capacity in old age. Under the Scheme, a weaver is provided an insurance cover of Rs. 10,000 for an annual premium @ Rs. 120. The premium is shared equally between the beneficiary, the Central Government and the State Government.

During the Eighth Five Year Plan, a total sum of Rs. 339.27 lakhs was released to State Governments to cover approx. 10,68,646 weavers under this Scheme. During the year 1997-98 a sum of Rs. 39.61 lakhs was released to the State Governments to cover 1,06,432 weavers under this Scheme.

For the current financial year 1998-99, a budget provision of Rs. 800.00 lakhs is kept under the Welfare Package Schemes and out of this a sum of Rs. 200.00 lakhs has been earmarked for this Scheme.

New insurance scheme for handloom weavers

In order to provide relief to the weavers in the 50th year of Independence, the Government of India has introduced a New Insurance Package Scheme for the weavers through United India Insurance Company for the 9th Five Year Plan. The New Insurance Scheme will provide enhanced coverage against various types of risks at the same premium of Rs. 120.00 only.

The share of the Central Government has been increased from Rs. 40 p.a. to Rs. 60 p.a. and consequently the financial burden on Handloom Weavers towards payment of premium has been reduced from Rs. 40 p.a. to Rs. 20 p.a.. This is also in conformity with the directives issued under the Common Minimum Programme of the Government in which special reference has been made for initiating the steps for welfare of "underprivileged and deprived section of the community".

Handloom Weavers are among the most backward of the deprived sections of the community. By reduction in payment of premium from Rs. 40 to Rs. 20 per year, the financial burden on Handloom Weavers will be about six paise per day (365 x 0.06 = Rs. 21.90).

During 1997-98, a sum of Rs. 36.27 lakhs was released to United India Insurance Company to cover 60,453 handloom weavers of the states.

For the current financial year 1998-99, a budget provision of Rs. 50.00 lakhs has been kept under the New Insurance Scheme for Handloom Weavers and out of this a sum of Rs. 16.19 lakhs has bee released to the United India Insurance Company to cover 26,983 weavers of the State Governments.

Health package scheme

The Government of India had introduced, Health

Package Scheme for handloom weavers during the year 1992-93. Under the Scheme the weavers are to be provided financial assistance treatment of diseases like asthma, T.B. and inflammation of the respiratory system, cost testing eyes and spectacles, supply of drinking water, maternity benefits to women weavers, payment of additional compensation for permanent measures of family planning and infrastructure for primary health care.

During the 8th Five Year Plan a total sum of Rs. 2243.38 lakhs was released to the State Governments to cover approximately 4,55,044 weavers under this Scheme. During the year 1997-98, a sum of Rs. 281.09 lakhs was released to the State Governments under this Scheme to cover approx. 67463 weavers.

For the current financial year 1998-99, a budget provision of Rs. 800.00 lakhs has been kept for the Welfare Scheme and out of this Rs. 300,00 lakhs has been earmarked for Health Package Scheme.

Research and development/market surveys & studies

Research & Development activities are being carried out with a view to improve the basic engineering design and concept of the looms/methods used in handloom sector so as to bring about increase in productivity, improvement in quality of products and reduction in drudgery.

Projects have been sanctioned to State Handloom Corporations, Apex Societies, Educational Institutions, Research Institutions and Handloom Organisations. During 1997-98, a sum of Rs. 50 lakhs was released under the Scheme. In 1998-99, five new projects have been sanctioned till January, 1999 to Weavers' Service Centres, Indian Institute of Technology, Delhi, NIFT, Hyderabad, J&K state, etc. An amount of Rs. 15 lakhs approximately has been released so far.

Market development assistance

The Government of India has introduced from the financial year 1989-90, the Market Development Assistance Scheme for providing assistance to the handloom sector. This is in lieu of Share Capital Assistance Scheme to Apex

Societies and Corporations, Share capital and managerial subsidy to Primary Societies and Special Rebate Scheme. The new scheme apart from providing assistance to State Handloom Weavers Cooperative Societies also envisages providing assistance to national level handloom organisations viz. All India Handloom Fabrics Marketing Cooperative Societies Ltd., Delhi; North Eastern Handicrafts and Handloom Development Corporation, Guwahati; Rehabilitation Industries Corporation, New Delhi, etc.

The MDA assistance to the state organisation is shared equally by the respective State Governments and Central Government. The assistance to the National Handloom Organisations is borne entirely by the Central Government. The releases made under the above Scheme during 1998-99 (till December 1998) is Rs. 1874.86 lakhs. The guidelines of the MDA Scheme in respect of Primary Cooperative Societies and the rates of MDA thereof have been revised we.f.1.4.1995 in order to bring more and more such societies under the ambit of the Scheme.

The Scheme was to be discontinued w.e.f.1.4.98. However, on persistent demand from the State Governments, the Scheme has been restored with partial modifications up to March 31, 2000.

Marketing through ACASH

The Association of Corporations and Apex Societies of Handlooms, New Delhi (ACASH) was registered in 1984 under the Societies Registration Act to coordinate and promote marketing in the handloom sector. It serves as the nodal agency for supply of handloom goods to be purchased by Central Government Departments/ Agencies/Public Sector Undertakings, etc. During the year 1998-99 (till 30th November 1998) ACASH received orders worth Rs. 4.45 crores and executed orders of Rs. 3.80 crores and is expected to complete supplies of goods worth of Rs. 10 crores by March, 1999.

Apart from supplies under STS, ACASH is also providing marketing of handloom goods by organising exhibitions at regular intervals. ACASH has also been participating in the international fairs along with state handloom organisations at Heimtextil Fair at Frankfurt and in other places.

All India handloom fabrics marketing cooperative society

The All India Handloom Fabrics Marketing Cooperative Society Ltd., Delhi is a national level cooperative society registered under the Multi-State Cooperative Societies Act, 1984 and comes under the jurisdiction of the Central Registrar of Cooperative Societies, New Delhi.

The procurement of handloom products from Apex and Primary Cooperative Societies and the promotion and marketing of handloom fabric, both within the country and abroad are the main activities. Towards these objectives, the Fabrics Society has set up 27 retail outlets. The Society has its Export Houses at New Delhi, Salem, Chennai and Calcutta. Also, the Society has showrooms at Singapore and Mauritius and Export Promotion Offices at New York for giving an impetus to marketing of Indian handlooms in the foreign markets.

The Society has a Board of Directors including three government nominees. Membership of the Fabrics Society consists of State Level/Regional Level Apex Handloom Weavers Cooperative Societies ('A: class), Primary Level

Handloom Weavers Cooperative Societies ('B' class) and Public Trusts, Government and Government owned/ controlled organisations ('C' class). The number of shares were 1,49,243 in 1996-97 against 1,43,843 in 1997-98. The paid up share capital of the Fabrics Society has declined to Rs. 763.61 lakhs in 1997-98 from Rs. 790.61 lakhs of the previous year.

The Fabrics Society's purchases during 1997-98 amounted to Rs. 4249.21 lakhs against Rs. 5742.58 lakhs in 1996-97. The Society's total export during 1997-98 was Rs. 2018.85 lakhs as against Rs. 2880.58 lakhs in the previous year. During 1997-98, the Society has been able to achieve a profit of Rs. 13.40 lakhs as against Rs. 67.68 lakhs during the previous year. The Society was also able to achieve a sales turnover of Rs. 56.01 crores during 1997-98 as against the turnover of Rs. 71.32 crores during the previous year. During 1998-99, the target has been kept at Rs. 61.97 crores. Till November, 1998, the actual sales were Rs. 30.33 crores.

Census of handloom

As the earlier handloom census was conducted almost a decade ago many changes in the database have taken place since then. Keeping in view these changes, it has been decided to conduct joint census of handlooms and powerlooms throughout the country. The draft Census Report prepared by the National Council of Applied Economic Research is being examined.

The joint census of handlooms and powerlooms will help the Ministry of Textiles in ascertaining the requirement of these sectors in an accurate manner and formulation of more useful and effective schemes for the benefit of handloom and powerloom weavers.

6

Raw Materials

Cotton

Cotton is one of the major crops cultivated in India. It accounts for about 81 % of the total fibre consumption in the spinning mills and about 66% of the total fibre consumption in the textile sector. The Textile Policy Statement of 1985 assured off-take of the farmer's produce at remunerative prices and also laid down that cotton needed by the domestic textile industry would be made available in adequate quantity at reasonable prices. The twin objectives are sought to be achieved through timely announcement of remunerative Minimum Support Price (MSP) to the farmer and through appropriate export-import intervention as and when necessary.

Production and consumption

During the last four decades, the production of cotton rose from 30 lakh bales in 1950-51 to 177.90 lakh bales (170 kgs each) in 1996-97 (including loose cotton of 6.40 lakh bales) and there has also been an increase in the area under cultivation from 58.91 lakh hectares in 1950-51 to 91.22 lakh hectares in 1996-97. The average yield per hectare also rose from 88 kgs in 1950-51 to around 332 kgs in 1996-97. However, there has been a fall in production and productivity and also a slight decline in the area in 1997-98. For the cotton season 1997-98, the production of cotton has been estimated at 158 lakh bales and area at 88.09 lakh hectares. The average yield per hectare works out to 305 kgs. The low yield is mainly because 65% of the area under cultivation is still rainfed. In the Cotton Advisory Board's meeting held on 18-02-99 for the cotton season 1998-99, the production of cotton has been estimated at 161.50 lakh bales (inclusive of 6.25 lakh bales of loose cotton), area at 91.12 lakh hectares and the average yield per hectare at 301 kg.

The largest share in the total production of cotton is of medium staple variety (50%) followed by long staple (41.66%). In contrast, the share of short staple is 8.3% and of extra long staple around 3%. The main cotton producing states are Gujarat, Maharashtra, Andhra Pradesh, Punjab, Madhya Pradesh, Rajasthan, Haryana, Karnataka and Tamil Nadu.

Consumption of cotton has been increasing over the last few years. As against a total consumption of 115.50 lakh bales during 1990-91 (Mill and Non-Mill), the consumption level including consumption by spinning units in the Small Scale Sector has been to the tune of 170.16 lakh bales in 1996-97 but declined to about 159 lakh bales in 1997-98 due to poor crop followed by less demand by a recession hit textile industry. The variety-wise demand for cotton follows the same pattern as the variety-wise production in that the major demand is for medium staple variety. The demand for short staple and extra long staple is relatively lower.

Prices of cotton

The Government announces Minimum Support Price (MSP) for varieties of cotton every year to ensure remunerative prices for the cotton growers. The Cotton Corporation of India (CCI) is the only agency for implementation of this policy. CCI enters the market and makes purchases of cotton under support price operation whenever prices tend to decline and come below MSP level. Since the market prices of all varieties of kapas ruled well above the support prices during the year 1997-98 there was no occasion for the Corporation to undertake any support price operation during the year. However, commercial operation of the Corporation continued as it was during previous years.

The Government of India has fixed the Support Price of two basic varieties of cotton, viz. F-414/H-777/J-34 and H-4 of new crop kapas of Fair Average Quality for Cotton Season 1998-99. The Support Price for F-414/H-777/J-34 variety has been fixed at Rs. 1440/- per quintal, an increase of Rs. 110/- per quintal over 1997-98 Support Price.

Similarly, the Support Price for H-4 (Long Staple variety has been fixed at Rs. 1650 per quintal, an increase of Rs. 120 per quintal over Support Price of 1997-98. For other varieties, the Minimum Support Prices are announced by the Textile Commissioner based on market differentials.

In the cotton season 1997-98, the Government released an export quota of 720 lakh bales of cotton comprising 5.75 lakh bales of staple cotton and 1.45 lakh bales of Bengal Desi and Assam Comilla cotton to State Federations, private trade, CCI, general ginners and modern ginning and pressing units. Due to lower cotton crop in that year and the prevailing lower international prices coupled with poor response for Indian cotton from abroad the Government did not release any further export quota during 1997-98.

As against the above quota released, the actual export quantity shipped was 3.4647 lakh bales including 0.8747 lakh bales as spill over shipment of 1996-97. Further a quota 1,05,000 bales of cotton waste was also released 1997-98. However, the actual shipment was or 0.4878 lakh bales of cotton waste.

For the cotton year 1998-99, the Government has, till 24.02.99, released an export quota of 5 lakh bales of raw cotton. A quota of 1,27,000 bales of cotton waste has also been released, till 24.02.99, for export during the cotton year 1998-99.

Cotton advisory board

The Cotton Advisory Board is a representative body of Government/Growers/Industry/Trade. It advises the Government generally on matters pertaining to production, consumption and marketing of cotton and also provides a forum for liaison among the cotton textile mill industry, the cotton growers, the cotton trade and the Government.

The Board reconstituted as on 21.4.97 has 30 members (as amplified on 26.11.97), of which 5 are Central Government nominees, 3 State Government nominees, 6 representatives of cotton growers, 6 representatives of the textile industry, 5 representatives of the cotton trade, 2 representatives of the cotton research and development, and I representative each of the Powerloom Sector, Handloom Sector and Ginning and Pressing Sector. The members will serve on the reconstituted Board up to 20.4.1999.

International Cotton Advisory Committee (ICAC)

The International Cotton Advisory Committee is an association of governments having an interest in the production, export, import and consumption of cotton. It is an organization designed to promote cooperation in the solution of cotton problems, particularly those of international scope and significance.

The functions of the International Cotton Advisory Committee, as defined in the Rules and Regulations, are

— To observe and keep in close touch with developments affecting the world cotton situation.

— To collect and disseminate complete, authentic, and timely statistics on world cotton production, trade, consumption, stocks and prices.

— To suggest, as and when advisable, to the governments represented, any measures the Advisory Committee considers suitable and practicable for the furtherance of international collaboration directed towards developing and maintaining a sound world cotton economy.

— To be the forum of international discussions on matters related to cotton prices.

The 57th Plenary Session of ICAC was held in Santa Cruz de la Sierra, Bolivia from October 1216, 1998. The Indian delegation, led by Secretary (Textiles) presented the country statement inter alia covering the cotton production, availability, consumption, import, export, price trend and steps taken by the Government to improve cotton development in the country.

For the fiscal year 1998 (July, 1998-June, 1999), India's contribution to ICAC was US $24;300 (approximately Rs. 10, 00,000).

Cotton technology mission

In view of a long felt need to have a co-ordinated approach to cotton development, a Cotton Technology Mission has been proposed to be implemented jointly by the Ministry of Textiles and Ministry of Agriculture. The main objectives are productivity, improving research, marketing and post harvest activities.

The Mission will comprise four mini missions dealing respectively with research, extension of technology, marketing arrangements and improvement in ginning and pressing. The proposal is at an advanced stage of consideration.

Man-made fibre & yarn industry

The man-made fibre and yarn industry comprises fibre and filament yarn manufacturing units of cellulosic and non-cellulosic origin. The cellulosic fibre/yarn industry is under the administrative control of the Ministry of Textiles while non-cellulosic industry is under the control of Ministry of Chemicals and Fertilizers (Department of Chemicals and Petrochemicals). This industry has a vital role to play in the textile industry in the sense that over 30% of the raw material consumed is manufactured by the man-made fibre/yarn industry.

The production of man-made fibre/yarn in general, has increased during 1997-98 as compared to production during 1996-97 The production of viscose staple fibre during 1997-98 had increased by 5% as compared to 1996-97. The production of polyester staple fibre and polyester filament yarn during 1997-98 had increased tremendously by 35.1% and 35.4% respectively, over the previous year.

The production of acrylic staple fibre had decreased marginally by about 4%. The production of viscose filament yarn during 1997-98 remained more or less at the previous year's level. The production of nylon filament yarn declined significantly by about 21%.

Imports

Though the production of man-made fibres and yarns has increased in the past, the production of these fibres and yarns is found inadequate to meet the requirements of the textile industry and other user industries. As such to meet the requirements of user industries adequately, the Government has liberalised imports and all the items of man-made fibres and yarns now stand placed under OGL. Such imports are, however, constantly and carefully monitored to ensure that the indigenous producers are not adversely affected due to unfair competition or unfair trading practices by foreign suppliers.

Exports of man-made fibre/filament yarns

The man-made fibre and yarn industry has contributed to a great deal in the export of man-made textiles. Further, in order to encourage the exports of various fibres and yarns, the Government reviews, from time to time, the export policy for fibres and yarns. While the export of all other man-made fibres and yams is freely allowed., the export of viscose staple fibre is subject to licensing primarily with a view to safeguard the interests of the textile industry.

Research and development

There are two research associations in this sector whose activities are directed and funded jointly by the Government and the industry on the basis of an agreed formula. These research associations are:

(i) Silk & Art Silk Mill's Research Association (SASMIRA), Mumbai and

(ii) Man-Made Textile Research Association (MANTRA), Surat.

7

Woolen Industry

The woollen industry in the country is small in size and widely scattered. It is basically located in the states of Punjab, Haryana, Rajasthan, U.P., Maharashtra and Gujarat. 40% of the woollen units are located in Punjab, 27% in Haryana, 10% in Rajasthan, while the rest of the states account for the remaining 23% of the units.

The woollen industry today presents the following scenario:

(a) Total no. of registered units : 665

(b) Total no. of persons employed in the Woollen Industry : 12 lakhs. (Approx.)

(c) Total exports (excluding man-made carpets, rugs, durries etc.) Rs. in crores

1997-98 : 1128.80

1998-99 : 887.55

(d) Total imports of raw wool

1997-98 : 57.124

Million kg

The woollen industry in India broadly falls under two sectors:

(a) Organised Sector

i) Composite Mills

ii) Combing Units

iii) Worsted and Non-Worsted Spinning Units.

iv) Machine Made Carpet Manufacturing Units.

(b) Decentralised sector

i) Hosiery and Knitting

ii) Powerloom

iii) Hand knotted Carpets, Drugget, Namadahs

iv) Independent Dyeing and Processing Houses.

Since indigenous production of fine quality wool required by the organised mills and the decentralised hosiery sector is very limited, India depends almost exclusively on imports. Import has been mainly from Australia and New Zealand, the major supplier being Australia. New Zealand wool is being imported mainly for carpet sector for blending with indigenous wool. Similarly, for the shoddy sector, import of pre-mutilated woollen/synthetic rags is allowed under OGL.

(A) Indigenous production

The production of indigenous wool in the country has been as under:

Year	Quantity (in million kg.)	
1993-94	39.88	
1994-95	40.62	
1995-96	41.10	(provisional)
1996-97	430	(provisional)
1997-98	44.50	(anticipated)

(B) Import

The figures of import of raw wool and rags (Woollen/ Synthetic) have been as follows:

(a) Raw wool

(Merino/New Zealand-Greasy/scoured)

Year	Quantity in million kg.
1993-94	57.12
1994-95	36.73
1995-96	45.53
1996-97	58.46
1997-98	57.12
1998-99	31.40

(b) Rags (Woollen / Synthetic)

Year	Quantity in Million Kgs.
1993-94	61.45
1994-95	83.02
1995-96	79.87
1996-97	75.28
1997-98	94.42
998-99	44.08

(C) Installed Capacity (as on 31.12.98)

i)	a) Wool Combing	29.28 m. kg.
	b) Synthetic Fibre Combing	3.57 m. kg
ii)	Worsted Spindles	5.74 lakh nos.
iii)	Non-Worsted Spindles	4.11 lakh nos.

iv)	Powerloom	7220 nos. (approx.) (including decentralised sector)
v)	Machine made carpet sector	8.1 lakh sq. mtr. 2.27 m.kg.

Capacity permitted by way of information memorandum and letter of intent as well as for 100% EOU from 1-4-1998 to 31-12-1998:

		Nos.	capacity
(a)	Application for Industrial Licence received from SIA for setting up New Units.	1	6000 Spindles

		Nos.	yarn	fabrics
(b)	Industrial Entrepreneur's Memorandum received from SIA (in terms of Notification No. SO.477 (E) dt. 25.791) for the manufacture of woollen Worsted blended fabrics, tops, Yarns, blanket, etc.	7	1250 Spindles + 1895 MT 750 MT Wool Tops	5.05 Lakh -Sq.m. + 9.00 Lakh.m. 30 Lakh pairs liners

	Nos.	Yarn	Acrylic Mink
(c) 100% EOU	2	1132 tonnes	10.00 Lakh pieces

(D) Production of woollen items

Terms	unit	1994-95	1995-96	1996-97	1997-98 eati.	98-99 esti.
Worsted yarn	mn.kg.	34.0	37.8	37.5	42.00	43
Woollen Yarn (non-worsted)	mn.kg.	56.0	61.6	58.0	31.50	32
Worsted Wearable	mn.mts.	55.0	60.5	60.0	66.00	67
Woollen /Acrylic Knitted goods Hosiery	mn.kg.	12.0	13.2	12.0	13.50	14
Non-Worsted Fabrics.	mn.mtr	12.0	13.2	14.0	17.00	18.00

Central wood development board

The Central Wool Development Board (CWDB) which started functioning from 1989 has been registered as a Society under the Societies Registration Act of Rajasthan to promote growth and development of wool and woollen products through various activities like marketing intelligence, marketing of wool and woollens, price stabilisation, standardisation of wool and woollen products and quality control. The Ministry of Textiles has allocated Rs. 4.50 crores to the Board for 1998-99.

The Board has been administering the following schemes for development of wool industry either with the help of the State Government departments/ bodies or through non-governmental organisations.

Integrated sheep & wool development project

Starting as a pilot project in the year 1991-92, the Integrated Sheep & Wool Development Project covers the aspects of breed improvement, health coverage, product development, marketing assistance and training to sheep breeders in sheep husbandry and productivity. The programme he been extended to all major wool producing states and is being implemented through their Sheep & Wool Department/Animal Husbandrary Departments or other State Governmental Organisations.

During 1998-99 (up to December, 1998) the Board had released Rs. 60.30 lakhs for new scheme; to be taken up in Rajasthan and Gujarat. For ongoing schemes Rs. 9.61 lakhs have been released

Integrated angora rabbit development project

The Integrated Angora Rabbit Development Project was taken up by the Board in 1994-95 in Himachal Pradesh initially and was extended to other hilly areas of western Uttar Pradesh and Darjeeling. The Project is aimed at encouraging rabbit farming in remote hilly areas thereby increasing the production of angora wool resulting in saving of foreign exchange.

Generation of employment in the remote hilly areas is an important component of the project. The projects are implemented through State Government organisations as well as through NGOs.

Under the aegis of the Country Co-operation Framework (UNDP) a programme for angora development is being taken up. The project will commence from 1999-2000.

During 1998-99 (up to December, 1998) the Board had sanctioned one new project to cover 50 families in Himachal Pradesh (Solan District). The Board released Rs. 3.90 lakhs to DRDA, Solan. To expand further this programme, the Board has taken up the matter with the research institutions and agricultural universities for taking up such projects under transfer of technology programme of these institutions.

Machine shearing-cum-training project

This project was taken up by the Board from the year 1993-94 for popularising machine shearing through demonstration and in the process training sheep breeders to take it up as an economically viable activity. The objective was to increase wool production and to generate employment amongst the rural youth. 46 shearing machines have been provided by the Board to the State Government Departments/Organisations and the operational cost of machines as well as stipend and honorarium of trainees and instructors are being financed by the Board under this scheme.

During 1998-99, the CWDB has initiated a process of procuring 20 machines at a cost of Rs. 25 lakhs for distribution to states concerned.

Wool scouring plant & mini wool scouring plant

During the VIIIth Five Year Plan, the Board set up on a pilot basis a Wool Scouring Plant at Beawar, Rajasthan for providing scouring facilities to small and cottage industries engaged in wool sector. In addition, the Board funds have been released to concerned organisations for setting up mini scouring plants in Rajasthan, Himachal Pradesh, Gujarat, Karnataka, Jammu & Kashmir. These are in the process of being established.

Industrial service centre

Although each segment of the woollen industry has its own programmes and priorities about development of technology and improvement of quality of products as well as reduction of the cost, such programmes by the individuals are rather inadequate. To remedy this situation, the Board has set up Industrial Service Centres near the manufacturing heartland equipped with the latest technological know-how at Bikaner (Rajasthan), Amritsar (Punjab), Pithoragarh and Pashulok (Uttar

Pradesh), Bhuj (Gujarat) and Srinagar (J&K). An Industrial Service Centre is being set up at Kullu (Himachal Pradesh) which will provide testing facilities for fibre yarn and woollen fabric and also dyeing facilities for yarn and computer colour matching facilities for woven printed woollens at a cost of Rs. 78.25 lakhs during 1998-99.

Wool testing centre

To provide wool testing facilities to wool growers, wool merchants and the wool industry, the Board has taken up this scheme. During 1998-99, the Board will set up one Wool Testing Centre at Beawar (Rajasthan) at a cost of Rs. 12.95 lakhs. The Board also runs a centre at

Bikaner which was established in 1993-94. In addition, funds have been released to the Government of Karnataka to set up a centre at Dharwar. It is expected that this centre will become functional during 1998-99.

Area based project for wool & woollens development

The scheme taken up by the Board in the year 1994-95 aims at providing common facilities for weavers and spinners, training to wool growers, weavers, upgradation of technology and skills, breed improvement of sheep and marketing of wool and woollens by cluster of 100 to 300 families in a compact area with financial allocation of Rs. 14.48 lakhs. Six such projects have been taken up by the Board in Gujarat, Andhra Pradesh, Maharashtra, and Himachal Pradesh. The scheme is being implemented through the State Government Departments.

Weaving & designing training centre

From the year 1992-93, a Weaving & Designing Training Centre has been working at Jaisalmer (Rajasthan) which was set up by the Board with the objective of training weavers and dyers engaged in woollen handloom production activities in rural areas. The centre has now been shifted to Kullu (Himachal Pradesh) during 1998-99. During 1998-99 (up to December, 1998) 45 weavers have been trained at a cost of Rs. 2.83 lakhs.

Market intelligence network

To create Market Intelligence Network in the country and to build a reliable information system, the Central Wool Development Board has established 10 functionary centres in the main wool producing states of the country. The Board is collecting information on prevailing market rates of wool and yarn, latest trends and transaction of wool and woollen products on a weekly basis through these agents appointed for this purpose. These centres are at Bikaner, Beawar, Panipat, Ludhiana, Shimla, Jammu, Jamnagar, Mirzapur, Mahboob Nagar and Hubli. The Board is compiling and analysing the information received from these centres and this is being disseminated through a Wool Bulletin among the wool growers, wool merchants, wool users and concerned departments/organisations of the Central and State Governments. Till December, 1998 Rs. 1.92 lakhs has been spent.

Woollen expo

To promote sale of wool and woollens and to provide better marketing facilities to weavers and societies in the country, the Central Wool Development Board has been organising Woollen Expos. In the year 1998-99, the Board has decided to organise 5 woollen expos at different places of the country. The Board has made a provision of Rs. 56.25 lakhs.

Up to December, 1998, 4 Expos were organised at Chandigarh, Darjeeling, Jammu and Jodhpur at a cost of Rs. 20.41 lakhs. The Board has organised one Expo at Delhi as a part of Handloom Expo organised by the Development Commissioner (Handlooms), New Delhi in January, 1999.

Promotional activities

Since inception of the Central Wool Development Board, the Board is carrying out various important activities for promotion of wool and woollens in the country like organising seminars and workshops, conducting survey and study, publication of quarterly news magazine-WOOLWAYS, organising fairs, sales cum exhibitions. During 1998-99 a provision of Rs. 8.75 lakhs is proposed for promotional activities.

Human resource development

It has been felt that human resource development aspects have rather been neglected in the wool sector. Since the wool industry has been recognised as thrust area by the Government, it is necessary to make efforts for human resource development to meet the requirements of the wool industry. The following areas have been identified for undertaking training programmes in the country as well as abroad in collaboration with other wool producing countries.

(i) Farm management

(ii) Sheep shearing

(iii) Testing and report writing

(iv) Wool marketing

(v) Processing of wool & woollen products

(vi) Quality control.

In the year 1998-99, the Board intends to depute 50 persons to train/study under this scheme with financial provision of Rs. 5.00 lakhs.

8

Sericulture

India continues to be the second largest producer of silk in the world. Among the four varieties of silk produced during 1997-1998, mulberry accounts for 92.2%, eri 5.3%, tasar 2.1% and muga 0.4% of the total raw silk production in the country.

Sericulture is an important labour intensive and agro-based cottage industry providing gainful occupation to about six million persons in the rural and semi urban areas in India. Of these, a sizeable number of workers belong to the economically weaker sections of the society. There is substantial involvement of women in this industry

Physical progress

The physical progress is as under:-

S.No.	Particulars	1997-98 Achievement	1998-99 Anticipated achievement
I.	Area under Mulberry (lakh hec.)	2.82	2.90
II.	Production of Raw Silk (tonnes)	15,236	15,236
III.	Employment (lakh persons)	60.57	60.57

The central silk board (CSB)

The Central Silk Board was constituted by an Act of

Parliament. The Board currently provides research and development, training, extension and basic seed support to the industry. It also discharges the function of certifying silk goods for export and extends support to states in the form of joint projects and offers developmental schemes.

Research and development

The main Research & Training Institutes of the CSB function to provide R&D and training support for the development of sericulture. The Institutes at Mysore (Karnataka), Berhampore (West Bengal) and Pampore (J&K) deal with mulberry sericulture and the one at Ranchi (Bihar) deals with tasar. A main Research Institute is being established at Jorhat (Assam) for muga. Research on muga and eri is now being carried out by the Institutes located at Boko (Assam) and Mendipathar (Meghalaya) respectively.

Regional Sericultural Research Stations (RSRS) for mulberry and non-mulberry have been tackling the regional field issues of industry. Besides, a network of Research Extension Centres for mulberry and non-mulberry also function to disseminate the research findings. In order to provide R&D support in post-cocoon technology, the Board has established a Central Silk Technological Research Institute (CSTRI) at Bangalore. CSB has also setup a Silkworm Seed Technology Laboratory (SSTL) in Bangalore (Karnataka), a Silkworm & Mulberry Germplasm Station (SMGS) at Hosur (Tamil Nadu) and a Seri-Bio Technology Laboratory (SBRL) at Bangalore.

Research work on the on-farm side is directed mainly to evolve mulberry varieties which give high leaf yield with stress tolerance, breeding superior silkworm races, besides evolving improved techniques of silkworm rearing, control of pests and diseases of both mulberry and silkworms. During the year 1998-99, 9 silkworm hybrids were tested at the Race Authorisation Test Centres. Evaluation is under process. The NRDC has offered the bed disinfectant "Vijetha" to M/s. Vetcare, Bangalore for commercialisation and sales of the same have commenced. Two other products are in the process of commercialisation by NRDC.

Patenting of fifteen technologies in pre and post cocoon areas is being followed up by NRDC. Thirteen new technologies in post-cocoon sector and from the pre-cocoon areas are expected to be offered to NRDC for patenting during 1998-99.

Research work on tasar, muga and eri silk is directed towards improvement of productivity potential and to develop an Integrated Pest Management Technique for prevention of pests. Under in-situ condition, 5 Eco-races of tasar have been raised under different habitats for adaptability.

An integrated technology for grainage operation, covering preservation, oviposition, incubation and transportation of eggs has been developed for tasar culture, and it is under process for patenting. An oviposition device has been developed in case of muga culture and field trials are being conducted.

On the post-cocoon side, efforts are being made to popularise a multiend reeling package for reeling quality silk from bivoltine and crossbreed cocoons, as per a scheme sanctioned by Government of India during July, 1997. Around 50 entrepreneurs, who have applied for the machinery so far are expected to obtain equipment supply in 1998-99.

The Central Silk Technological Research Institute, Bangalore has also fabricated a low-cost multifuel drying chamber, a tail end cutter and slit buttons which are being field tested. Silk knitted fabrics i.e., pique, interlock, single and double jersey, plaited fabrics have been developed and being analysed for various fabric properties.

The Research Institutes of CSB have developed low-cost improved pedal-cum-motorised reeling-cum-twisting devices for tasar and muga and improved spinning wheel for muga and eri, which will produce better quality silk/spun yam with less wastage, thereby fetching better income. These improved reeling/ spinning devices are being popularised through the Demonstration-cum-Technical Service Centres and through NGOs/Cooperatives under the CDP programmes, being implemented in 9th plan.

A network of Demonstration-cum-Technical Service Centres imparts training in silk reeling and spinning. Besides, in some important weaving centres, these Centres provide technical services in post cocoon areas. Besides these, Silk Conditioning and Testing Houses are functioning for testing of raw silk, Eco-Testing laboratories at Bangalore, Varanasi and Bhagalpur have recently commenced trial testing of physical, chemical and eco-parameters of textile products. One more Eco-Testing Laboratory at Jammu is being setup.

A second phase project of five year duration initiated from 1.4.1997 with assistance from the Japanese International Co-operation Agency (JICA) for verification of technologies evolved in the first phase and for demonstration of bivoltine technology packages is in progress. Under the project, JICA has made available so far in the second phase, ,he services of Team Leader, Coordinator, long-term experts, 10 short- term experts and accepted 9 Indian scientists for training under the counterpart training component. Up to December 1998, four bivoltine technology verification trials with farmers were conducted and the performance of cocoon crops have shown gradual improvement.

In the first phase, JICA made available 12 long-term experts, 28 short-term experts and trained 28 counterparts, apart from providing equipment valued at about 352 million Japanese Yen.

Silkworm seed organisation

Under the National Silkworm Seed Project, a network of Basic Seed Farms (BSF) (to produce and supply the basic seed for production of commercial silkworm seed by CSB and State department units) and Silkworm Seed Production Centres (SSPC) are functioning in different States to support industry. These Commercial Silkworm Seed Production Centres have produced 165.47 lakh dfls during 1998-99 (up to December, 1998). Similarly, on the tasar side, the CSB has established 19 Basic Seed Multiplication & Training Centres (BSM&TC) with 3 sub-units for supply of tropical tasar basic seed and I oak tasar grainage and 3 BSM&TCs for supply of oak tasar basic seed. Under muga sector 7 Basic Seed Farms (BSF) and 2 Silkworm Seed Production Centres are functioning.

For production and supply of eri seed, CSB has established I Silkworm Seed Production Centre. In the year 1998-99 (up to December, 1,998), 12.07 lakh tasar basic seed, 0.76 lakh oak tasar basic seed and 1.35 lakh muga basic seed have been produced and supplied to states. The muga and eri SSPC set up in VIII plan have produced up to December, 1998, (in the year 1998-99), 0.44 lakh & 0.45 lakh commercial seed respectively.

Training

The CSB organises a number of training programmes at its Research and Training Institutes. The total number of persons trained during 1997-98 and 1998-99 (up to December, 1998) is detailed below:

	No. of candidates trained					
	1997-98			1998-99 (up to December, 1998)		
Training Course	No. of Courses conducted	Nos. trained	Category	No. of courses conducted	Nos. trained	Category
1. Structured Course	6	60	DOS	2	32	DOS
2. Capsule	34	828	CSB/DOS/ NGO	30	556	CSB/ DOS/ NGO
3. Adhoc Training	1	331	College Student/Staff/ Entrepreneur	1	897	College Student/ Staff/ Entrepreneur
4. Foundation Course Induction/Re Orientation	1	15	CSB Officers/ Staff	1	10	Officials (Bangladesh)

Catalytic development schemes initiated during IX plan (1997-2002)

Based on the suggestions of the Working Group for IX Plan and findings of several studies, the profile of the developmental schemes of the CSB for the IX Plan have been substantially altered. Thirty six catalytic schemes of the CSB had received approval from July, 1997 up to November, 1998 at a cost of Rs. 89.27 crore. These are targeted to motivate State efforts towards productivity, quality and market support.

Central Silk Board has so far received and approved 190 proposals from 21 states for a total value of Rs. 75.70 crores of which CSB's share is Rs. 38.62 crore under the above schemes. The states have initiated implementation of these schemes in 1998-99.

The CSB is also implementing joint projects for development of sericulture in specific areas. These are discussed hereunder.

Poorvanchal semiculture development project in Uttar Pradesh

A Poorvanchal Sericulture Development Project is being implemented jointly by Central Silk Board and the Department of Sericulture, Government of Uttar Pradesh in three Eastern Districts viz. Varanasi, Gazipur and Bhadohi at a total cost of Rs. 5.64 crore between 1993-94 and 15th June, 1999. Of the total project cost, Rs. 3.01 crore is borne by Central Silk Board and the remaining Rs. 2.63 crore by the Government of Uttar Pradesh.

The project envisages raising of 3000 acres of mulberry plantation.

The project also envisages an incremental raw silk production of 77.1 metric tons by the end of the project period. An expenditure of Rs. 2.67 crore has been booked up to December, 1998 under the Central and State share. Under the project, 8 TSCs, 18 CRCs, 1 REC, 1 Cocoon Market, 3 Project Sub-Offices and I Project Monitoring Cell have also been set up besides strengthening of 2 State grainages.

The REC at Varanasi set up under the project has been organising regular field days and demonstrations of package of practices for mulberry cultivation, silkworm rearing and disease control, and has from inception (1993-94) up to December, 98, organised training for 506 farmers and taken 114 farmers on study tour.

The plantation raised and surviving up to January, 1999 is of the order of 1844 acres and the CSB has fielded the extension team.

Action plan for north eastern states

The Central Silk Board, in collaboration with the 7 North Eastern States has launched during 1995-96 an Action Plan for intensifying mulberry sericulture development in the North Eastern region at a total cost of Rs. 12.89 crore, of which, CSB's share is Rs. 6.03 crore. The States other than Tripura bear Rs. 2.31 crore. The State of Tripura has an assistance of Rs. 1.31 crore. In addition a contribution of Rs. 3.24 crore for the Action Plan was also received from Ministry of Human Resource Development.

The completion of the project is expected to result in expansion of mulberry plantations by 7000 acres to produce 73.26 metric tons of raw silk and employment to 28,000 persons (excluding Meghalaya State which did not sign the MOU).

Under the mulberry component of the Action Plan, 5592 acres of mulberry plantation has been raised up to November, 1998, besides setting up 6 Project Offices and I REC, 6148 farmers and 250 reelers have been trained. 1909 nos. rearing kits were supplied to farmers. Besides trainers', training has been imparted to 55 persons. One P2 Farm-cum-Grainage is being established at Tripura. An expenditure of Rs. 3.07 crore. is anticipated up to the end of December, 1998.

Under the non-mulberry part of the Action Plan, the following components were completed in 1996-97 at a cost of Rs. 3.12 crore over the VIII plan period.

Muga

a. Augmentation of muga food plants.

b. Establishment of 2 muga SSPCs.

c. Survey of muga growing areas.

d. Product development and diversification of muga.

Eri

a. Augmentation of eri food plants.

b. Establishment of one eri SSPC.

c. Product Development and Domestic Marketing of eri.

d. Assistance to Agencies for Marketing of eri cocoons.

Government of India have extended the Action Plan in North Eastern States up to 31.3.99. Two evaluation teams have been fielded by CSB.

Silk exports

To enable exporters of silk goods access to quality silk at international prices, the Government has allowed silk exporters the facility to import raw material requirements on duty-free basis under the Advance Licensing Scheme (ALS). In the current policy, the input output norms have been liberalised and value addition rationalised.

Under the EPCG "Zero Duty Scheme", the threshold level for duty exemption on import of capital goods has been brought down from Rs. 5 crore to Rs. 1 crore. Besides, assistance for garment design is being provided to NIFT by CSB through the Indian Silk Export Promotion Council.

Silk goods certified for exports during the years 1996-97, 1997-98 and 1998-99 (up to September, 1998) is as follows:

Year	Certified Exports (in Rs. crores)
1996-97	880.44
1997-98	926.29
1998-99 (till December 1998)	768.55

The Government have also permitted import of mulberry silk under SIL with the condition that the value of the surrendered SIL shall be three times the CIF value of the imported goods.

Indian silk export promotion council

The Indian Silk Export Promotion Council continues to undertake activities relating to promotion of exports of natural silk goods from India and to act as the registering authority for silk exporters.

The Council produces and disseminates information to its members about market developments in the world, changes in the trade policies etc. through its weekly bulletin known as the "SILK NET". The silk sample catalogues containing sample swatches of the full range of silks available in India brought out by the Council are available to potential buyers, importing textile agents and Indian Missions abroad.

Tribal sub-plan

Sericulture being an agro-based cottage industry plays an important role in the rural economy of the country. The major programmes being implemented by CSB are towards Research and Development and basic seed supply. Programmes for specific target groups are implemented by the States.

Miscellaneous

To plan for optimal use of infrastructure created under the NSP and to reassess the manpower requirements of CSB, Ministry of Textiles has commissioned a study by National Institute of Science Technology & Development Studies (NISTADS).

The Draft Report on optimum utilisation of Infrastructure and Manpower of Central Silk Board was presented by NISTADS on 28th July 1998 to Secretary (Textiles) in Udyog Bhavan. After detailed discussions, NISTADS have been advised to recast the Report. The process of restructuring will be undertaken in the Central Silk Board.

An International Conference on Wild Silk Moths was held in Bhubaneswar between 11-14, November, 1998. Eminent scientists from India and abroad attended the Conference. Under the aegis of the Country Co-operation Framework I of UNDP, a programme in the non mulberry sector will be taken up during 1999-2000. The programme is presently under finalisation.

9

Handicrafts

The Handicrafts sector enjoys a special significance in the country's economy in terms of employment generation as well as earnings of foreign exchange through exports. This sector alone employs around 81.5 lakh persons at present. However the exact figure of artisans would be known only after the completion of the all India Census of Handicraft artisans. The majority of this work force belongs to the women, SC/ST minority and other weaker sections of the society.

During the last few years the growth of this sector has been phenomenal which is evident from the fact that the employment has increased from 48.25 lakhs persons during 1991-92 to 81.5 (estimated) lakhs in the year 1997-98. The promotion of handicrafts industries is primarily the responsibility of the State Governments. However, the office of the Development Commissioner (Handicrafts) has been implementing various developmental schemes at the central level to supplement state activities in the handicrafts sector besides exploring the new thrust areas.

Development programmes

The Office of the Development Commissioner for handicrafts implements Plan schemes covering various areas like training, design development, technology upgradation, market promotion, exhibition and publicity, exports, etc. Some of these are outlined below:

Training

Training is given for upgradation of skills of the existing craftsmen as well as to unskilled ones with a view to expanding employment and the production base of crafts with high potential for economic growth and for revival of languishing crafts.

Training is given through:-

— Departmentally-run-training centres.

— Apprenticeship training scheme under mastercraftsmen following the 'Guru-Shishya tradition'.

— Other organisations like Central/State Handicrafts Corporations, Apex Cooperatives and voluntary bodies.

Departmentally run training centres

Handknotted carpets

The Handknotted carpet industry in India employs over 15.5 lakhs of weavers in a number of States including Jammu and Kashmir, Uttar Pradesh, Rajasthan, Madhya Pradesh, Bihar, Andhra Pradesh, Karnataka and Tamil Nadu. More than, 90% of the carpets produced in India are exported. Exports amounted to more than Rs. 2151.86 crores (US M$ 55.3,46) during 1997-98. During 1998-99 the export of carpets have been targeted at Rs. 2527 crores. The achievement till December 1998 was Rs. 1423.41 crores (P).

As a step towards rationalisation, 68 Carpet Training Centres have been closed. At present 261 Departmental Basic Training Centres and 107 Advance Training Centres are in existence all over India. The peripatetic character of these centres has made it possible to bring a wider area under the programme. A programme has also been successfully initiated to expand the carpet production base in the country through institutional training in the hilly areas of Western U.P., Northern Madhya Pradesh and some places of South India. Its target is to train 3500 trainees during 1998-99 in carpet weaving.

Besides, there are seven centres for washing and finishing of carpets where training in post-weaving operation is imparted. Apart from imparting training, these centres also ensure finishing of carpets before disposal.

In order to provide modern facilities in pre-loom and post-loom operation in carpet weaving, an Indian Institute of Carpet Technology has been set up at Bhadohi, Uttar Pradesh. The institute will impart training to practising craftsmen in upgrading their technical knowledge with reference to weaving, dyeing, designing, finishing etc.

Printed textiles

To promote handprinting of textiles and upgrade the skills of artisans, 9 Handblock Printing Training Centres are being run by the office of the Development Commissioner (Handicrafts) throughout the country. In each centre 25 trainees get training for a period of one year duration. I operation of this scheme, during 1998-99, Rs. 70.50 lakhs has been allocated.

For technology upgradation in handprinting, a National Craft Institute of Handprinted Textiles has been functioning at Jaipur to study the present technique of production and suggest improvements in design, styles and techniques of handprint During the year 1998-99, a total allocation of Rs. 22.50 lakhs has been made, out of which 1 December, 1998, a sum of Rs. 12.92 lakhs has I utilised. The Institute has undertaken a survey of three identified clusters for ascertaining the census of the craft/ craftspersons. The institute organises workshops, training programmes etc., in the remaining part of the year. There are two Common Facility Service Centres at Farrukhabad and Ahmedabad.

The main objective of centres is to provide pre and post printing facilities to local craftspersons in order to improve quality of their printed fabrics and ensure fastness of colour. During the year 1998-99, a total amount of Rs. 24.50 lakhs was allocated out of i Rs. 10.00 lakhs has been utilised till December 1998. The Office of the Development Commissioner (Handicrafts) has conducted a survey of these centres to evaluate the n continue the set up in future in view of sub-c performance observed in the recent past.

The Regional Design and Technical Development Centres (RD&TDC), Bangalore has expanded the Dye Research Laboratory by which detailed experiment and research are being conducted to find out the usefulness of using various materials. An amount of Rs. 16.10 lakhs has been sanctioned for the scheme during 1998-99 and till December, 1998 a sum of Rs. 3.98 lakhs has been utilised.

Extension unit in textiles weaving under regional design & technical development centre

The objective of this scheme is to conduct research and dissemination of information on handprinted textiles. This Design centre also has 4 extension units which impart training in handblock printing apart from demonstration in techniques evolved/developed in handprinted textiles. During 1998-99 an amount of Rs 29.02 lakhs has been sanctioned for operation of this scheme. So far till December, 1998, a sum of Rs. 3.40 lakhs has been utilised.

Art metalwares

In Art metalware, 19 training centres are functioning in

the country to impart training in different processes of the metalcraft production like moulding, casting, sheet metal fabrication, scrapping, polishing, welding, engraving and icon making etc.

Out of 19 centres, 13 centres are functioning in Uttar Pradesh, 3 in Andhra Pradesh and I each in Haryana, Tamil Nadu and Kerala; Majority of the centres are situated in minority dominated areas. The duration of the training course is for one year. 8393 trainees have been trained till 1997-98, out of which 380 trainees were trained during 1997-98. A majority of the trained persons are gainfully employed in their respective crafts. Candidates belonging to reserved categories are encouraged for training in these centres.

The Metal Handicrafts Service Centre set up at Moradabad with UNDP assistance provides facilities for Silver Plating, Powder Coating, Lacquering, Research and Development, Testing of metal and training of artisans in the higher skills.

Cane and bamboo

Thirty five Departmental Training Centres in Cane and Bamboo crafts have been set up since 1978-79 in different parts of the country. These centres are shifted from one place to another depending upon the availability of raw material and adequate number of candidates for training etc. The duration of the training is one year. During the year 1997-98, 788 trainees were trained. During the year 1998-99, up to December 1998, 242 trainees have been trained and approximately 638 trainees will be trained during 1998-99.

To monitor the activities of these training centres, there are 3 Field Administrative Cells located at Bangalore, Guwahati and New Delhi.

Bamboo and development institute, Agartala

This Institute was set up at Agartala during the year 1974 with a view to developing proper techniques for treatment and preservation of Cane and Bamboo handicraft items by using suitable chemicals and lacquer to protect them from insects, fungus and to disseminate these techniques to the various pockets of this craft by giving practical demonstrations. Besides this, there is also a training centre located in the premises of Bamboo and Cane Development Institute (BCDI) Agartala.

The training course is advanced in nature and duration of the course is six months with each batch consisting of 40 trainees. Thus this centre imparts training to 80 practising craftpersons in a calendar year. The trainees are selected from all over India as well as outside India (i.e., from centres, which fall under the purview of the Colombo Plan).

A stipend of Rs. 400 per month is paid for the local trainees and Rs. 500 for those coming from outside Tripura, Besides this, TA/DA is also given for the trainees coming from outside Tripura for to and fro journeys, for joining the training course and going back to their respective places after completion of the training. During the IXth Plan, upgradation of the institute is proposed.

Woodwares

There are three departmental training centres in Lacquerware craft: two centres at Channapatna (Karnataka) and one at Tirupati (Andhra Pradesh). The duration of training in each centre is of one year and 25 trainees are enrolled in each centre. 63 trainees will be trained during 1998-99.

Apprenticeship training scheme

With the objective of preserving and reviving languishing crafts and to impart training in crafts which need specialised skills, an Apprenticeship Training Scheme under mastercraftsmen on the pattern of 'Guru-Shishya Parampara" has been implemented. Training is imparted in wooden lacquerware, ornamental textiles, wood, grass, leaves, reed and fibre, stone and pottery, toys and dolls and other craft. About 5 to 15 trainees per session, depending upon the crafts discipline are placed under a mastercraftsman for training.

During the year 1997-98, 1200 trainees have been trained. Up to December 1998, 510 trainees have been trained and up to March 1999, 3480 trainees will be trained.

Training through other organisations

Training in various crafts are also imparted through other organisations viz. Central/State Corporations, apex societies and voluntary organisations engaged in development and of handicrafts. The objective of the scheme is to (i) increase the production base of crafts having high market demand, (ii) upgrade skills of existing craftpersons and (iii) revive languishing crafts. The duration of the training course under this scheme is 6 to 12 months depending on the craft.

During 1997-98, under Training Scheme A (Crafts other than Carpet), 690 trainees have been trained. Under Training Scheme B (Carpet) 325 trainees have been trained. Up to December, 1998, 285 trainees have been trained and up to March, 1999, 720 trainees will be trained under scheme A.

Training of trainers and master craftsperson

It is a training module prepared for the craft training instructors (trainers) who are working in Government Departments or with NGO's and State Corporations who are not very exposed to the change taking place in the crafts world because of volatility of the market demand.

Besides, the techniques of production are also undergoing changes so as to achieve perfection in skills and quality. Presently, there is no scheme to organise refresher courses for the Instructors. The Task Force has therefore recommended formulation of a Scheme for organising training workshops for a duration of 2 weeks in the Regional Design and Technical Development Centres (RD&TDCs) located in Bangalore, Guwahati, Bhopal, Calcutta and Delhi, in other reputed Institutions/Engineering Colleges, etc. to acquaint them as well as other practising mastercraftsmen with the latest developments that have taken place in the field of design technology and production workshops as a part of visiting facility. The scheme will address:-

a) new design concepts;

b) use of improved tools;

c) new production techniques;

d) new technologies;

e) production management and costing;

f) economic & commercial intelligence and

g) packaging.

The Design Centres will organise 5 such training programmes during the year in various crafts, for a group of 20 artisans in each course. The expenses on account of TA/DA, wage compensation, reading material and other training aids will be provided by the Office of the DC (Handicrafts). The target during 1998-99 is to train 140 artisans.

Design and technical development

Keeping in view the need to make handicrafts a viable economic activity by making the products more acceptable in the market, six Regional Design and

Technical Development Centres at New Delhi, Bhopal, Mumbai, Bangalore, Calcutta and Guwahati are functioning to provide design and technical guidance accompanied by training facilities in different crafts to artisans in their respective regions.

The main activities of the design and technical development in handicrafts are :

a) To make crafts a success in the contemporary market and thus enhance income and employment opportunities and

b) To preserve the craft's traditional beauty which is the main source of strength to a designer.

These centres are concerned with the development of new designs and products in certain crafts in collaboration with outside designers. Various Design Workshops in various crafts are being organised from the empanelled designers and alumni of NID/NIFIF in the craft pockets by these centres. Besides this, the workshops are also being conducted through the department. 42 Design workshop have been sanctioned to six RDTDC's for 1998-99, for which Rs. 32.46 lakhs have been allocated. Total amount sanctioned under the scheme for 1998-99 is Rs. 48.55 lakhs.

Design assistance is also extended to State Corporations/ Apex Societies as well as Voluntary Organisations through a scheme of grant-in-aid for engaging professional designers to evolve new designs/products. Under the approved scheme an amount of Rs. 1.00 lakh per workshop is being given as assistance and payment is being made in two instalments

During the year 1997-98, 1478 designs in various crafts were developed by the Design Centres including Voluntary Organisations in different crafts. During the current financial year i.e. 1998-99, it is expected that 1800 new designs would be developed. To upgrade the Regional Design & Technical Development Centre, Bangalore, the study had been entrusted to National Institute of Design, Ahmedabad.

A new Scheme "Supply of Modern Tools & Kits", has been formulated during 9th Plan and action has been initiated to identify modern tools for various crafts in collaboration with Indian Institute of Technology, New Delhi. The design Centres have also been endeavouring to develop improved tools and equipment for improved productivity by craftsmen and upgradation of products.

During the year 1998-99, various proposals had been received from Corporations/ Voluntary Organisations under the approved scheme. Till December, 1998, 19 Design Workshops have been sanctioned. During 1998-99 (till 31.12.98), 11 Design Workshops have already been conducted.

Own premises are being acquired for RDTDC, Guwahati at total cost of Rs. 85.00 lakhs from HOUSEFED, Guwahati.

NID had been engaged to suggest modernisation of RDTDC, Bangalore.

Marketing

During the year 1998-99, the marketing centres are organising 6 crafts bazaars, six product promotion programmes, 30 State level Marketing Workshops, 47 Local Level Marketing Workshops, 30 Fairs and Festivals and 5 National Level Melas. Besides these, the Office of the DC (Handicrafts) is organising 2 National Handicrafts Expos and 2 Mini-Handicrafts Expos at various places in the country.

During the year 1998-99 so far till December 1998, 20 programmes have been organised benefiting 1252 persons with a sale of Rs. 173 lakhs.

The main objective of the marketing schemes is to provide ample opportunity to artisans to market their products directly to customers and get a fair price for their crafts. With a view to boost the domestic market, Dilli Haat has been set up in Delhi, in which craftspersons/NGOs/Voluntary Organisations participate from different parts of the country from time to time. Keeping in view the excellent response, efforts are being made to set up similar types of permanent Haats in other important cities.

Special efforts are being made to explore new foreign markets. The two Export Promotion Councils initiated a number of measures during 1998-99 to this effect which includes organisation of Buyer-Seller Meets, participation in fairs and festivals, sponsoring of sales-cum-study teams abroad and organisation of Indian Handicrafts Fair and Carpet Fair annually in India.

Master Creation at Dilli Haat was organised from 8th to 14th December 1998 with an aim to provide opportunity to the National Award winners in selling their exquisite masterpieces.

Financial assistance to central/state handicrafts corporations and apex societies

(A) Share participation in central/state handicrafts corporations and apex co-operative societies

With a view to enhancing the working capital base of the beneficiary organisations, the office of the Development Commissioner for Handicrafts provides equity to State Handicrafts Development Corporations and Apex Co-operative Societies in order to enable them to undertake procurement of handicrafts directly from artisans and distribute raw materials.

During the year 1998-99 a sum of Rs. 145.00 lakhs has been allocated to State Handicrafts Development Corporations/Apex Societies.

(B) Scheme of financial assistance to various central/ state corporations, apex cooperative societies and non-government organisations for setting up new emporia and renovation of existing emporia under market development scheme.

The objective of this Scheme is to financially assist the implementing agencies to enable them to open new emporia and renovate/expand the existing emporia. The Scheme has been modified on the basis of the recommendations of the Sub-Group on Handicrafts.

Under the modified scheme, 50% of the capital expenditure (non-recurring) is provided by the Office of the DC(H) as grant in aid and the remaining 50% is contributed by the concerned State Government/ Corporation/Apex Societies/ Voluntary Organisations, subject to the maximum limits as under:

1. Rs. 5.00 lakhs for renovation of existing emporium.
2. Rs. 20.00 lakhs for a new emporium to be housed in its own premises in a metropolis and Rs. 15.00 lakhs at other places.
3. Rs. 10.00 lakhs for a new emporium to be opened in rented premises.

During 1998-99 an amount of Rs. 150.00 lakhs will be released for renovation of 10 emporia, opening of 15 new emporia to a number of State Corporations/Apex Societies/Voluntary Organisations. So far till December 1998, a sum of Rs. 31.05 lakh has been released.

(C) Financial assistance for setting up of craft development centres

To meet the persistent need of craftspersons in the areas of design guidance, raw material depot, common facility services and marketing, a scheme of Craft Development Centres to offer a package of services to a cluster of craftsmen is in operation. During 1997-98, 30 Craft Development Centres were sanctioned and an amount of Rs. 145.50 lakhs was given as financial assistance to various organisations. During the year 1998-99, 18 Craft Development Centres will be sanctioned and an amount of Rs. 60 lakhs will be released. So far till December 1998, a sum of Rs. 22.56 lakhs has been released. In all, so far 158 Craft Development Centres have been established.

Training programs for members of primary handicrafts co-operative societies

With the sponsorship from the Development Commissioner (Handicrafts), The National Cooperative Union of India organised Members Education Programme in different parts of the country at the grassroot level. During 1998-99 it is targeted to benefit 8000 persons through course programmes. Till December, 1998, 2242 persons have benefited through these courses.

Publicity

In order to promote sales of crafts abroad and in the domestic market, publicity arrangements were made by printing folders, brochures and catalogues on crafts provided in different states through the State Handicrafts Corporations, Apex Co-operative Societies and Voluntary Organisations. 24 new proposals for printing of brochures, folders and catalogues and 5 proposals for making video films were cleared during the financial year 1997-98. These Video films are under production. Besides 24 new proposals for printing of folders, brochures and catalogues have been received during the year 1998-99 along with production of five more new video films namely: -

1. Jute Handicrafts of India
2. Musical Instruments

3. Sankhera of Gujarat
4. Nirmal Craft of A.P.
5. Bamboo Craft of North East

"Handicrafts Week" to popularise handicrafts, was celebrated from 8-15 December, 1998 by printing and distributing posters, by releasing advertisements in newspapers, journals and by announcing a rebate of 10% on purchase of handicrafts during the week. Publicity by Radio Spot through AIR was also done.

Exhibition

Financial assistance is also given as grant-in-aid to Corporations, Co-operatives and Voluntary Organisations to organise exhibitions. The office also sponsors exhibitions in India and abroad under the Cultural Exchange Programme with different countries. Under the agreed Cultural Exchange Programme with different countries, this office sponsored exhibitions on handicrafts abroad and deputed master craftspersons to give liv, demonstrations.

The following Handicrafts Exhibitions were conducted during 1998 - 99 under the Culture, Exchange Programme:

(i) Tunisian Handicrafts Exhibition in Delhi from 24 October - 2 November 1998.

(ii) DPRK (North Korea) Exhibition in New Delhi from 24 November - 3 December 199

During the year 1998-99, it is anticipated that 350 exhibitions with an estimated expenditure Rs. 402 lakhs, will be organised through state handicraft corporations/ voluntary organisations/apex societies and till December 1998, 97 exhibitions with an estimated sales of Rs. 2.91 crores have been organised through various organisations.

To have a regular system of feedback on the economic, social, aesthetic and promotional aspects of various handicrafts and craftspersons in this sector, efforts are being made under this scheme to buildup a reliable data base. Though a number of area/craft specific surveys have been undertaken in the past, these could not provide sufficient information for national level policy formulation.

A complete census of the handicrafts sector was undertaken. The findings of the Census Report, which are expected to be ready shortly, would provide reliable and exhaustive data on employment, production, earnings, etc. at the district/state/national level. Based on the results of the census, follow up studies on various aspects will be undertaken in the coming years.

During 1998-99, it is proposed to conduct an evaluation of NGO's and a concurrent evaluation of a few existing schemes of the office-

Scheme for survival of languishing crafts

A scheme for identification, survey and revival of languishing crafts through such measures as design development, training, pilot projects, exhibitions and publicity has been introduced. Financial assistance is being given to Voluntary Organisations, Apex Co-operative Societies and Corporations under this scheme.

During 1998-99 it is proposed to revive 2 languishing crafts from each region.

National awards to master craftspersons

'A scheme of National Awards to outstanding master craftspersons focusing attention on their high level of skills and their exquisite creations was initiated in 1965. Each award-winner gets Rs. 25,000/- in cash, a tamrapatra, an Angavastram and a certificate. Since its inception, 714 craftspersons/we avers have received National Awards by 1997.

Besides, 501 National Merit Certificates were given to outstanding master craftspersons and weavers for their excellence in crafts up to the year 1997. Each Merit Certificate winner is given Rs. 5000/- in cash and a certificate.

Pension to master craftspersons in indigent circumstances

A scheme for pension to master craftspersons unable to work due to old age, has been in operation since 1973-74. 206 master craftspersons under the above pension scheme, are availing pensionary benefits @ Rs. 500/- per month during 1998-99.

Social security schemes

Social security and welfare of artisans is another area which is being given special attention. Three new schemes namely:- (i) Workshed-cum-housing/ Workshed, (ii) Health package for artisans and (iii) Group Insurance for artisans have been introduced during 1994-95. These Schemes have been further modified on the basis of the recommendations of the subgroup on handicrafts to suit the changing requirements of the artisans. These schemes have become a very popular measure for providing a security net to the craftsmen. In the coming years, all State Handicrafts Corporations and leading NGOs will be encouraged to avail the financial assistance from the Government and bring more and more craftspersons under this security net.

During 1998-99 it is proposed to construct 2,100 worksheds and 275 workshed-cum-houses. So far till December 1998, 800 worksheds and 375 workshed-cum-houses have been sanctioned to be constructed. 6000 and 9000 artisans are sanctioned to be covered under Group Insurance and Health Package Schemes respectively.

New schemes proposed to be introduced during 1998-99

Urban haats

Under the Scheme, Dilli Haat type infrastructure would be created at prime locations where artisans and weavers would get an opportunity to sell their products to the consumers. In IXth Five Year Plan, setting up of 20 such Haats is contemplated out of which five would be set up during 1998-99.

For creating the needed infrastructure, the State Governments shall provide land and the total cost of the project shall be borne by the Central Government to the extent of 70% (to be shared equally by the office of the DC (Handicrafts), and DC (Handlooms), the balance 30% being the share of the State Governments.

National level design centre at Moradabad

National Level Design Centre is proposed to be set up at Moradabad to cater to the design needs of the area.

Export of handicrafts

Export of handicrafts including handknotted carpets were recorded at Rs. 6457.69 crores (prov.) during 1997-98 representing an increase of 14.73% over the export of Rs. 5628.62 crores (prov.) recorded during previous year. The export target for the year 1998-99 has been fixed at Rs. 7776.00 crores. The main items which exhibited increase in exports during 1997-98 are Zari and Zari goods (14.49%), Art metalware (12.37%), Woodware (20.90%), Handprinted textiles and scarves (25.16%) and embroidered and crocheted goods (89.68%).

Export promotion activities

During the year 1997-98, 3 Exhibitions have been held respectively at Houston, San Francisco and Washington DC in which Indian Handicrafts/Antique Designs were displayed which were greatly appreciated by the foreign buyers at all the three places. These handicraft items attracted a very large number of buyers and new trade enquiries were made. There was a provision for sale of these handicrafts items at Washington DC and handicrafts items worth of Rs. 7.50 lakhs were sold.

During the period one Indian Handicrafts and Gifts Fair, '98 was held at Pragati Maidan, New Delhi where a large number of buyers attended the fair. It is estimated that the orders worth Rs. 540 crores were booked during the fair. The 15th Carpet Expo 1998 was also organised by the Carpet Export Promotion Council, New Delhi during the month of February, 1998 at Pragati Maidan, New Delhi. A large number of foreign buyers also attended the fair and orders worth Rs. 300 crore were booked.

Export promotion measures

1. Participated in Hong Kong Gift and Houseware show during 15- 18 April, 1998.
2. Participated in International Houseware show, Japan during 25- 27 June, 1998.
3. Participated in Regala Gifts and Premier show, Argentina during 6- 10 August, 1998.
4. Participated in International Tokyo Gift Show, Japan during 2- 9 September, 1998.
5. Organised Indian Handicrafts and Gifts Fair (Autumn) 1998 at Pragati Maidan, New Delhi during 10- 13 October, 1998.
6. Participated in International Heim and Handwork, Munich during 28.11.98 to 6.12.98.
7. Participated in International Spring Fair Birmingham during 7- 11 February, 1999.

8. Likely to participate in Import Shop, Berlin during March, 1999.
9. Likely to sponsor sales- cum- study team/ technical study team to U.K., France, Germany and Holland.
10. Likely to organize Indian Handicrafts and Gifts Fair (Spring), '99, Carpet Expo during February-March, 1999.
11. Organised Export Promotion Programme/ Workshop/Training in Handicrafts Industry.
12. Launched commercial publicity abroad to apprise Indian Handicrafts in C/WIHGF.

Carpet export promotion council (1998-99) (CEPC)

1. Organized Indo-Carpet Expo in Brazil and Chile.
2. Participated in the Dynamic Asia Small and Medium Enterprises Fair at Osaka, Japan from 9-11 September, 1998.
3. Participated in the Domotex 1999 at Hanover, Germany from 16-19 January, 1999.
4. Special projection of child labour in Germany during Domotex 1999 and Atlanta, USA during Atlanta Fair, 1999.
5. Proposal for organizing promotional campaigns for exports of Indian carpets into USA in association with M/s ABC Trade Am.

Training programmes in packing and packaging of handicrafts

To acquaint manufacturers/exporters with the latest techniques in packaging of handicrafts, it is proposed to conduct 12 training programmes during 1998-99. So far till December 1998, 10 training programmes have been organised.

Training programme in business enterprises and export management for educated craftspersons

The scheme envisages the creation of export consciousness among educated craftspersons and to acquaint them with export policy and procedures so that they may be able to enter the export business. During 1998-99 it is targeted to organise 12 training programmes. So far fill December 1998, 11 training programmes have been organised.

UNDP Projects

Jute handicrafts

The Government of India and UNDP approved the programme in 1995 for implementation within a period of 3 years, which will expire in December, 1999. The project aimed at creating an expanded production base in jute Handicrafts through training for creation of new skilled hands, training of trainees for upgrading skills, association of NGOs with design workshops for development of new designs and product prototypes and lastly domestic marketing of jute Handicrafts.

For the year 1998 (January- December, 98) details of target/ achievement is given here as under:

Training

Trainees to be trained	:	1425
Trainees trained	:	980
Under Training	:	445

Out of the trainees trained, 760 persons got employment.

Design

Design Workshop	:	4
Artisans participated	:	154
Prototype Designs developed	:	454
Designs commercialised	:	408

Wood handicrafts

For promotion of export of wood based handicrafts, UNDP assisted wood project is being executed by the Office of the Development Commissioner (Handicrafts). The development objective of the project is to increase the export of wood based handicrafts on a sustainable basis as a part of the larger national effort to increase exports and generate income and employment for artisans.

Experts in various fields from overseas countries have been appointed in consultation with the UNDP/ITC Geneva, who have been working in the field of design, marketing, etc. The project envisages UNDP assistance of $1009371 and counterpart assistance of Rs. 185 lakhs as per project document approved by Central Government.

Carpets & cane & bamboo

From April, 1999 under the aegis of Country Co-operation Framework-I (Fibres & Handicrafts Programmes) projects in collaboration with UNDP in two sectors namely, carpets and cane and bamboo, will be taken up. The projects are presently under finalisation.

Computerisation of office of the development commissioner (Handicrafts)

A computer centre has been established by NIC in the office of the DC(HC). Software packages for monitoring the progress of various schemes like departmentally run training schemes, marketing development schemes, financial assistance to State Corporations/Apex Co-operative

Societies and progress of Marketing & Service Centres are operational. Database on State/ National Awards and crafts are also maintained. Five Pentium based Computers have been installed at Headquarters at New Delhi and three Computers have been installed, one each at Regional Offices; CR Lucknow, NER Guwahati and SR, Chennai. The internet connection has also been provided to the office and a web page is being developed on' handicrafts.

Keeping in view the use of CAD and other sophisticated computer software for development of new designs, it has been decided to install CAD centres in the RD&TDCs, BCDI Agartala, ICT Bhadohi, MHSC Moradabad and at the headquarters at New Delhi. A detailed plan has already been worked out and NIC has agreed to assist in this regard. During 1998-99, funds have been transferred to NIC to implement the CAD scheme.

10

Textile Experts

Profile of textile exports

The export of Indian Textiles plays a pivotal role in the Indian economy. Textile exports account for about 30% of Indian exports of all commodities, making Indian textiles the largest single net foreign exchange earner for the country.

Indian exports of all textiles in 1997-98 including Jute, Coir and Handicrafts were of the order of Rs. 46278.81 crore as against Rs. 41828.15 crore in 1996-97, which represented an increase of 10.6%. In dollar terms, the same has increased from 11839.13 million US$ in 1996-97 to 12389.91 million US$ in 1997-98 representing an increase of 4.6%.

The exports during the current financial year for April-December, 1998 are of the order of Rs. 38458.8 crore as against Rs. 33962.8 crore during the corresponding period of the previous year. The major chunk in export has taken place in the field of apparel and cotton textiles. Sector wise break up of export performance during April-December, 1997 and April-December, 1998 is given hereunder.

Sector-wise analysis of textile exports

(i) Cotton yarn

The export of cotton yarn, including sewing thread had shown an increase in 1997-98 over the previous year with exports being Rs. 5865.64 crore (1596.79 Million US$) as against Rs. 5330.17 crore (1501.50 Million US$) in 199 6-97. The exports during the current financial year (April-December, 1998) have, however, registered marginal increase to Rs. 4476 crores as against Rs. 4448.7 crore during the corresponding period of the preceding year, it amounts to a 13.2% fall in $ terms mainly due to the currency and financial crisis in the South East Asian region which accounts for almost half of our cotton yarn exports.

The export of cotton yarn of below 40s counts is subject to specific ceiling keeping in view the interests of the decentralised sectors of handlooms and powerlooms. Ministry of Textiles (MOT) permits a specific quantity of this count group yarn for export every year.

For the year 1998 the ceiling for export of up to 40s count was kept at 175 million kg; for 1999 the ceiling is 200 million kg. However, the export in respect of the following is exempted from the purview of the ceiling:

(i) Export to quota countries viz. the EEC & USA.

(ii) Export by 100% EOUs/EPZ units.

(iii) Exports under ALS and against raw cotton imported by spinning units under OGL.

(iv) Exports of processed yarn viz, mercerised, bleached, dyed and melange yarn and

(v) Exports within the minimum annualised limit of additional export obligation (excluding the obligation towards maintaining the average annual export performance), in respect of the EPCG licence-holders.

In addition, the export of yam of counts above 40s is freely allowed except the quantity covered under bilateral agreements, where there is a quantitative limit.

(ii) Cotton mill made/powerloom textiles

The export of Mill Made/Powerloom, Cotton fabrics and made-ups amounted to Rs. 7,251.50 crore in 1997-98 registering an increase of 11.1% as compared to the achievement of Rs. 6,526.12 crore in 1996-97. The export during (April- December, 98) amounted to Rs. 6313.8 crore as compared to Rs. 5224.5 crore during the corresponding period of the previous year. The main markets for Cotton Textiles remain the same as in the previous year, such as U.S.A., EU, and the Middle East.

(iii) Cotton handlooms

The export of Handloom Textiles increased from Rs. 1758.89 crore in 1996-97 to Rs. 1859.53 crore in 1997-98. In terms of US dollars, the exports increased to a level of 505.93 million US$ during 1997-98 from 495.48 million US$ during 1996-97. The exports during the current Financial Year (April- December, 1998) were of the order of Rs. 1491.2 crore as against Rs. 1402.4 crore during the same period of last year thereby representing an increase of 6.3%. The main destinations of Indian Handloom Textiles are U.S.A., EU, Japan, Hongkong and Malaysia.

(iv) Readymade garments

Readymade garments have the largest share of export amongst all textile items. The garment sector has witnessed phenomenal growth. The export of garments, which was merely of a few lakhs of rupees during the seventies, touched the level of Rs. 18389.57 crore in 1997-98. Export during April- December 1998 reached the level of Rs. 15469 crore as against Rs. 13024.7 crore during the corresponding period of the preceding year.

(v) Silk textiles

The export of Silk textiles during April-December, 1998 was of the order of Rs. 746.5 crore (178.3 million US$) as against Rs. 641.9 crore (177.7 million US$) during the corresponding period of the previous year. Export in 1997-98 was Rs. 901.57 crore (245.32 million US $) as against Rs. 880.62 crore (248.06 million US$) in 1996-97.

(vi) Wool & woollen textiles

The export of Woollen textiles in 1997-98 substantially increased to Rs. 1128.80 crore from Rs. 103 6.78 crore in 1996-97, thereby registering an increase of 8.9%. In US$ terms, the export increased to 305.08 million US$ from 296.22 million US$. Exports during the current year (April-December, 1998) have marginally increased to Rs. 887.55 crore as compared to Rs. 887.00 crore during the corresponding period of the previous year.

(vii) Man made textiles

The export of man-made fibre textiles in 1997-98 increased to Rs. 3730.00 crore from Rs. 3216. 10 crore in 1996-97, thereby registering an increase of 16.0%. Exports during the current financial year April - December, 1998, have registered an increase over the corresponding period of the previous year. Exports were of the order of Rs. 2960.3 crore during April-December, 1998, as against Rs. 2737.7 crore during April-December, 1997.

Quota administration

The international trade in textiles and clothing was regulated by a special arrangement for 40 years outside the rules of General Agreement on Tariff and Trade (GATT). The framework of Multi Fibre Arrangement (MFA) applied to international trade in textiles and clothing for the period 1974 to 31.12.94. India has entered into bilateral agreements under MFA with USA, Canada, EU, etc. exports to which account for a major share of total exports of Indian textiles.

Consequent upon the establishment of the World Trade Organisation (WTO) with effect from 1.1.1995, the quantitative restrictions in the bilateral agreements under the MFA are being governed by the Agreement on Textiles and Clothing (ATC) contained in the final Act of the Uruguay round negotiations. The quota regime in the textile sectors is scheduled to be completely phased out by the end of 2004 .

In order to achieve maximum utilisation of quota levels and better unit value realisation, Government has been announcing a long term export quota policy. The current quota policy is for a three year period from 1. 1. 1997 to 31.12.1999. The Textile Commissioner exercises day to day supervision over matters relating to the allocation of export entitlements. There is a Quota Co-ordination Committee under the chairmanship of the Textile Commissioner with representatives of Export Promotion Councils as members, to review the operation of the policy periodically.

Under the export quota policy, the available quotas are distributed under different systems of allocation, such as Past Performance Entitlement (PPE), First Come First Served (FCFS), Manufacturer Exporters Entitlement (MEE), Non-Quota Entitlement (NQE), Powerloom Exporters Entitlement (PEE), New Investors Entitlement (NIE), etc. The Garment Export Entitlement Policy is implemented by the Apparel Export Promotion Council (AEPC), whereas the Textile Export Entitlement Policy is implemented by the Cotton Textiles Export Promotion Council (TEXPROCIL).

The break up of quota allocation under various systems for export of cotton yarn, readymade garments and other textiles is given on previous page.

Non-tariff barriers

The Indian textile sector also faces non-tariff barriers by importing countries. Colombia had initiated safeguard action against imports of denim fabrics inter-alia from

India on 20th April 1998, invoking the Agreement on Textiles & Clothing. The matter was immediately taken up by India before the Textiles Monitoring Body under the WTO. The TMB recommended on 31st July 1998 that Colombia should rescind the safeguard measures. The Colombian Government accepted the recommendations of the TMB, on August 5, 1998.

The European Union (E.U.) had imposed provisional anti-dumping duties on imports of Unbleached Cotton Fabrics from India. This was the third back-to-back measure initiated on this item. India took up the case bilaterally with the European Commission (EC). The Ministerial Councils of the EU decided on 5th October, 1998 to drop the proceedings.

The European Commission has initiated two parallel investigations, namely, anti-subsidy and anti-dumping proceedings concerning the import of Polyester Texturised Filament Yarn (PTFY) originating inter-alia from India. The Synthetic & Rayon Textiles Export Promotion Council is coordinating the defence of producers and exporters in the PTFY anti-dumping case. However, the anti-subsidy proceedings are being contested by the Government of India also, besides the producers and exporters.

The EC had initiated anti-dumping investigations in September, 1996 concerning import of cotton type bed-linen items originating inter-alia, from India. Subsequently the EC imposed definitive anti-dumping duty on imports of cotton type bed-linen originating from India. Government of India has had one round of consultations with the EC's on the subject and the process is on.

Steps to boost textile exports

Government has been operating several Schemes and has

undertaken some new initiatives with a view to helping the textile exporting industry to overcome some inherent disadvantages and to facilitate growth in exports of textile and textile products from the country. The central objective of most of the Schemes is to ensure availability of capital goods and raw material to the manufacturers at globally competitive rates.

Cotton yarn

A number of steps have been taken to arrest the downslide of cotton yarn exports. Firstly, the precondition of fulfilment of Hank Yarn Obligation for cotton yarn exports was removed, although the Obligation continued without any reduction of level. Secondly, such 100% EOUs that were manufacturing cotton yarn and are subject to count restriction were permitted to export cotton yarn without any count/domestic cotton use restriction initially up to 31st December 199 8, which has been extended up to 31st December 1999. Thirdly, in regard to the composite units manufacturing cotton yarn as well as fabrics- both existing and new- under the 100% EOU sector, the flexibility to export cotton yarn was extended without any count restriction/sourcing of domestic cotton condition. This dispensation is contingent upon the unit being completely balanced for spinning and weaving capacity, after such capacity is fully installed and commercial production started and the unit undertaking a commitment to ensure that at least 50% of its total value of export obligation is in the form of fabrics.

As far as capital goods are concerned, mention may be made of the following:-

Export promotion capital goods scheme (EPCG) Under the Export Promotion Capital Goods Scheme textile machinery, both new and second hand, can be imported at concessional rates of duty, subject to time bound discharge of the prescribed export obligations. The Scheme has two windows, namely, 10% concessional duty and zero duty. The threshold limit for availment of zero duty EPCG scheme has been lowered from Rs. 20 crores to Rs. I crore in respect of the garment sector from 13th April, 1998.

Among the various Schemes/provisions intended to facilitate availability of raw material at globally competitive rates are the following:

Special schemes under EXIM policy

a) Advance licensing scheme

This scheme permits duty-free import of raw materials, intermediates, components, consumables, parts, accessories, mandatory spares and packing material required for the manufacture of textile and clothing export products. With a view to facilitating exporters' access to duty-free inputs under the scheme, standard input-output norms for about 300 textiles and clothing export products have been prescribed. The Standard Input-Output Norms for a number of apparel items have been revised upwards, based on large garment size.

b) DEPB scheme

The objective of the DEPB scheme is to neutralise the incidence of customs duty on the import content in the export product. DEPB credit rates have been prescribed for 74 textiles and clothing products. In pursuance of an initiative taken by Ministry of Textiles, the value cap on DEPB rates for certain textile products has been suitably increased.

c) Special import licence

The special import licences (SIL), are valid for import of items appearing in ITC (HS) classification of Export and Import items subject to payment of normal customs duty.

The Textiles Committee has already brought out model manuals and has been conducting a country-wide campaign to encourage textile sector units to acquire ISO-9000 standard certification.

d) 100% EOU/FTZ scheme

Under the scheme, units undertaking to export their entire production of goods can be set up. They are entitled to import of all inputs as well as capital goods on a duty-free basis. There are now more than 300 EOUs manufacturing textiles including yarn and clothing.

e) Duty drawback scheme

Duty Drawback is a mechanism for refund of Central Excise and Customs duty chargeable on any imported materials or excisable materials paid by the exporters while undertaking export production. The objective of the scheme is to reduce the burden of indirect taxes on exports and make them more competitive in the international market.

f) Duty free import of trimmings and embellishments

Earlier, seven items of trimmings and embellishments namely labels, tags, stickers, buttons, printed bags, belts and hangers were allowed to be imported on a duty-free basis by bonafide garment exporters. Deptt. of Revenue extended the facility for duty-free imports to "All types of fasteners" and "Polywadding" also.

In addition, mention needs to be made of some other steps taken by the Government:

Government has reduced interest rates on pre- and post-shipment credit from 11 % to 9% for the remaining period of 1998-99.

An important development has been the constitution of the Export Promotion Board (EPB). under the Chairmanship of the Cabinet Secretary. The basic objective of the EPB is to coordinate efforts of all concerned Ministries to create a more favourable environment for maximising export earnings.

Among the other existing institutional arrangements, the most important are the Export Promotion Councils for different sectors, such as Apparel Export Promotion Council, Cotton Textiles Export Promotion Council, Synthetic & Rayon Textile Export Promotion Council, Handloom Export Promotion Council, Wool and Woollens Export Promotion Council, Carpet Export Promotion Council, Indian Silk Export Promotion Council, Export Promotion Council for Handicrafts and jute Manufacturers Development Council.

These Textile EPCs function under the sponsorship and direction of the Ministry of Textiles. These Organisations have been taking a number of steps, including sponsoring Buyer-Seller Meets, participation in fairs in major markets, releasing advertisements in foreign trade magazines, product development and quality upgradation through appropriate training programmes, etc.

For redressal of grievances of exporters, a High Level Committee chaired by Secretary (Textiles), with representatives from Ministry of Commerce and Department of Revenue, has been constituted. The Committee also takes up inter-ministerial matters like DEPB rates, Drawback rates, steps to counter Anti-subsidy, Anti-dumping measures targeted against Indian textile, exports etc. to redress exporters' grievances/problems.

Textile committee

The Textiles Committee, established by the Textiles Committee Act, 1963, has the primary objective of ensuring quality of textiles both for internal marketing and exports. Its functions include promotion of textiles and textile exports, research in the technical and economic fields, establishing standards for textiles and textile machinery, setting up of laboratories and data collection.

The Textiles Committee, besides its headquarters at Mumbai has 29 Regional Offices. It has set up Laboratories at 15 important centres to assist the industry and trade in testing their products. The Committee has the following functional divisions at headquarters, Mumbai -(1) Textiles Inspectorate Wing (2) Textiles, Laboratory Wing (3) Market Research Wing (4) ISO Wing (5) Vigilance Cell (6) Accounts Wing, and (7) Administration and Co-ordination.

In exercise of the powers conferred on it, the Committee has been levying and collecting cess from all textile and textile machinery manufacturers at the rate of 0.05% with effect from 1.5.1977. The Cess thus collected is deposited into the Consolidated Fund of India. During the year 19971998, the Committee remitted to the Government of India Rs. 3018 lakh towards the cess collection.

The Inspectorate Wing continues to carry out the statutory and voluntary inspection of textiles, inspection of material for establishing the loom origin, issue of GSP and other special certificates during the year.

The laboratories of the Textiles Committee continue to render services to the trade and industry, under the Commercial Testing of Samples Scheme. During the year 33,180 samples were tested under the commercial testing scheme and Rs. 70.58 lakh testing charges were collected.

The Market Research Wing of the Committee continued the data collection regarding purchases of textiles from 10, 250 households, selected on a random sampling basis from all over the country. Reports on Consumer Purchases for the years 1993, 1994, 1995 and 1996 were published.

A survey on the quality of man-made fibre cloth manufactured by the powerloom sector in and around Surat was conducted. A report on the findings, giving recommendations for improving the quality was published. A survey on the quality of cotton cloth manufactured by the powerloom sector in and around Ichalkaranji in Maharashtra was commenced.

The programme of computerisation of the working of the Textiles Committee at Headquarters, Mumbai was taken up vigorously with the National Informatics Centre (NIC) of the Planning Commission, as the Consultant. The NIC has developed software application programmes for Consumer Panel Household Project, Cess Collection Work, Information System on Sampling Testing, GSP Certification System, Quality Inspection Monitoring System, Ginning Survey, Surat Survey, Ichalkaranji Survey, Library Information System, etc. The software so developed are put to common use.

Apart from its regular activities, the Committee undertook the following developmental activities during 1997-98.

(i) Activities relating to ISO 9000 Quality System Standards

Seminars were conducted at seven places-Kanpur, Hyderabad, Ahmedabad, Amritsar, Coimbatore and Chennai, which were attended by persons not only from the textile industry but also from other industries too.

41 textiles companies engaged the Textiles Committee for rendering consultancy services in implementation of ISO 9000 Quality Systems in their companies. During the year 1997-98, eight companies

were awarded ISO 9000 certificates under the consultancy services provided by Textiles Committee, thus bringing up the number of units certified so far to 20. Ten companies engaged Textiles Committee as consultant for implementation of ISO 9000 Quality System in their companies.

As a part of the implementation strategy various programmes were conducted during the year 1997-98, the details of which are as under:

— Awareness Programme in 10 units attended by 254 participants.

— Statistical Process Control Training Programmes in 3 units attended by participants.

— Internal Quality Audit Training Program in 8 units attended by 112 participants.

— Pre-Assessment Audit Programme in 6 units

— Apart from conducting various programs in client units, the Textiles Commit conducted Third Party Audit at M/s. Go Mills Ltd., Gokak as a part of services to textile trade and industry.

(ii) Eco-friendly textiles

In order to promote the concept of Eco-friendly textiles, the Committee organised seminars at (i) Hyderabad, (ii) Coimbatore, (iii) Amritsar (iv) Kanpur and (v) Ahmedabad during 19971998. The officials of the Textiles Committee have also presented papers in seminars organised by other organisations at Mumbai, Surat and Cannanore recently.

The Textiles Committee has forwarded to the Ministry of Textiles, feedback obtained on the prohibition of some of the sensitizing Disperse dyes and Trichlorobenzene (Dyestuff carrier) from experts and dyestuff manufacturers.

The Textiles Committee proposes to take up a project on "Natural Dyes" jointly with other organisations.

Publications on "Eco-Friendly Textiles: Challenges to the Textile Industry", and "Guidance for the Manufacture of Eco-Friendly Textiles" were reprinted and distributed among the trade, industry and exporters.

Textiles Committee has set up as many as 8 eco-laboratories throughout the country, which includes 5 laboratories, set up recently. About 2000 samples have been tested for different eco parameters at the eco laboratories of the Textiles Committee at Mumbai, Tirupur, New Delhi and Chennai. The remaining 4 eco laboratories of the Textiles Committee at Cannanore, Jaipur, Ludhiana and Madurai will start functioning shortly.

The Textiles Committee has taken steps for additional eco testing equipments required by the 11 Eco laboratories set up during 1995-1996. The Committee has also arranged for training on eco testing in India and abroad, to the officials from the Textiles Committee and Textile Research Associations, which have set up eco laboratories.

The Textiles Committee has also arranged for performance evaluation of the 11 Eco laboratories during the year 1995-96 in order to ensure the proper utilisation of the eco-testing facilities created.

(iii) Consumer related matters

Consumer awareness and consumer interests in the textile field is of utmost necessity today. Accordingly the Textiles Committee has set up a Standing Committee under the chairmanship of the Textile Commissioner. The Standing Committee comprises representatives of NGOs involved in consumer protection programmes and representatives from the trade and industry. The Standing Committee meets periodically. Complying with the decisions of the Standing Committee, the regional offices of the Textiles Committee, in co-ordination with the offices of the Textile Commissioner and consumer protection organisations of each region, conducted 19 awareness programmes.

National institute of fashion technology (NIFT)

The National Institute of Fashion Technology (NIFT) was registered as an autonomous Society in 1986. It is a 100% Government funded institution under the Ministry of Textiles with Secretary (Textiles) as Chairman of the Board of Governors (BOG). Besides the Chairman, there are 17 members on the Board of NIFT, including the Executive Director who is the Chief Executive Officer of the organisation.

NIFT was established in collaboration with the Fashion Institute of Technology (FIT), New York. The genesis of NIFT was in the idea of an apex institution to cater to the growing needs of India's evolving fashion industry. Over the years, NIFT has emerged as the premier training institute in India nurturing and creating bright professionals in different areas of fashion technology, meeting the Human Resource requirements of this vital industry. Its high level of interaction and collaboration with the leading fashion institutions of the world has enhanced the stature and scope of the fashion industry in India to meet the challenges of industrial competitiveness on a global plane.

Beginning from July, 1995 NIFT has set up under its umbrella six other Centres located at Bangalore, Calcutta, Chennai, Gandhinagar, Hyderabad and Mumbai. Each of these Centres have a Director in-charge who is assisted by a Registrar and a nucleus staff. The Executive Director is responsible for the overall coordination and monitoring of the activities of these Centres, which are under the common management of the BOG.

The State Level Management Committee (SLMC) of each Centre, consisting of representatives from the State Government, Industry and having the Chief Secretary as its Chairman, acts as a link between the Industry - NIFT Centre -Government. The Registrar of the Centre is the designated Member-Secretary of the SLMC.

Major landmarks of NIFT during 1998-99

NIFT has taken the initiative to form the International Foundation of Fashion Technology Institutes (IFFTI). A conference for formation of this Foundation, discussion on modalities of working of the Foundation, the ways and means of financing the activities of the Foundation, etc., was held in the first week of November, 1998. The Conference decided to establish the Headquarters of IFFTI at New Delhi and elected Secretary. (Textiles) as Chairman of the Board of Directors of IFFTI and the ED, NIFT as Chief Executive Officer.

Steps were initiated for formation of the Fashion Designers Council of India. This was registered as a Society under the Societies Registration Act, 1860 and has started functioning since December 1998.

NIFT has started two regular courses of Post Graduate Diploma in Leather Garment Design & Technology and Post Graduate Diploma in Knitwear Design & Technology in the Calcutta and Mumbai Centres, respectively, keeping in view the demand for these courses in these regions.

Various interaction sessions were organised during this year with the Directors and Registrars of the NIFT Centres to involve and integrate the NIFT Centres in the activities of NIFT, Delhi and this has brought about a greater level of cooperation amongst all the Centres and has helped remove the communication gap. Steps have been taken to add to the library and resource facilities of all the Centres. The NIFT Centres are making all out efforts to enrich the Resource Centres keeping in view the financial position.

Systematic efforts have also been made to, enhance the hardware as well as software facilities.

Building and other facilities at NIFT Centres

Construction work for building of the permanent facilities for NIFT at Hyderabad is progressing and the first phase of the building is expected to be completed shortly and the Centre will start functioning in its own building thereafter.

Construction work for building of the permanent facilities for NIFT at Calcutta is also making progress and the same is expected to be completed by June, 1998.

NIFT, Bangalore was allotted land at the HSR Layout area in Bangalore. The construction work on this land is also expected to commence shortly.

11

Jute

On the whole, the first nine months of 1998-99 has turned out to be a favourable period for the jute sector. With a moderate sized crop currently estimated by Jute Advisory Board at around 80 lakh bales, the carryover stock of around 27 lakh bales from 1997-98 season and estimated import of 3 lakh bales, the raw jute supply position has become comfortable. As a result, the industry has faced no problems in maximizing production of jute goods to cope with the demand in the domestic market. Jute goods market continued to display volatility and show mixed trends with prices of all goods showing fluctuations.

The market is expected to rule steady in the coming months as all foodgrain procuring agencies have finalised their advance purchase of a massive quantity of 4.5 lakh bales of B.Twill bags for the forthcoming Rabi season and generation of demand from sugar sector.

An encouraging trend during 1998-99 is that farmers have generally received a remunerative price for their produce in the post harvesting period by staggered release of their crop in order to take advantage of the favourable price trend in the market.

Production of jute goods

Production of jute goods during 1997-98 was an all time record of 16.78 lakh tonnes as against 14 lakh tonnes in 1996-97. Production during 1998-99 (April/October) also recorded a marginal increase by 1% to reach 9.37 lakh tonnes from 9.32 lakh tonnes during the same period of last year. This increase in production is attributable to comfortable raw jute availability at reasonable rates at the beginning of the current year, stable domestic demand and consequent normal functioning of jute mills. If the current trend is maintained, production of jute goods is likely to touch around 16 lakh tonnes.

Domestic off-take of jute goods and related developments

Internal off-take of jute-goods during 1997-98 recorded a substantial growth (by 22%) to 13.84 lakh tonnes from 11.36 lakh tonnes in 1996-97. This was attributable mainly to the sharp rise in the off-take of jute bags on Government account for packing foodgrains due to higher procurement of grains. This impressive development had taken place despite the fact that the cement industry had discontinued totally the use of jute bags and still lower percentage of use of jute bags by the fertilizer (urea) industry.

The internal off-take during 1998-99 (April/Oct.) has also increased by 8.4% to 787 lakh tonnes from 7.26 lakh tonnes during the same period of last year. The domestic demand scenario is expected to remain as good as the current situation in the remaining period of the current year due to a number of favourable developments, most remarkable of which are the planning of advance purchases of B.Twill bags on Government account for the coming rabi season.

As per ILO convention regarding maximum permissible weight to be carried by an adult, a decision was taken by the Government for switch-over to packaging of foodgrains procured for central pool in 50 kg bags. According to this decision, all state foodgrains procuring agencies including FCI have agreed to purchase 50 kg bags for the coming rabi season and, accordingly, the indents have been placed by them for 50 kg bags entirely.

Since the earlier standardised 50 kg bags having a weight of 650 gms per bag have not been found free from complaints, a new bag with a weight of 665 gms has been developed which is expected to be suitable for this purpose.

The Standing Advisory Committee set up under the jute Packaging Materials (Compulsory Use In Packing Commodities) Act, 1987 analysed all the issues relating to projected requirements of jute bags for packing different specified end-user sectors covered by this Act, the supply scenario for jute goods, etc. in its 7th meeting held in three phases on 30.4.98, 15.5.98 and 2.6.98 in order to have a fresh look into the reservation order for jute packaging valid up to June, 1999.

While the performance in using jute bags by Foodgrains and Sugar sectors as per provisions of the Reservation Order has been totally satisfactory, utilisation of jute bags by fertilizer (urea) sector is still lower by 10 to 15% of the specified level. The Cement industry has been exempted from the provisions of this order.

Export of jute goods and related developments

Export of jute goods during 1997-98 (April/March) was 250,000 tonnes valued at Rs. 755 crores. During 1998-99 (April-December), the exports have been 159,000 tonnes valued at Rs 482.4 crores as against 243,000 tonnes valued at 683 crores during the corresponding period in 1997-98.

For promoting export of jute goods, Government have taken various measures which include the following:-

(a) The External Market Assistance Scheme operated by JMDC was revised w.e.f. 01.04.97 for a period of three years for giving added thrust to export of value added and diversified jute products with recent inclusion of Hydrocarbon free bags in the EMA list;

(b) Special thrust is being provided to re-orientation of R & D activities with special emphasis on enlargement of production base for diversified and value added jute products;

(c) Acceleration of export promotion programme by JMDC under UNDP assisted jute sector programme and also under its own budget allocation;

(d) Increase in rates of cess on jute manufactures to the maximum levels specified in the Cess Act, 1984 w.e.f. 2703.97 for augmenting the resource base of JMDC for funding, among others, approved market promotional activities; and

(e) Imposition of export obligation on jute mills.

Program in the product diversification of jute goods

Under the programme of jute diversification being funded by UNDP with a matching share from the Government of India, a large number of projects are being implemented by various institutions.

The National Centre for Jute Diversification (NCJD) is actively engaged in consolidating R & D results and transmitting these to the entrepreneurs by providing technical, financial, infrastructural and marketing support in order to encourage them to take up production and marketing of various jute based diversified products.

NCJD is also implementing various programmes like jute Entrepreneurs Assistance Scheme Jute Yarn Bank Scheme Jute Service Centre Scheme, Design Development Scheme, Market Support Scheme, HRD Support Scheme, NGOs Support Scheme, etc. for promotion of the diversification programme.

In addition, JMDC has accelerated promotion of export of such products under UNDP assisted jute sector programme and also under its own budget allocation from cess collection on various jute products.

The Council has been organising domestic workshops, seminars, exhibitions/fairs, fashion shows, etc. and participating in various international fairs from time to time for market promotion of such products.

The jute industry has also taken up the diversification programme seriously. A number of mills have made substantial investment for development and production of export yarn, floor coverings and home furnishings which has large growth potential within India and abroad.

There has been an impressive growth in production of shopping bags and wall coverings of various designs and the industry is now fully geared to meet the entire requirements of cloth and yam for production of these articles in the decentralised sector.

The research outfit IJIRA, in association with Indian jute Industry, has recently developed foodgrade jute bags and cloth namely Hydrocarbon Free Jute bags conforming to international standard specifications. These bags and cloth have a large demand in export markets for packing cocoa beans, coffee beans, shelled nuts and other food products.

Support prices for raw jute

Minimum Support Prices are being fixed by the Government every year on the basis of recommendations of the Commission for Agricultural Costs and Prices so as to ensure a reasonable return to the farmers after covering the costs of all inputs. The minimum support price for TD-5 grade of jute grown in Assam has been raised from Rs. 570.00 per quintal for 1997-98 season to Rs. 650.00 per quintal for 1998-99 season.

The gradewise price differentials have been fixed in such a manner as to motivate farmers to improve quality outturn of their produce. The corresponding minimum support prices for all grades of jute and mesta for various upcountry markets in different states for 1998-99 season have, accordingly, been revised upward and widely publicised for information of all concerned.

Industrial and labour scenario

There are 73 jute mills in the country, of which 59 are situated in West Bengal, 3 each in Bihar and UP, 4 in Andhra Pradesh and I each in Assam, Orissa, Tripura and Madhya Pradesh. At the end of October, 1998, the total number of looms installed in the industry stood at 44,035 and installed spindles at 5,46,836 on the fine side and 84,612 on the coarse side. These jute mills employ around 2.32 lakh workers.

The maximum achievable spinning capacity in the organised mill sector is estimated to be of the order of 18.6 lakh tonnes per annum. As on 23.11.98, only six mills were lying closed. Out of these six mills two mills namely, Kanpur jute Udyog in UP and Katihar jute in Bihar are lying closed for more than 12 years. These two closed mills had employed a total of 2340 workers before closure.

Raw jute scanario

On account of inadequate rainfall from March, 1998 onwards, delayed sowings, both area and production of raw jute have declined in the 1998-99 season. The Jute Advisory Board in its last meeting held on 26th October, 1998 projected the crop size at 80 lakh bales. Accordingly, the projected jute budget for 1998-99 season and that estimated for 1997-98 season are indicated below:

Estimates of supply and distribution position of raw jute

Qty: In lakh bales

A. Opening Stock	*Estimated* (1997-98)	*Estimated* (1998-99)
i) At Mills' godowns	5.66	12.00
ii) With JCI	0.01	2.00
iii) With traders	12.83	13.00
Total: (A)	18.50	27.00
B. Supply		
i) Raw Jute Import	2.50	3.00
ii) Crop Estimate	109.00	80.00
Total: (A+B)	130.00	110.00
C. Distribution		
i) Consumption by jute mills	26.40	92.00
ii) Rural & industrial Consumption	7.00	7.00
iii) Export	Neg.	Neg.
Total: (C)	103.40	9.00
Closing carryover stock (A+B-C)	26.60 or say 2700	11.00

According to the above estimate, the carryover stock at

the end of the current season i.e., June, 1999 is likely to be of the order of 11.00 lakh bales which may be sufficient to meet the normal consumption requirement of the industry for one and a half months. In view of the moderate sized crop, a quantity of 3 lakh bales consisting of high grade jute for export production of various diversification products is expected to be imported by Indian Jute Mills from Bangladesh in the current season.

Price situation of raw jute

The 1998-99 season began with prices of raw jute ruling well above the support levels in the all upcountry markets fixed on the basis of Rs. 650.00 per quintal for TD-5 grade ex-Assam. Prices started registering an abnormal increase from the beginning of October, 1998 and touching the level of Rs. 1020.00 per quintal (basis TD-5 grade of West Bengal). This spiralling trend in prices is caused due to various reasons like looming prospect of a shortage situation, irregular movement of raw jute from North Bengal to mills due to severe flood, cornering of stocks of raw Jute by a section of traders with a view to realising still higher prices, etc.

In order to arrest this unusual rising trend in prices, the jute Commissioner had issued Purchase and Stock Regulation Order under jute (Licensing & Control) Order, 1961 to all jute mills and a directive to stockists/traders of raw jute holding stocks in excess of 500 quintets to declare their stocks. These measures have produced a salutary impact on raw jute prices and at present the raw jute prices are hovering at Rs. 900.00 to Rs. 920.00 per quintal of TD- 5 grade Ex-West Bengal (at Calcutta).

UNDP jute programme

The UNDP Jute Programme approved by the Government in 1992 under the National Programme for Jute Sector with financial assistance from UNDP, continued during the year. The programme which was earlier scheduled to conclude in May, 1998 has been further extended up to March 1999 to facilitate completion of ongoing projects. The Government of India funds for the various projects under the programme are provided from Special Jute Development Fund (SJDF) as a matching contribution to the UNDP assistance of about US $ 20 million. During the current year, 1998-99 (April-December, 1998) GOI released an amount of Rs. 108.00 lakhs for the various ongoing projects under the programme.

The major objectives of the UNDP Jute programme are to enhance the welfare of jute farmers by implementing schemes to improve productivity, facilitate the diversification of the jute sector by developing new technology, promote employment opportunities by encouraging new entrepreneurs to set up manufacturing facilities for jute based items, assist development of the indigenous machine manufacturing sector for catering to the diversified products programme both in the textile related and non-textile areas and the strengthen R&D efforts in these fields.

Some of the ongoing projects are for the use of jute for paper production, human resource development, jute for packaging, jute textiles, jute blended yarn, electronic application in jute, jute handloom and handicrafts, improvement of fibre jute crop, jute denier fibre, machinery development for jute and steam explosion technology for jute. Major initiatives have also been undertaken in the field of geo-textiles and jute reinforced products and composites. Initiatives have been taken for setting up of jute retting tanks in various jute growing states with JCI as the nodal agency.

The present phase of UNDP Jute Programme is scheduled to be taken over by a successor programme in the second phase under CCF - I. In the next phase it is proposed to extend assistance to areas relating to jute, wool, silk and certain handicrafts under the fibres and handicrafts programme. The programme is scheduled for a period up to March 2002. The sub-programme for the jute sector is presently under finalisation.

During the current year an amount of Rs. 200 lakhs has been released so far for the Jute Entrepreneur Assistance Scheme (JEAS) from SJDF to transfer the benefit of R&D and test marketing efforts to a large number of entrepreneurs in different parts of the country. The operation of the Scheme has been extended up to March, 1999. The Scheme has been under implementation since November, 1995. So far, 63 entrepreneurs have benefited from the scheme as on September, 1997.

The Scheme is designed to increase the demand of jute fibre, ensure remunerative price to jute growing farmers and help traditional jute industry as well as the new class of entrepreneurs to find fresh end uses and markets for various products.

National centre for jute diversification (NCJD)

National Centre for jute Diversification (NCJD) was registered in January, 1992 under the Societies Registration Act, 1860 and established in June, 1994 under the Chairmanship of Secretary (Textiles) in order to give focused attention to the diversification efforts in the jute sector. NCJD is required to consolidate R&D results of various -institutes in jute and textiles and transmit these to the entrepreneurs for commercial products. It coordinates with various agencies and helps the entrepreneurs in arranging technical, financial and infrastructural support to encourage them to take up production and marketing of jute diversified products.

The Council of Governors of NCJD has been reconstituted with effect from 24th September 1998 for a period of two years. It consists of 25 members, drawn from various sectors like Jute Entrepreneurs, Banking, International Institutions and the Government.

The NCJD is implementing the following schemes for development of the jute sector:

(1) Jute Yarn Banks Scheme

(2) Jute Service Centres Scheme

(3) Jute Entrepreneurs Assistance Scheme

(4) Design Development Scheme

(5) Market Support Scheme

(6) Workshops, seminars and exhibitions.

The above schemes of NCJD have generated considerable enthusiasm amongst small entrepreneurs, and NGOs. NCJD is helping these entrepreneurs, women/NGOs to consolidate their production activities and enhance their production of such diversified products.

NCJD is also providing liberal assistance to these entrepreneurs in order to strengthen the marketing efforts in this direction and helping such diversified products to find foothold in the market. The jute Entrepreneur Assistance Scheme implemented by NCJD in this direction has popularised jute diversification and received tremendous response.

NCJD has been working in close co-operation with the Programme Management Unit of UNDP assisted National Jute Programme initiated in June, 1992 towards computerisation, JEA Scheme and Design Development.

All along it has been the spirit behind the programme according to the programme document that NCJD will take over the activities run by the Programme Management Unit after the UNDP Programme is over.

Jute manufactures development council (JMDC)

JMDC was setup as a statutory body with effect from 1.5.84 under the Jute Manufactures Development Council Act, 1983. The Act provided for establishment of a council for the development and production of jute manufacture by increasing efficiency and productivity in the jute industry and the financing of activities for such developments and for matters connected therewith. JMDC has been delegated with all functions relating to export promotion in the jute sector and also to perform other activities in the domestic market of jute sector, as are performed by a commodity board. The activities of JMDC are wholly financed by the Government of India out of the cess collected on various jute manufactures.

The major activities undertaken by JMDC during 1998-99 (up to November, 1998)

1) JMDC in coordination with IJMA organised an international workshop in February, 1998 on behalf of IJO for establishing an international standard specification for jute bags used in the packaging of food materials.

2) A 10 member Indian Jute Delegation led by the Minister of Textiles visited selected South African and West European countries in August 1998 to promote Indian technology for producing food grade jute bags/cloth.

3) It entered into an agreement with Central Cottage Industries Corporation jute consumer products will be on display and sale in the Cottage Emporia in 4 metropolis. Similar agreement has' been reached with Andhra Pradesh Handicrafts Development Corporation for display of jute diversified goods in its showrooms at Tirumala.

4) The Council was provided funds to the tune of Rs.

26.6 crores during 1997-98. A major part of the funds is utilised for external market assistance for promotion of the export of diversified jute goods.

5) Up to November, 1998 in the current year the Council has organised 6 jute exhibition cum sales, 2 workshops/interactive meetings and organised participation in 2 product specific fairs and in 4 general exhibitions and participated in 2 foreign fairs.

12

Public Sector Undertakings

National textile corporation limited (NTC)

NTC was set up with the main objective of managing the affairs of the Sick Textile Undertakings taken over by the Government. It was also proposed to rehabilitate and modernise these mills after the takeover and expand them wherever necessary with a view to making them economically viable.

NTC was incorporated in April, 1968 and started functioning in October, 1968. At present there are 119 mills, controlled by 9 subsidiary corporations of the holding company, namely, NTC (APKKM), NTC (DPR), NTC (MP), NTC (MN), NTC (SM), NTC (GUJ.), NTC (TN&P), NTC (UP) & NTC (WBABO).

Capital structure

The NTC Ltd. (Holding Company) started with an Authorised Capital of Rs. 10.00 crores, which was raised from time to time. It stands at Rs. 600 crores as on date. The paid up capital as on date is Rs. 512.10 crores.

Capacity

The installed capacity of the mills under the NTC as on 31.03.98 was 31.83 lakh spindles and 29621 looms. The commissioned capacity was 27.12 lakh spindles and 17658 looms.

Performance during 1998-99

Financial results

During the period April-September, 1998 the NTC Group has reported a provisional net loss of the order of Rs. 414 crores. The Group's anticipated loss for the year 1998-99 is expected to be of the order of Rs. 826 crores (Prov.).

The cash loss suffered by the Group before depreciation, tax and interest on Government loans is of the order of Rs. 305 crores (Provisional) for the period April-September, 1998. Looking at the trend, the cash loss for the year 1998-99 as a whole is likely to be of the order of Rs. 610 crores (Prov).

Four major factors, namely, shortage of working capital, stoppage/curtailment of activities, payment of idle wages to employees and lack of modernisation put together, are responsible for deteriorating performance of NTC mills.

Performance parameters

a) production

During the period April- September, 1998, NTC mills have reported a production of 16.30 million kgs. of market yarn (own) and have undertaken job work of yarn to the extent of 12.31 million kgs. Based on this trend, the annual production is estimated to be of the order of about 60 million kgs., including job, work.

Similarly, NTC mills have produced 2 1. 10 million mtrs. of cloth (own) during the period April-Sept. 98. In addition, NTC mills have undertaken job work for cloth production to the tune of 1.91 million mtrs. during this period. If this trend continues, the annual production of cloth, both own production as well as job work, is expected to be of the order of about 45 million mtrs.

b) Turnover

The sales of market yam (own) in value terms for the period April-September, 1998 is approx. Rs. 160 crores. During this period, the mills have also earned Rs. 31.00 crores by undertaking job work of market yarn. On this basis, it is estimated that for the whole year 1998-99, the turnover for yam, both own production as well as job work, would be around Rs. 380 crores.

Similarly, the sale of cloth (own) for the period April-September, 98 is of the order of Rs. 62 crores. In addition, the mills have earned about

Rs. 1.17 crores during April-September, 1998, by way of doing job work for cloth production. If the same trend continues, the turnover for cloth for the whole year is expected to be of the order of about Rs. 130 crores.

Based on the above indications, the total turn over of NTC group is expected to remain at about Rs. 510 crores.

The average sales realisation of market yarn and cloth for the year 1998-99 is expected to be Rs. 96.60 per kg. for market yarn and Rs. 26.00 per mtr. for cloth respectively.

c) Exports

Exports in value terms are of the order of Rs. 9.30 crores for the period April-September, 1998 which is expected to touch Rs. 19 crores for the whole year 1998-99.

d) Employment

At the end of September, 1998, there were 92,703 employees on roll. As per the Turn Around Strategy, 1995, 62,086 workers and 7,385 officers and staff totalling 69,471 employees were identified as surplus. Since September, 1992 when the Voluntary Retirement Scheme was introduced, 55,654 employees have opted for VRS up to September, 1998.

e) Working status

Due to acute shortage of funds of working capital and other reasons, the mills under NTC Subsidiary Corporations have not been able to utilise their full capacities. Most of the mills are dependent on job work for private parties. The working status of the mills during the month of September, 1998 was as under

Mills with no activity	:	34
Mills with partial activities	:	61
Mills with normal activities	:	24
No. of mills doing job work	:	56

Rehabilitation

The overall provisional accumulated net loss of z Group as a whole as on 31.12.1998 is Rs. 5379.32 crores. 8 out of the 9 subsidiary corporations have been referred to BIFR which has declared them as sick industrial companies under the provisions of the Sick Industrial Companies (Special Provisions) Act, 1985.

The BIFR has also appointed Operating Agencies for drawing up rehabilitation plans, which have in turn drawn up the rehabiliation/modernisation schemes.

The rehabilitation plans for all the 8 subsidiary corporations of NTC were placed before the BIFR for their approval before implementation. The BIFR has issued show cause notices for winding up of NTC (MP) Ltd., NTC (GUJ.) Ltd., NTC (WBABO) Ltd. and NTC (UP) Ltd. Rehabilitation Schemes in respect of NTC (APKKM) Ltd., NTC (DPR) Ltd., NTC (SM) Ltd. and NTC (MN) Ltd. asking for reliefs and concessions from the Government of India, State Governments and other institutions have been published. The BIFR is yet to take a final decision in the matter.

Government had approved on 9.5.1995 a revised Turn Around Plan for the NTC Mills involving restructuring of 36 unviable mills into 18 viable mills and modernisation of 79 mills at an estimated cost of Rs. 2005.72 crores. The funds for the revised Turn Around Plan were expected to be generated by sale of surplus lands and assets of NTC mills.

The funding of the Turn Around Strategy as approved by the Government in 1995 was dependent primarily on resources to be available out of the disposal of surplus land and other assets available in the mills, which has not materialised so far, for many reasons. As such, the same could not be implemented.

To arrest further deterioration in the working conditions in the mills, NTC has carried out a mill-wise analysis on the financial viability taking into account various technical parameters, work culture, etc. The revival plan, prepared in 1998, is under further review and consideration of the Government.

The British India corporation limited, Kanpur

The British India Corporation Ltd. was taken over by the Government of India on 11.6.1981 by acquisition of all private shares. The BIC has two woollen mills, namely, Cawnpore Woollen Mills branch (Lalimli) and New Egerton Woollen Mills branch (Dhariwal) under its direct control. Besides, it has two cotton subsidiary companies, namely, Elgin Mills Co. Ltd. and Cawnpore Textile Ltd.

The two woollen mills have 10,176 woollen spindles, 22,092 worsted spindles, 518 powerlooms and 162 handlooms. The total share capital of the BIC is Rs. 44.65 crores out of which the share holding of the Government of India is Rs. 42.96 crores. The total number of employees in the BIC is 4,519.

Financial performance

The anticipated cash loss for 1998-99 is Rs. 31.85 crores. The cash loss incurred in 1997-98 is Rs. 32.24 crores. Up to September, 1998 the cash loss is Rs. 16.25 crores.

Physical performance

The capacity utilisation for the year 1997-98 is 15.0% in worsted spindles and 6.0% in woollen spindles, while the capacity utilisation in weaving sector is 16.35%. The value of production is Rs. 9.32 crores. During 1998-99 (up to Nov. 1998), the corresponding figures are 6% in worsted spindles, 10% in woollen spindles while the capacity utilisation in weaving sector was 37%. The decline in production has been due to shortage of working capital, excess man power and obsolete machinery etc.

Reference to the BIFR

In 1993, the Company was referred to the BIFR which declared it as a sick industrial company. The BIFR passed orders on 31.10.94 recommending the winding up of the company. Against these orders of BIFR, the company filed an appeal before the AAIFR on 26.12.1996. The AAIFR also dismissed the appeal of BIC at its hearing held on 9.5.97 as the AAIFR felt that no rehabilitation scheme was feasible for the BIC Ltd.

The Government asked the Wool Research Association (WRA) to prepare Techno-Economic Viability Reports of the two woollen mills separately to consider the feasibility of reviving the units/company. The report was submitted by WRA to Ministry of Textiles in February, 1998. The matter regarding the future strategy for BIC is presently under consideration of the government.

The Elgin mills company limited, Kanpur

The Elgin Mills Company Ltd., a Cotton Textiles subsidiary of BIC has under it two mills located in Kanpur. It has an installed capacity of 1,18,092 spindles and 2,376 looms and employs 3036 workers and staff as on 30.9.1998.

Physical and financial performance

The capacity utilisation both spinning and weaving for the year 1997-98 was Nil (Since the operation has been totally stopped since December, 1995). The Company incurred a loss before charging interest and depreciation of Rs. 14.31 crores in the year 1997-98 while loss before interest and depreciation for 1998-99 is expected to be Rs. 14.00 crores. The accumulated net loss as on 31.3.98 stood at Rs. 529.42 crores including interest of Rs. 221.74 crores on Government loan, and anticipated net loss up to 31.3.99 is projected to be Rs. 597.42 crores.

Voluntary retirement scheme.

Till November, 1998, 4426 employees have been covered under the Voluntary Retirement Scheme at a cost of Rs. 43.07 crores provided by the Government.

Reference to the BIFR

BIFR on September, 1994, recommended winding up of the Elgin Mills Company Ltd., before the Hon'ble High Court, Allahabad. The appeal preferred by the Company against the orders of BIFR has been dismissed on 9th May 1997. The matter is subjudice in the Allahabad High Court.

Cawnpore textiles limited, Kanpur

The Cawnpore Textiles Ltd., is a cotton textiles subsidiary of the British India Corporation Ltd. located at Kanpur. It has an installed capacity of 37800 spindles and 604 looms per shift and employs 1468 workers and staff per day as on 8.12.1998.

Physical and financial performance

The average capacity utilisation of the plant both of spinning and weaving during the year 199798 was 3.36% and 5.49% The lower utilisation of the plant was on account of total stoppage of mill operations since 12th May, 1997 The Company incurred losses, amounting to Rs. 7.43 crores before interest and depreciation during the year. The expected losses before interest and depreciation during 1998-1999 would be Rs. 6.74 crores. The accumulated net losses as on 31.3.98 stood at Rs. 82.60 crores with interest amounting to Rs. 38.63 crores on Government loans and anticipated net losses to Rs. 97 77 crores as on 31.3.99.

Voluntary retirement scheme

The Voluntary Retirement Scheme was implemented in the Company since August, 1992 and the employees who retired under the Scheme as on 31.3.98 are 1061. The Ministry of Textiles has released a sum of Rs. 16.50 crores up to 31.3.98 for the said purpose and the payment of Rs. 9.58 crores has been released against the retirement of the aforesaid 1061 employees.

Reference to the BIFR

The BIFR on January, 1995 recommended winding up of the Cawnpore Textile limited before the Hon'ble High Court, Allahabad. An appeal was preferred by the Company before AAIFR against the aforesaid orders.

However the same has also been dismissed by AAIFR on 9th May, 1997 and the matter is subjudice in the High Court Allahabad (Company Bench).

Birds jute and exports limited, Calcutta (BJEL)

Birds Jute & Exports Limited (BJEL) is a pioneer in processing for jute, jute Cotton/Viscose blended fabrics used as decoratives and furnishing. It was initially a subsidiary of Bird & Company Ltd. and following nationalisation of Bird & Company Limited on October 25th 1980, Bharat Process Mechanical Engineers Limited (BPMEL) took over the assets of Bird & Co. Ltd. and became holders of 58.94% of BJELs equity shares. By virtue of a decision of the Government of India, the equity shares held by BPMEL (Under Ministry of Industry) were transferred to National jute Manufactures Corporation Ltd. (NJMC) (Under Ministry of Textiles) with effect from 20th November 1986 and BJEL became a subsidiary of NJMC Ltd.

The activities of BJEL which remained suspended since 25th October, 1980 due to stoppage in operations arising out of financial stringency for non-availability of Working Capital started production after Memorandum of Settlement was signed on 8th April, 1998 by and between the Management of BJEL, BJEL Workers' Union and BJEL Shramik Union and after necessary repairs and renovations.

Modernisation & diversification

BJEL had taken up a Modernisation and Diversification programme in the year 1993-94 with the object of increasing profitability. The features of the programme were:-

a) Updating of existing process technology by way of installation of some modern and balancing machinery.

b) Installation of new project of Composite Lamination Plant to produce thermoplastic/ thermosetting Composite jute Sheet as a substitute for plywood and decorative paper laminates.

e) Diversification of the process for new outlet of jute decoratives.

However, on account of lack of working capital and non-installation of balance machinery, the profitability of the Company did not improve.

Production & productivity

Installed capacity:

Bleaching & dyeing plant	60 Lakh mtrs. Per annum
Composite lamination plant	2.83 J.R.P. Sheets per annum.

The reason for low productivity is due to old and outdated machinery in the context of modern processing techniques. But on account of acute financial crunch arising out of inadequate Cash Loss reimbursement, proper maintenance of Plant and Machinery could not be adhered to for the last couple of years resulting in drop in productivity. Working result of last five years, up to 30th November, 1998 and anticipated figure up to 31st March, 1999 are given to the next page.

During 1998-99 the anticipated production is 3.75 lakh metres as against 5.38 lakh metres of fibres and 0.34 lakh kg. of raw dyed jute in 1997-98. Up to November, 1998, the production was 2.75 lakh metres. The anticipated cash loss during 1998-99 is Rs. 3.25 crores as against cash loss in 1997-98 of Rs. 3.64 crores. Till November, 1998 the cash loss is Rs. 2.24 crores.

From the beginning the Company has been carrying surplus labour, which also accounted for cash loss to a substantial extent. In order to reduce the surplus manpower, Voluntary Retirement Scheme (VRS) was introduced. During 1997-98 and 1998-99, 18 persons and 12 persons were retired respectively under VRS fund at a cost of Rs. 45.44 lakhs.

Financial results

1993-94	1994-95	1995-96	1996-97	1997-98	1998-99 upto	1998-99 upto Nov '98	Mar '99
Sale Value	132.42	128.67	79.23	103.93	48.90	19.98	31.63
Cost of Sales	395.27	392.85	418.08	453.03	438.49	276.45	407.43
Operating loss	262.85	264.18	334.85	349.10	389.59	256.47	375.80
Other Income	21.13	20.66	21.67	20.88	17.55	26.49	40.77
Net Loss	241.72	243.52	313.18	328.22	372.04	229.98	335.03
Cash Loss	221.63	234.89	304.88	319.21	363.73	223.58	325.43
Cash loss	34.00	35.00	35.00	35.00	10.00	-	-
					(Till Date 1998)		

National jute manufactures corporation limited, Calcutta (NJMC)

National jute Manufacturers Corporation Limited (NJMC) was incorporated in 1980. There are six nationalised jute Mills under its management of which five are located in and around Calcutta and one at Katihar, Bihar. NJMC is the only Public Sector Undertaking engaged in jute goods manufacture. The Undertakings of the six sick jute mills viz. National, Kinnison, Khardah, Alexandra, Union and RBHM, the management of which were earlier taken over by the Government under the Industries (Development & Regulation) Act 1951 were nationalised and vested in NJMC.

The Mills produce traditional jute goods like hessian, sacking, jute twine and also jute Carpet Backing Cloth (CBC). The plant and machinery of the six Jute Mills were installed about a century back resulting in poor condition of plant and machinery due to normal wear and tear coupled with age-old technology. Prior to nationalisation all NJMC Mills were lying closed for a long time and were taken over under the Industries (Development & Regulation) Act 1951.

The condition of machinery and other equipment such as generators, boilers, etc. were in very poor state and needed urgent repairs/replacement. Most of the mills had also problems of layout and other infrastructural deficiencies.

Modernisation

After nationalisation, NJMC took a Modernisation & Renovation Scheme (M&R) in the year 1981-82 with a total outlay of Rs. 28.34 crores for five of the six jute mills of NJMC with the object of increasing productivity by achieving higher capacity utilisation and improving profitability by changing product-mix with emphasis on renovation within existing technology. However, the flow of funds for the said scheme was suspended by the Financial institution (IRBI) for four years from 1983 to 1987 The time overrun of 4 years resulted in cost overrun, necessitating pruning and re-orientation of the original schemes. After reviewing the schemes afresh, the financial institutions resumed funding in 1987 with the Government of India agreeing to increase its participation in the funding and sanction financial reliefs to NJMC.

The setback in the implementation of M&R Schemes for 4 years resulted in further deterioration of the condition of the existing machineries apart from time and cost over run. A Rescue-cum-Rehabilitation programme of the 6th Unit i.e. RBHM at Katihar was undertaken in the year 1988-89 for replacement of obsolete machinery by the existing technology with total outlay of Rs. 3.75 crores. The Government of Bihar contributed Rs. 1.50 crores for implementing the scheme and the balance amount was given by the Government of India.

Performance

Due to shortage of working capital as mentioned above NJMC could not procure raw material to build up stock of jute timely and economically. As a result within the initiating factors the savings and benefits achieved in quantitative terms are being steadily eroded by steep escalation of cost of inputs, specially raw materials, labour, power and fuel, interest charges, etc.

The unbridged gap between Cash Loss incurred and reimbursement thereof amounting to around Rs. 226.61 crores up to 31.03.98 has resulted in an avoidable reduction in capacity utilisation due to non-procurement of raw materials, stores, etc. Due to accumulation of past losses, the net worth of the Corporation has become negative. In addition nonreimbursement of a substantial portion of the cash losses by the Government of India has severely affected the working capital and it has become extremely difficult to maintain the day to day operations of the mills. Due to such nonreimbursement cash losses from the Government of India, the Corporation could not liquidate its dues to JCI, CCI Provident Funds, ESI, Sales Tax, Raw Jute Tax, etc.

Failure to build up stock of raw materials for want of capital had resulted in decrease of drawing power from the cash credit account with the Banks which caused further erosion of working capital. Banks are insisting on Government Guarantee for restoring the drawing power limit and smooth operation of accounts.

The anticipated production and capacity utilisation for 1998-99 is 78294 metric tonnes and 50% respectively. During 1997-98, the corresponding figures are 76450 metric tonnes and 48% respectively. Up to November, 1998 the production and capacity utilisation is 47199 metric tonnes and 45% respectively. The anticipated cash loss during 1998-99 is Rs. 102.25 crores as against cash loss of Rs. 83.24 crores in 1977-98. Up to November, 1998 the cash loss was Rs. 86.21 crores.

NJMC has installed a fine yarn project at its Unit - Kinnison with the support and guidance of UNDP. The proposal for the installation of new technology in the spinning system has been thoroughly examined from the aspect of skills to handle the new technology, supporting infrastructure, availability of raw materials, domestic and export market and the economic viability of the project. The target production of the said project is 6 MT. per day of Fine Export Yarn.

Labour rehabilitation

From the pre-Nationalisation period NJMC units have been carrying a large surplus work force which accounted for cash loss to a substantial extent. In order to reduce the surplus manpower in the PSUs, the

Government of India introduced Voluntary Retirement Scheme (V.R.S.) as communicated by DPE through O.M. No.2(36)/86-BPE(WC) dated 05/10/88. With the approval of the Ministry of Textiles, the Corporation adopted the Voluntary Retirement Scheme. Till November, 1998, 3258 workers have been covered under VRS at a cost of Rs. 48.10 crores.

Reference to BIFR

NJMC has been suffering cash losses since inception on account of the various reasons mentioned above. In view of continuous cash loss and complete erosion of net worth, NJMC was referred to the Board for Industrial and Financial Reconstruction (BIFR) on 11th Aug., 1992. Thereupon BIFR declared the company a Sick Company under the provisions of Sick Industrial Companies (Special Provisions) Act 1985. Revival Plan for Rs. 343.83 crores was prepared by IJIRA and financially vetted by IRBI.

On the advise of the Committee of Officers headed by the Secretary, Expenditure, Government of India, a Revised Revival Scheme was prepared in consultation with Indian Jute Industries Research Association IJIRA) and Industrial Investment Bank of India (IIBI)- the Operating Agency (OA) with the total financial outlay of Rs. 182.14 crores and submitted to the Government of India. In the course of the hearing on 21st March, 1996, BIFR directed the O.A. to update the package further by analysing the Company's projection and the assumptions forming the basis of the same. The Bench directed that the cutoff date would be 3lst Dec., 1996 and JCI's dues to be provided in the scheme.

However the above Turn Around Plan was subsequently revised. The Plan is presently under consideration of the Government.

The jute corporation of India LTD., Calcutta (JCI)

The Jute Corporation of India Ltd. is the official agency of the Government of India in implementing its policy of providing minimum support price to the jute growers and to serve as a stabilising agency in the raw Jute sector. However, in years when prices of raw jute had ruled above the minimum support level the JCI had also undertaken commercial operation. It has completed 27 years of service to the jute growers in April '98.

JCI has set up a field network of 208 procurement centres in 45 jute producing districts in 8 eastern States of India and provided sustenance to 4 million small jute farmers when the prices rule at or below the minimum support rates fixed by the Government of India. The jute so procured was sold in the years of scarcity with the resultant stabilising effect in raw jute prices in other years when MSP operations were not called for.

The Ministry of Textiles had, however, advised the JCI to reduce its manpower by 25% and bring down the establishment expenses by pruning its purchase centres. Accordingly, to make the JCI more cost effective, a detailed study was undertaken for restructuring the purchase centres of JCI through assessment of their performance for seven years for the period from 1985-86 to 1992-93 (1985-86 & 1986-87 were years of highest procurement of 28 lakh bales and 22 lakh bales respectively by JCI). On the basis of this study it was decided to close down 43 centres of JCI on an objective basis and in a transparent manner looking at its commercial viability. Through implementation of the Voluntary

Retirement Scheme as well as natural wastage by way of superannuation, death, resignation, termination, etc. it has since been possible to bring down the manpower of the Corporation by over 15% and any fresh recruitment from outside has been banned by the Ministry in 1992. Reduction in manpower and establishment cost on the lines stated above has inevitably led to curtailment of infrastructure of the Corporation and this, in turn, has lowered the procurement capability of JCI to around 15% of the total market arrivals from the past level of 20%. Currently the JCI is operating through 165 purchase centres situated in seven eastern States.

The range of services provided by the Corporation is as under:

i) MSP operation for the benefit of marginal jute farmers and commercial operation at prices above support level depending on the raw jute market situation. The Corporation procured 9.85 lakh bales under MSP operation in 1997-98. Up to end December 1998 the JCI purchased 0.53 lakh bales (0.09 bales under MSP operation and 0.44 bales under commercial operation). In the current season the procurement is still continuing.

ii) procured at minimum support prices or higher in a phased manner to ensure that inventory level is kept at the minimum without adversely affecting the raw jute price situation. The JCI has also created a buffer stock from time to time in years of surplus.

iii) Pioneering the establishment of BIS standards for raw jute grading. Due to strict quality control, jute purchased and packed by the Corporation fetches a premium in the raw jute market.

iv) Export and import of raw jute depending on domestic availability and international prices.

v) Acting as Inspection Agency of the Government prior to export of raw jute as and when called for.

vi) Spearheading the marketing of non-traditional jute

products in collaboration with the jute Manufactures Development Council (JMDC). The JCI had first set up an emporium named 'SONALI' at Calcutta in association with the JMDC for promoting production and sale of non-conventional jute products like jute utilities and specialities. Subsequently another emporium was set up at Bhubaneswar in Orissa. Following the lead given by JCI, a number of other Government emporia and private concerns have since taken up the sale of diversified jute products. A growing number of production units in the decentralised sector producing various jute based handicraft products have since entered this field thereby opening a new horizon for self employment. Recently as per decision taken by the Government the emporia at Bhubaneswar has been closed down and the other at Calcutta is under process of being handed over to the CCIC.

vii) Dissemination of knowledge to jute growers in respect of jute quality improvement through better techniques has been undertaken by the Corporation envisaging various extension services especially designed for the jute growers in increasing productivity and quality of jute through a package of measures like sale of certified jute seeds, etc. Under the Jute Quality Improvement (Retting Technology Project) undertaken by the JCI with the financial assistance of the Government of India and UNDP, 7 pucca community retting tanks in various growing states (4 in West Bengal and 1 each in Assam, Bihar and Orissa) have been constructed and field level demonstrations of improved jute retting technology were undertaken. This project also included the development of simple and cost effective mechanical devices for extracting fibre. Besides, and industrial Retting for jute has also been set up. On successful completion of this project, the Government of India has again entrusted JCI to function as the nodal agency for implementation of two more projects - one for construction of 14 cost-effective community retting tanks in jute growing districts in India on a 50 : 50 cost sharing basis between the Government of India and the respective State Governments. Construction of five retting tanks under this projects has already started in five important jute growing districts in Assam. A project on further development of a manual/power driven ribboner machine for extraction of fibre from green jute plant.

viii) Providing services in the field of market research and acting as a decision support system in the field of agricultural marketing.

The cotton corporation of India Ltd., Mumbai (CCI)

The CCI was set up in 1970. It came into existence with the objective of acting as the canalising agency for import of cotton and undertaking purchase of raw cotton for giving necessary price support to enterprising cultivators growing new varieties of cotton developed as substitute for imported Long and Extra Long Staple Cotton and also for procuring raw cotton for textile mills both in public and private sector. Over the years its operations have undergone significant changes in keeping with the developments which have taken place in the Indian cotton economy during the past two decades. Subsequent to the announcement of the Textile policy of 1985, CCI's role was expanded to carry out commercial operations for meeting the cotton requirements of institutional buyers and to fulfil the export quota allotted to it by the Government.

The sales turnover of the Corporation is expected to be around Rs. 1254 crores during the year 1998-99 as compared to Rs. 1048 crores in the previous year. The net profit after tax was Rs. 28.17 crores in the year 1997-98 as against Rs. 49.13 crores in the previous year. The ratio of operational profit to turnover of the Corporation worked out to 4.02 percent in 1997-98.

The CCI's sales of cotton to the quality conscious mills in the private sector (particularly the 100% Export Oriented Units) increased from 56.8 per cent during 1996-97 to 65.04% during the year 1997-98. The sales to NTC mills registered a decrease of 16.62% during the year under review, mainly on account of reduced cotton requirement of these mills due to financial crunch faced by these mills which had forced them to work below their capacity.

The CCI intensified its developmental activities during the year while continuing the existing activities and taking up new ones during the year. These were basically aimed at increasing production, productivity of cotton and also for improvement in the quality of cotton.

The developmental activities involved a Village Adoption Programme for dissemination of technology to the farmers to increase the yield per hectare, production and distribution of genetically pure certified seeds, distribution of pesticides to cotton growers, production of genetically improved parental lines of DCH-32 variety, funding Research Projects for genetic improvement of parental lines of DCH-32 Hybrid cotton in Karnataka, crop surveillance, Research Projects on naturally coloured cotton, promotion of medium staple cotton, bringing new areas under cotton, etc. For the various developmental activities listed above, the Corporation spent an amount of Rs. 2.10 crore during 1997-98. The Corporation has targeted an expenditure of Rs. 11.00 crores during 1998-99 on various developmental activities.

The CCI also implemented an Action Plan to modernise the Ginning & Pressing Factories with a view to ensuring contamination free processing of cotton for improvement in quality and also for ensuring that processing of cotton conforms to BIS norms. The CCI spent about Rs. 83.59 lakhs on improvement of infrastructure in Ginning Pressing Factories in Madhya Pradesh, Gujarat, Punjab, Haryana and Rajasthan during 1997-98.

The Corporation has been able to achieve all the targets set under the Memorandum of Understanding (MOU) signed by it with the Ministry for the period covering 1997-98. The performance of CCI as per MOU for 1997-98 has been rated as 'Excellent'. The MOU for 1998-99 has also been signed with the Ministry in April, 1998.

Contamination-free processing of cotton

With a view to meeting the growing demand for quality cotton from the quality conscious export oriented private sector mills, the Corporation has taken up the processing of contamination-free cotton from 1997-98. The Corporation processed 5500 bales in the first year and intends to process about 10 per cent of its total cotton purchases in future.

Handicrafts & handlooms export corporation, New Delhi (HHEC)

The Handicrafts & Handlooms Export Corporation of India Limited (HHEC) was set up in June, 1962 with the twin objectives of (i) Export promotion, and (ii) Trade development of handicrafts and handloom products. HHEC is a trading house in the field of handicrafts and handloom products (including handknotted woollen carpets and ready made garments) besides undertaking export of gold and silver jewellery/ articles. In the year 1997-98, vide Government notification No. 80/97-Customs dated 21st October, 1997, HHEC along with other ten agencies was nominated for import of bullion under OGL and sale in the domestic market.

Capital

The authorised share capital of HHEC remained Rs. 20 crores and paid up capital is Rs. 10.82 crores as on 31st March, 1998.

Turn over

The turn over of the Corporation during the year 1997-98 amounted to Rs. 318.28 crores as against Rs. 99.25 crores (excluding gold jewellery exports through its associates) during the corresponding period last year, which includes exports to the extent of Rs. 8720 crores and Rs. 97.03 crores respectively. Targets for 1998-99 are at Rs. 446.10 crores which includes export of Rs. 143.95 crores.

Working results

During the year 1997-98, the gross profit amounted to Rs. 18.64 crores as against Rs. 13.29 crores during the corresponding period in the previous year. The overheads during the year 1997-98 amounted to Rs. 20.15 crores as against Rs. 1740 crores during the corresponding period in the previous year. The year ended with a net profit of Rs. 2.00 crores as against a net loss of Rs. 1.65 crores during the corresponding period in the previous year. The Company also declared a 4% dividend amounting to Rs. 43.28 lakhs and paid the same to the Government of India.

Export promotion and trade development

The Corporation continued its export promotion and trade development activities during the year by developing new samples, engaging professional designers from India's prime fashion technology institutes i.e. NIFT, including a foreign designer from Japan, the promotion of exclusive samples in the international market by participating in international trade fairs and shows, for example in Uzbekistan for promotion of handicraft items and in Israel for handlooms.

Attention is being paid to entering the South American and Candian markets with handicraft and handloom products. In addition we are planning to explore the scope of markets for export of gold jewellery in countries like Lebanon, Canada, Brazil, Turkey and South Africa.

Silk

The Government of India has allowed import of mulberry raw silk without any import licence by HHEC along with six other designated agencies in October, 1998. As in the case of bullion again we are one of the first few to start operation of import of raw silk. However the permission has been withdrawn we.f. 30th October, 1998. During the year, HHEC took note of Government notification nominating eleven agencies for import of bullion and we were one of the first few to initiate import of buillion under the new Exim Policy of the Government. As early birds catch the best worms we achieved a sales of Rs. 229 crores to our taking margin.

North eastern handicrafts and handlooms development corporation, Shillong (NEHHDC)

The NEHHDC Ltd. was established in 1977 as a regional nodal agency for the promotion and development of handicrafts and handlooms in the region. The areas identified for undertaking promotional and devleopmental activities included infrastructural and input support for research, design development, training of craftsmen and weavers, technical upgradation, supply of raw materials through appropriate budgetary support. The Corporation was also required to market the products outside the region and promote.

Activities

The main activity of the Corporation is developmental covering different spheres mentioned above. Its secondary activity is related to marketing. Its marketing operation is being conductxed through a network of emporia located in mentropolitan and other cities. These emporia also organised and participated in a variety of exhibitions, Handloom and Handicraft Expos, N.E. Crafts Fair, etc. The Corporation has also been participating in I.I.T.F. and other Trade Fairs and Gifts Fairs, etc. on a regular basis. Despite financial and operational constraints the Corporation successfully conducted 26 exhibitions up to Dec. 98. N.E. Crafts Fair, Bangalore has been conducted from 21st November, 1998 and IITF from 14th November, 1998.

The functioning of the Dye House was stopped from 1st April, 1994 under the direction of the Government of India. In February 1997, the Government further ordered winding up of the Dye House and disposal of plant, machinery and other assets by auction or leasing to other institutions. However, complete winding up of the Dye House has not been possible in absence of Government decisions on the treatment of outstanding secured and unsecured loans availed in the setting up of the Dye House. Due to closure of the Dye House the manpower numbering 63 have been rendered idle. However, Government has sanctioned funds in March '98 to the Dye House, which will facilitate use of the Dye House building and also redeployment of about 25 staff of the Dye House.

The authorised share capital of the Corporation is Rs. 2 crore which is fully paid up and subscribed by the Government of India. The Corporation has submitted a proposal to enhance the share capital to Rs. 15 crore to accommodate enhanced equity captial after the conversion of outstanding loans/interest into equity proposed under the Capital Restructuring Plan.

Performance

Up to December, 1998 the turnover and gross profit was Rs. 211 lakh and Rs. 52 lakh respectively. During 1997-98 the turnover and gross profit was Rs. 3.26 crores and Rs. 0.89 crores respectively.

Central cottage industries corporation India, New Delhi (CCIC)

The Central Cottage Industries Emporium was established in Delhi in the year 1952 under the Management of the Indian Co-operative Union and was later on taken over by the Central Cottage Industries Association in 1964.

The Central Cottage Industries Corporation of India was incorporated on 4.2.1976 as a wholly owned subsidiary of the Handicrafts and Handlooms Export Corporation of India Ltd. However, with effect from 273.1991, CCIC has ceased to be a subsidiary of HHEC of India Ltd. and has been brought under the administrative control of the Ministry of Textiles.

The main object of the CCIC is to act as dealer, exporter, manufacturer and agent of Indian quality handicrafts and handlooms and to develop markets for these products in India and abroad. However, it also engages itself in export activities and is an eligible export house.

The Corporation has six showrooms viz; at Delhi, Calcutta, Mumbai, Bangalore, Secunderabad and Chennai. Besides this, the Corporation has its own production centre at NOIDA for manufacture of readymade garments and accessories. The production centre also has a printing unit where sarees, fabrics, etc. are printed.

The authorised capital of the Corporation is Rs. 12.00 crores and the paid up capital is 10.85 crores. The total sales of the Corproation for the financial year 1997-98 were of the order of Rs. 4865.77 lakhs as against Rs. 4568.11 lakhs during the year 1996-97. Thus during 1997-98, the sales were increased by 6.52% over the previous year. Cumulative sales during April-December, 1998 were of the order of Rs. 3582 lakhs. The Corporation has set for itself an ambitious target of turnover of Rs. 555-3 lakhs for the financial year 1998-99. The net profit before tax for the year 1998-99 is anticipated to be around Rs. 188 lakhs.

The Corporation continues to strive for excellence in the field of its operations. To promote traditional crafts of the country, the Corporation purchases bulk of the merchandise directly from the artisans. The Corporation proposes to open more branches in the major cities of India in future.

National handloom development corporation Ltd., Lucknow (NHDC)

National Handloom Development Corporation (NHDC) Ltd., Lucknow was set up in February, 1983 as a Public Sector Undertaking by the Government of India as an autonomous body under the Companies Act, 1956, in pursuance of the imperative need for a National Level Agency to assist the speedy development of the Handloom Sector by co-ordinating all action covering the procurement and supply of inputs at reasonable prices, augmenting the marketing efforts of the state handloom agencies and initiating development activities for upgrading the technology in the handloom sector and improving productivity.

Main objective of the corporation are:

1. To carry on the business of all types of yarn for the benefit of the handloom sector.

2. To organise supply of quality dyes and related materials needed by the handloom sector.
3. To promote marketing of handloom fabrics including exports.
4. To aid, assist and implement the projects connected with the production of handloom fabrics including taking up modernisation programme, introduction of appropriate technology for the handloom sector.

The total authorised capital of NHDC Ltd., is Rs. 20.00 crores and its paid up capital is Rs. 13.00 crores besides Rs. 1.00 crore as share application money as on 31/3/98. During the year 1998-99 a further amount of Rs. 1.00 crore has also been released to NHDC for equity participation.

The turn over and profit account of the Corporation for the last 3 years are as under :

Year	Turnover	Profit (Rs. in lakhs)
1995-96	11065.69	40.41
11996-97	10883.19	40.66
1997-98	14569.62	61.16

During the year 1997-98, the Corporation has declared dividend @ 21.25% of post tax profit and accordingly paid dividend of Rs. 13.00 lakhs to Government of India.

The Corporation has shown improvement in its performance as compared to the last year's performance. The NHDC has supplied yarn worth Rs. 12902.30 lakhs during 1997-98 as against Rs. 8899.91 lakhs worth of yarn supplied in 1996-97. Dyes and chemicals with Rs. 1240.54 lakhs were supplied during 1997-98 as against Rs. 1174.76 lakhs during the previous year. In terms of quantity

131.00 lakhs kg. of yarn was supplied to user agencies while in the field of dyes and chemicals the supply was 6.61 lakhs kg.

During the year 1998-99 (up to October, 1998) the Corporation has supplied yarn of 85-99 lakh kg. worth Rs. 8500.074 lakhs and 3.96 lakhs kg. of dyes and chemicals worth Rs. 723.756 lakhs.

13

Quality Control

Quality is related to the material and processing that are used in the products; high quality implies that expensive materials or processing or both have been used to achieve the desired characteristics. High price and quality are often associated because the particular end-use has stringent requirements, which are difficult, and hence expensive, to meet. In view of this relationship, quality in this sense can be referred to as 'expense quality'. Since the more expensive material and processing tend to give a greater range of properties, this title has a real meaning. It has, nevertheless, certain limitations in that inexpensive materials or processing may produce a product that is perfectly suited to a particular end-use. High- or low-expense quality does not imply any judgement on the merits of the product: it relates merely to the type of product.

In fact, of course, the aim is to produce an article that satisfies the demands of the end-use it was designed to serve. For this reason, it is preferable to use the term 'design quality' when the merits of a product are judged from the standpoint of end-use suitability. Whether a yarn or fabric has a high end-use suitability depends upon how the design has been translated into reality through production. This introduces the concept of quality measured in the degree of conformity to specification. Achieving conformance is a production problem and this aspect of quality can usefully be referred to as 'production quality'.

Circumstances will affect the relative importance of these two aspects. End-use suitability does not merely imply the presence of a certain quality characteristic; rather is it a combination of many separate or related characteristics or both. In certain cases, once the material has been chosen and the processing sequence decided upon, most of the characteristics are already uniquely determined. In others, the important characteristics may be quite different.

In general, however, the characteristics fall into three groups. First, there are those that depend solely on the raw materials and their reaction to acids, heat, etc. Secondly, there are those qualities that are a reflection of the design and maintenance of the machines used and the skill and attention of the operatives attending such machines. For example, if a roller forming part of the drafting system on a spinning frame is eccentric, the material being processed will contain a periodic wave. The size and intensity of the wave will depend on the diameter of the roller, the amount of attenuation, and the degree of eccentricity.

Finally, there are those that are the combined result of both the material and the processing. For instance, in cotton yarn the incidence of neps is largely dependent on the percentage of immature fibres present. At the same time, the condition of the carding engine, particularly the state of the clothing and the frequency of stripping and grinding, can also influence the number of neps in the finished yarn. As knowledge of materials and machines becomes greater, the interrelationships revealed increase the significance of this third group.

Quality control

As with quality, there are differing opinions as to the meaning of quality control. To some, quality control is merely a synonym for testing, whereas others associate it primarily with the application of statistical methods to quality problems. Both views are unnecessarily restrictive. Broadly, quality control is regarded from two different standpoints. First, it is regarded as the control of all the factors that play a part in determining the quality of the final product. In this sense, it is a fundamental part of management. Secondly, it is used to describe a series of techniques or procedures that enable management to discharge its quality responsibilities more effectively. To call the latter 'statistical quality control' is no solution, since this is concerned only with a few of the many techniques available.

Quality control cannot be achieved in a complex textile undertaking without both management and technique. In practice, the deciding factor is that of management. Effective control depends on managerial policy and action; the techniques, however precise, can serve to improve such action, but they cannot replace it, They spotlight differences between the actual and required standard and, where possible, measure such differences quantitatively. Control itself depends on the taking of specific action to remedy such differences and this, in turn, involves management.

If the above comments are borne in mind, quality control is defined as being concerned with all the procedures used and action taken to ensure that the quality characteristics of the product conform to the required standard. This standard may, or may not, be written down, and it may not be particularly precise; nor need it cover all the characteristics. The measure of the effectiveness of quality control is then simply the degree to which such conformity is attained.

Role of standards

Fundamental in quality control is the concept of a standard of quality performance. Here again, the word 'standard' is subject to several interpretations. It is important, however, to consider the various meanings in order to provide a basis for a realistic and consistent quality policy. There are at least three-types or aspects of standard that merit consideration. They all play an important part in establishing a yardstick against which the effectiveness of quality control can be measured.

Commercial standards

The first important standard is the commercial one. This is the quality level desired for the market in which the product is to be sold. In the textile industry, the practice is varied. Although cloth constructions are usually laid down, there is considerable variation in the amount of detail on performance characteristics. Specifications of the permissible level of fault incidence likewise vary from the exceptionally detailed to the conveniently vague. For yarns, it is still common to produce to a specification covering only average count and minimum strength, both these characteristics being judged by a somewhat haphazard series of tests on small samples.

It is worth noting, however, that in many sections of the industry the trend is towards more detailed specifications, embodying not only more characteristics but also more systematically defined permissible limits. There are many factors influencing this trend but only a few need be mentioned here. First, there is the growing importance and influence of integrated manufacturing units. Controlling as they do part, or all, of their processing, they appreciate how different levels of yarn or cloth quality are achieved and how they affect performance at subsequent processing. On those occasions when they supplement their supplies from outside sources, they tend naturally to lay down specifications as similarly detailed as those used within their own units.

Secondly, there is the increasingly important role of the large institutional buyers. Many of these organizations have a direct financial interest in some of the most modern spinning, weaving, and knitting units. In addition, their influence is increased, since they are also the largest customers of certain other units. Laying down detailed quality requirements for the garments they sell, they force the firms at earlier processes to impose similarly stringent demands on their suppliers.

Thirdly, one of the factors that has hitherto prevented the preparation of standards on many characteristics is that of inadequate instrumentation. Developments in recent years have enabled more characteristics than previously to be accurately measured and compared with reproducible standards.

Even so, the influence of these forces should not be exaggerated. Many textile firms, in many sections, are still working in a situation where the standards in use are very loosely defined. Again, where standards exist, they still fluctuate as cyclical trade fluctuations affect the relative bargaining strength of buyers and sellers. This situation has had a fundamental influence on both the level and the control of production quality.

Although there are often no clearly laid-down commercial standards, this should not be regarded as a reason for reducing efforts to control quality. When certain customers are not able to measure quality characteristics in a systematic and precise way, it is incorrect to assume that they do not regard them as important, even though this is not explicitly stated. Secondly, many of the quality characteristics are an index not only of the suitability of the product for subsequent use but also of the ease of processing in the producing mill itself. For instance, it may be worth while for a spinner to produce a yarn stronger than a particular weaver requires because such a yarn can be processed with fewer breakages at the spinning frame. With reference to many of the characteristics not closely determined by the raw material used, it is often expensive to process low-quality product.

Better product quality is often associated with better and cheaper processing at the producer's mill as well as at that of the purchaser. Without adequate control procedures and checks, however, it is not possible for a manufacturer to evaluate the gains made in his own processing. In short, a producer is not able to make a consistent decision on what quality to aim for if account is taken only of the demands made by his customers.

Mill standards

Commercial standards relate to the quality level desired for the particular market in which the product is to be sold. More simply, they arc those that arc referred to by the buyer and seller in connection with their commercial transactions. Whatever commercial arrangements are made, however, the individual producer should aim at laying down performance standards at each processing stage in as precise and detailed a form as possible. These constitute a second group, which can be called 'mill-quality standards'.

For instance, to evaluate the setting, scouring, and maintenance procedures at the doorframe, it is necessary to measure the regularity of the sliver produced, with regard both to its over-all level and to the incidence of periodicities. This could in no way be called a commercial standard, in that no one Purchasing the yarn would be directly concerned with its performance at an early stage of processing.

The purpose of mill quality standards is to Provide management with a measure of the mill's quality performance. When standards for different quality characteristics are laid down and agreed with the Personnel responsible for their attainment, management is in a strong position to locate weaknesses in staff, materials, or machines and to take appropriate action when and where standards are not met. Without objective quality indices, management cannot assess quality performance and its position is correspondingly weakened.

The setting of these standards, which must be realistic, is not easy. What is realistic in any particular situation depends on the inherent variation in the process and on what is feasible, bearing in mind the quality of the material or labour employed. To get this information very often requires complex process-capability studies and, as so often, the greatest enemy is wishful thinking. If the customer is demanding a standard higher than can be met with existing machinery or materials, no useful Purpose is to be served by arbitrarily tightening mill standards.

Commercial and mill standards tend to coincide, in the long run. This is because, in general terms, if the quality is lower that desired, the product will not be sold, and, if the quality is higher than that desired, it will adversely affect the firm's competitive position because the product will cost more. 'In general terms' is the key phrase here because the here, because the determination of these standards is taking place in a changing situation, and the actual position seldom, if ever, reaches equilibrium. Again, as has been previously stated, it may still pay in certain cases to produce a quality higher than is needed if the processing economies that result justify it.

The discussion has manufacturing one quality of implicitly assumed that the producer is manufacturing one product. In actual practice, this is rarely so, and often there will be several different quality levels in a mill. It will not always be possible or desirable to achieve coincident commercial and mill-quality standards, on all of them.

The quality of material and the length and type of processing can be varied, but the mill standards for operative performance and machine condition must be geared to the highest quality being produced. In these respects, long-term quality standards must be the dominant ones, for it is notoriously difficult to restore lowered quality. Many firms found that they paid dearly for condoning poor operative methods and inadequate machine maintenance in the period of lowered commercial standards immediately after the second world war.

Technological standards

Finally, mention should be made of the role of general technological and processing standards. These 'norms' which are Published in various technical Journals, as well as in machinery manufacturer' specifications, are useful to management despite their inevitable generality. They usually relate to what is feasible in the present state of technical knowledge and machine development. To illustrate, one may quote some of the performance features to be expected from a modern speedframe employed on the cotton system for coarse-medium counts. The coefficient of variation of weight per unit length within a bobbin should be less than 1 per cent; the Uster regularity percentage should not exceed 3.5 per cent and there should be no periodicities; it should be Possible to change the staple length Processed by 3/16 in.

Without changing settings, with a maximum

deterioration of 0.5 per cent. This information is useful in helping management to evaluate the Possible gain to be made in quality in relation to the capital expenditure necessary to achieve it. In addition, it gives an indication of the expected future level of competition in quality. Unfortunately, however, it does not Provide much assistance to a Particular firm in fixing its mill-quality standards.

Most firms are more interested in finding out how they compare With other firms using similar processing and machines of comparable age, rather than with some theoretical ideal. Such information is rarely available, and there is a tendency for managements to attribute all the quality differences to better machinery or different processing. Actual inter-firm comparison are so infrequent, and information is so scanty, that it is difficult to know if mill-quality standards are realistic.

There is undoubtedly a great deal of confusion over standards in many textile firms. This often results in an unwillingness or inability to lay down what is to be achieved at the various stages of manufacture. It is Important that the scope and aim in any particular case should be laid down and clearly understood by all concerned. Only then is it possible to devise a quality policy to meet these aims and, by measuring the results of such a policy, to evaluate its effectiveness. There are many difficulties in drawing up the various standards that form an essential part of a quality policy. One approach, which the author has found to be of value in widely differing circumstances, is that of 'quality audit'. It is not possible here to give a detailed description, and a brief outline only is included below.

A quality audit can be regarded as a logical application of the scientific method to the problem, of quality improvement. Initially, information is collected on all those factors that affect the final quality of the product. The central feature of this initial stage is the series of observations carried out by a team drawn from the mill staff. These observations provide details of the processing conditions on the various machines and the methods employed by the operatives attending those machines.

Concurrently, inspections are carried out to assess the mechanical state of the machines in question and to measure the environmental conditions in which processing is being undertaken. To complete the picture, the material itself is tested at various stages of processing. This provides more information on the effects of these various factors on the quality of the final product.

These observations, inspections, and tests are planned in such a way that it is possible to interpret and analyse the interrelationships that they reveal by the use of nothing more than the simplest statistical methods. This analysis forms the second stage of the audit, the object being to trace back significant quality differences to the relevant technical and operating conditions. From the results of the analysis a report is drawn up, this providing a complete account of the quality position of the mill. While the various types of remedial action are being undertaken, routine control methods are planned and installed to ensure that the improvements secured are maintained.

There are four main features of the approach that merit emphasis. First, the audit deals with all those factors that affect the final quality of the product and is not confined to the normal laboratory tests, which give only part of the picture. The usual difficulty in doing this is that there are so many factors that the data become unmanageable. The difficulty is alleviated in this method by building the data around investigation of one quality indicator. For spinning, doubling, and weaving, the number of 'end-down' is used. It is naturally much easier to study interrelationships between various factors if some sort of framework is available. The position is also eased by the use of very simple methods of quality assessment, such as the use of the + ; ± ; - scale to evaluate certain characteristics.

Obviously, other and more precise methods are employed, but often the simple methods are sufficient to reveal processing or technical weaknesses. The problem is the general one of trying to comply with the aims, which are sometimes mutually inconsistent, of keeping the data down to manageable proportions, getting them to be sufficiently accurate to be significant, and doing the job reasonably quickly with the type of observer available.

Since data are collected on all the factors affecting quality, the ensuing report thus provides a complete account of the quality position at one point in time. The interrelationship and interdependence of the various factors are clearly revealed, and such inconsistencies as may be present are highlighted. Managements are therefore able to see the whole picture and can then use this to establish a quality policy. Secondly, the audit brings together the various groups of people who have special responsibility for quality control. All learn to understand the contribution made by each other. In particular, the co-operation between laboratory and mill staff encouraged by the audit is likely to be continued afterwards. Several of the data-collection methods used can be adapted by the quality-control staff to help the supervisor to keep a check on the quality aspects of machine and operative performance.

The third feature is that of carrying out the whole

survey with the mill's own staff. This helps both in the collection of data and in the acceptance of results. Since all levels of mill staff have played some part in the final report, there is much greater likelihood that action to remedy particular faults will be taken. Essentially, the approach or method is aimed at helping the mill to help itself

Finally, the mill is being compared with itself. Although technological standards are used for comparison with regard to such characteristics as count, irregularity, etc., on many aspects none are available. In any case, to use such standards would be quite unrealistic, especially when an older mill is being considered. Mill standards, however, are always computed. For instance, if one group of frames is significantly worse than the rest in some respect, then attention can be directed to those frames, even though there are no 'technological standards' available for frames of that age and condition. Even if the long-term solution lies in re-equipment, some standards are necessary to ensure that an the frames are brought to a common level, however low this might be.

Framework of control

In a publication as general as this, the intention is not to describe particular control procedures but rather to provide some indication of the anatomy of control. Furthermore, although the various factors are interrelated, for ease of presentation they have been considered under three headings: Materials, Machines, and Operatives.

Materials

Initially, it is necessary to check whether the raw material, yarn, or cloth purchased conforms to the specification laid down. The importance of this aspect of control varies markedly from one section of the industry to another. For instance, in cotton spinning it is feasible and desirable to make on the raw cotton a range of tests covering such characteristics as staple length, maturity, percentage short fibre, fibre strength and fineness, and trash content. The whole of the subsequent processing will be affected by the results of such tests.

On the other hand, the weaver is often in the position of being unable to carry out more than the most rudimentary check on the standard of the incoming yam, particularly where beams are concerned. Unless the small sample reveals a major fault, the usual purpose is not so much to differentiate between good or bad batches but, over a period of time, to select good suppliers. Even apart from the sample-size problem, there is the difficulty of the characteristics to be tested. This is particularly so in weaving, where the factors that determine the performance of a certain set in the loom are just as likely to be found in the way it was prepared as in the inherent qualities of the yarn.

After the initial raw-material testing, the material may be tested after or during subsequent processing. These tests are to provide both a check on the running of the process and a basis for action where results differ from the standard. These checks are an important part of control in such process industries as spinning, rather than in assembly ones such as weaving or knitting. For instance, the regularity of a drawframe sliver may be tested on a daily basis. The over-all level provides an indication of the processing up to and including the drawframe process. The existence of certain periodicities of varying wave lengths also provides an indication of the areas where action needs to be taken.

In dealing with the final stage of material testing, i.e., the outgoing finished product, the aims of the procedures employed are threefold. First, they serve to provide a check on the characteristics of the product to see whether they conform to customer standards. The check may result in the despatch of the cloth or yarn, etc., as satisfactory or it may lead to its being withheld. Between these two extremes, there are an infinite number of possible courses of action, which may include price allowances. Where the product is supplied to customers with varying acceptance standards, the final testing may be used to provide a basis for allotting the product to the different customers.

Secondly, the degree of conformance of the final product to the standard laid down may be regarded as an indication of the effectiveness of quality control in the mill; for instance, with such characteristics as the variation in count, which reflects the ultimate effectiveness of a series of controls at various stages of processing.

Thirdly, the testing of the product can be regarded as a check on the final process. The regularity of yarn, for instance, taken in conjunction with that of the roving fed to the ringframe, indicates not only an important feature of the final product but also the degree of control in the ringroom.

Machines

Theoretically, were it possible to establish clearly the exact causes of variations from standard by examining the product, there would be no need to consider control procedures other than those related to material and product testing. In practice, however, this is not possible, and, even if it were, it does not necessarily follow that this would be the best thing to do. This is because the type of control procedure affects the likelihood that action will be taken on the results. For instance, if yarn is examined and periodicities are revealed, it is possible to conclude that an eccentric roller is causing the fault. At the same time, there may be a multitude of causes that have contributed, and the most direct way is to examine the rollers with an eccentricity gauge. This has the added advantage that it can be performed by the overlooker himself. With reference to machines, it can be argued that it is first necessary to check whether the postulated quality characteristics are consistent with the capabilities of the machine. This corresponds to the problem of selecting materials that can be expected to give certain characteristics in the final product.

For instance, just as it is impossible to spin yarns of a certain count and strength from certain cottons, it is equally impossible to produce yarn of a certain level of regularity from machines of certain age and design. There is also the question of whether it is possible to produce a certain quality by processing the material through a limited sequence of machines. These last two factors are interrelated with the process capabilities of the individual machines making up that sequence.

The action associated with these checks and process-capability studies will depend on both the results and the time factor. Small deviations from standard may lead to adjustment in the succeeding process or to changing the feeding procedures at the machine tested. Machine checks initially involve ensuring that the machine has been correctly set up, i.e., that the speeds and settings are consistent with obtaining the desired characteristics in the product. It is also necessary to check periodically that these speeds and settings remain as laid down. Checks should be made to ensure that the condition of the machines is being maintained at a level consistent with quality requirements. This provides a good example of how different levels of management are affected by the results of a particular control procedure.

It may reveal the need for relatively minor action, e.g., the fitting of new traveller cleaners in ring-spinning frames. The decision here can be made at departmental level. It may reveal the necessity for changes in the stipulated maintenance programme, e.g., increasing scouring frequencies. The appropriate action here involves the mill manager in that the effects of such a change will affect the balance of production in all departments.

Operatives

In relation to operatives, there are really three main areas of quality-control checks or procedures. Each must be covered to ensure that quality reaches, and is maintained at, the required level.

First, it is necessary to establish whether the operatives possess the level of ability required. Associated closely with this aspect of control, which is more accurately part of selection, is the question of training the operatives once they have been selected. It is fairly easy to do this with new operatives if systematic training procedures are adopted, but much more difficult with experienced operatives whose bad quality habits are deeply rooted.

Quality practices are by no means standardized, and it follows that each operative should be clearly informed of what he or she is supposed to do in very considerable detail. This can be illustrated by the possible ways of carrying out the apparently straightforward task of creeling in a can at the drawframe. There are two normal ways of doing this:

i. piece start of the full can to the end of the preceding can; this involves removing the remainder of the sliver from the old can while the frame is running, turning it over, and piecing the end to the start of the full can; and

ii. break the sliver and piece it to the start of a new can, a remnant being left in the bottom of the old one.

The piece that is created as a result of the adoption of the second method can, in turn, be disposed of in one of several ways:

a. it can be pieced to the top of the full can later;

b. it can be discarded as waste;

c. it can be placed in a special 'piece can'; or

d. the can containing it can be transferred to the front of the preceding head and used instead of an empty can at doff.

The quality of the product is clearly affected by the creation and use of these pieces. If the first or third means of disposal is employed, two further piecings are necessary to put the piece back into the system. The 'piece-can' method has an additional and obvious detrimental effect on quality. The last method requires only one join to put a piece back into the system, but, if the practice is continued, the piece will remain in the can for a long period of time.

This particular aspect has been given in some detail to illustrate the fact that there are often several ways of performing a relatively straight forward task in an individual situation. To ensure that the correct one is used involves not only a detailed breakdown of the task but clear instructions on each part of it, followed by regular checks to ensure that the stipulated procedure is adhered to.

The second area requiring attention is the work allocation. Does it permit the achievement of the quality standards ? This must be checked, for it cannot be assumed to be correct. In this respect, the role of techniques such as work study is important. For instance, it is just as important to calculate the amount of cleaning necessary as it is to discover the amount of time it takes to clean. Too often cleaning frequencies bear no relation to the standard of cleanliness of machines required for a given level of product cleanliness.

The work-study officer is not responsible for the decision on such frequencies: he merely takes them into account in calculating the over-all work-load. The precision in timing a particular operation is likely, however, to give an aura of objectivity, which conceals the fact that decisions on the nature and extent of cleaning are frequently made quite unsystematically.

If one considers work organization in the broader aspect, there seems little doubt that some systems of work allocation do adversely affect the quality of the product. For instance, it is customary in ring spinning for the operative to be responsible for patrolling the spinning frames both to repair broken ends and to replenish the empty supply packages. Some work-loading systems have aimed at separating these two jobs. Theoretically, there should be no overlap between the duties allocated to each group. In practice it is by no means so simple.

The division of responsibilities tends to have an adverse effect on quality, with respect both to the individual operative, who finds other people are playing a part in affecting the processing conditions, and to the supervisor, who finds it difficult to allocate responsibility. This is not necessarily to imply that these disadvantages may not be more than offset by increased machine efficiency, etc. In general terms then, it is wrong to consider standards of operative performance without regard to the particular work organization in which they are expected to operate. This should be interpreted in the widest sense and should not be confined to the division of duties.

It should also cover processing conditions at the operative's own and previous processes, together with machine settings and conditions. The last aspect of operative control is concerned with the establishment of check procedures to see whether operatives are carrying out their quality duties according to the appropriate standards.

The important thing is that these checks should be systematic and provide results in such a form that action can be taken. This framework covers the main areas that merit attention if quality control is to be effective.There will be marked differences of emphasis, depending on the section of the textile industry under consideration, and differences will also arise from firm to firm within a particular section.

Organization of control

The previous section was concerned with the framework within which techniques or procedures could be employed to achieve control of the quality characteristics of the product being manufactured. The range of subjects covered was considerably wider than that usually associated with quality control but was consistent with the wider definition of the subject given earlier. It is now necessary to consider the organizational implications of such a definition.

Management is responsible for laying down an integrated policy with respect to quality improvement and control. This policy should cover all the widely varying matters outlined in the previous section. Above all, it should be consistent with the production policy, and both should be regarded as equally important. The danger is that a clear quality policy is not produced and the quality programme is left to the various departments and sections, with their conflicting interests. It should be appreciated that production and quality requirements are often initially inconsistent, and, unless management takes its quality responsibilities as seriously as its production ones, quality will go by default. To label the head of the testing laboratory or inspection department a 'quality controller' often aggravates the difficulty, since it can mislead management into believing that, once it has made such an appointment or has set up such a department, it has discharged its quality responsibilities.

Almost every functional specialist has a part to play in assisting management to achieve the establishment and control of quality at the desired level. In the absence of a clear policy, these specialists and their departments tend to work independently of each other. Even where no actual differences arise, decisions are taken by one section that affect the success of decisions already made in others.

There are especial dangers in the situation where each functional specialist, such as the work-study engineer, the training officer, etc., believes that he has no direct responsibility with respect to quality, since this is the responsibility of another specialist section—the quality-control department. The laboratory staff are often well aware of those factors that make control difficult, but, since they are usually of a similar status to the personnel from the other sections, it is obviously difficult for them to take the initiative for the necessary co-ordination.

To avoid these difficulties, management should lay down a clear quality policy, together with the responsibilities of each section and department for the execution of such a policy. What is required is somebody able to give specialist advice on all aspects of control procedures relating to products, operatives, machines, work organization, etc. A possible title, and one found increasingly in the United States and on the continent, is that of 'quality analyst'. The word 'controller' has been deliberately discarded, since the actual control must remain in the hands of the management. The quality analyst occupies a position corresponding to that of a production engineer on the production side.

In practice, it may not be possible or economic to add a further specialist of this kind, and, if this is so, it will be necessary to increase the authority and broaden the activities of the testing department. Top management would certainly need to call upon the quality analyst to assist it in evaluating and assessing the over-all quality position, and it is therefore desirable to make him directly responsible to the board of directors or the general manager. Once the policy has been agreed upon, it should be implemented in the same way as the production policy associated with it.

Techniques of quality control

Quality control, as already defined, is concerned with both the procedures used and the action taken, to ensure that the quality characteristics of the product conform to the required standard. Consideration has already been given to standards, and the section on the framework of control has indicated the areas where control is necessary. Following this, the organizational aspects of control have been discussed. Finally, attention should be given to the actual procedures or techniques that the quality analyst and his staff can employ to assist management in taking corrective action.

Effectiveness of techniques

The major difficulty in describing such techniques is their number and variation, which represent, as they must, the requirements of widely different sections and processes. For instance, techniques employed in the spinning section of the industry are those associated with a process industry, whereas those in weaving are more analogous to those found in an assembly industry. Within each of these groups alone, there are a great number of procedures and checks. No useful purpose would be served by providing a catalogue of all the methods that could be employed in such a varied industry. It is more valuable to attempt to uncover the features common to effective control.

The first point to note is that there are very few so-called control procedures that do, in fact, control. With the exception of automatic-regulating devices that are built into the process, the effect of control procedures is indirect. They serve usually to detect differences between actual and standard, and, for certain quality characteristics, to measure such differences quantitatively. Although this is a necessary condition for control, it is clearly not a sufficient one.

Control depends on the taking of the correct remedial action. It follows that a procedure cannot be judged merely from the standpoint of whether or not it reveals a particular quality shortcoming; reference needs to be made to the likelihood that effective action will result from such a presentation. The first step in all control procedures involves the collection of data about the characteristics of the yarn or cloth being considered. It is at this initial stage that a serious problem is encountered.

To obtain accurate data often involves the use of testing instruments of increasing complexity. Not only are the instruments complicated, but many can be used only under specially controlled atmospheric conditions and hence must be placed in a room separated from the manufacturing process. It follows from this that the person who is carrying out the check is often different from the one who carries out the action demanded as a result of the check. This extra step tends to militate against action. It raises an immediate communication problem, aggravated by a physical and, in certain cases, a status separation. The more complicated the test procedures and the more specialized the interpretation of the results, the more difficult the problems become.

Types of control

Several points that follow from this directly affect the type of control procedures used. First, the best way to solve such a communication problem is to remove it by devising methods that can be employed by the people who are responsible for taking action on the results. For instance, yarn cleanliness is often an important quality characteristic. There are several sophisticated procedures in use in laboratories for judging this. It is difficult, however, to feed the assessment back to the mill in such a way as to promote remedial action.

It is more satisfactory to devise a means of enabling the supervisors to check the amount of cleaning that is being performed by operatives, so that the necessary action can be taken to remove the causes of dirty yarn. There are difficulties involved in drawing up such procedures. First, it is difficult to assess cleanliness, especially when the degree expected varies with both the fibre properties and the part of the machine inspected. Secondly, since cleaning is done periodically, to judge the operative objectively it is necessary to inspect the machines over a long period of time. Thirdly, the criteria of the assessment have to be sufficiently simple to allow the operative to appreciate in what way he or she is at fault and sufficiently quick to prevent the system from becoming too much of a burden for the supervisor.

The method below shows how these difficulties can be overcome, but of greater importance is the fact that it provides a demonstration of the type of procedure that sometimes has to be used to instigate action. Initial agreement is reached on what are the key points needing inspection and, depending on the time available, on the number of machines to be inspected per day or per shift. A simple + ; ± ; - scale of assessment may be found to be most useful.

From analysis, it is possible to see not only which operatives clean less frequently or less effectively or both than the others, but also which key points are being overlooked. It is also possible to judge whether work-study allowances for cleaning are appropriate for the degree of cleanliness required. The supervisor knows where to take action and the operative can understand on what basis it is being taken.

In many cases, it is not possible to use test methods that can be performed directly by supervisors. In these circumstances, it should be appreciated that whether action is taken or not on the basis of the results produced by the testing department depends on the confidence in, and understanding of, the results by line management. Every effort must be made to develop and use simple techniques. An illustration of this is found in the example of machine control below.

Simple machine-control methods are of great value to supervisors, especially in an industry where they are often responsible for a large number of machines. There are various statistical methods for revealing machine differences, but these are often too complicated for departmental supervisors to understand. Consider the case of cotton carding, where the carder or under-carder needs a means of determining maintenance and resetting requirements on upwards of 100 machines. A good indication of this can be obtained by observing the incidence of neps, small knots of entangled fibres, which appear in the web of material being produced by the machine. For a given quality and mixing of cotton, a deterioration of card condition tends, other things being equal, to reflect itself in an increased incidence of neps. By plotting the results of nep counts in histogram form and inserting the number of the machine in the appropriate square, it is possible for the supervisor to see at a glance where attention is needed.

It is not always necessary to calculate statistical limits, for, if a machine consistently appears at the upper extremity, it should be examined. All that is necessary is a form of spot-lighting, which will enable staff to concentrate their efforts where they are most needed. The results produced in the succeeding weeks enable a check to be made on whether action has been taken and also on whether it has been effective or not. As with the case of cleanliness, it is not necessary to work to any standard, and the object is to move the whole distribution, as it were, to the left.

One danger is that the machines will settle at too high a level, but normally this does not seem to happen and the process of correcting extreme results goes on until an optimum position is reached. It is then necessary to install a spot-check to ensure that the level is maintained, and this generally involves setting statistical limits. Normally, however, improvement comes before control. The introduction of such methods helps to take quality control out of the laboratory and build it into the mill. They are an attempt to place on an objective basis judgements that the supervisor is making every day, often in rather an ineffective way.

Statistical methods

In the textile industry, one of the most notable characteristics and one of the major sources of difficulty is the variability of raw material and product at different stages of processing. It is largely this factor of variation that necessitates the use of statistical methods in quality control. There is, however, a danger in equating statistical methods with progressive methods. In many branches of textiles, there is evidence that, although simple statistical tools are invaluable, there is a rapid falling off in effectiveness as more complicated statistical techniques are employed. This is not necessarily a criticism of the methods but is implicit in a realistic appraisal of the industrial circumstances in which they have to be applied.

There are certainly very special difficulties in enabling mill personnel to understand results with a statistical background, and there is ample evidence of a negative emotional response to symbols, but the tremendous advantages that can be obtained by having personnel with a basic knowledge of simple frequency distributions, measures of variation, etc., make the attempt to surmount such problems worthwhile.

Certainly one of the main tasks of the quality-control personnel is to train the supervisory staff in simple statistical procedures. Such training must start from a very simple basis, such as the drawing of graphs, and must relate closely to the particular product and processes with which the supervisor is familiar. It is not suggested that every supervisor or departmental manager should expect to be familiar with every test or method of analysis, even if this were possible, but that, if he is given sufficient understanding of some of them, he will have confidence in the others. Even if he does not understand certain aspects of them, he will nevertheless act in accordance with them. If this is not done, there is a real danger that a division will arise between the quality-control department and the mill.

Quite apart from these difficulties, the usefulness of statistical methods varies from case to case. In certain sections, they can and do make a significant contribution; in others, they play no real part. Even where they are applied, they have to be judged in relation to a whole series of problems of a non-statistical nature.

One of the most commonly used methods is that of control charts. The control chart is simply a graphical device for indicating when a particular process has moved away from specification. The limits that indicate such a change are based on a measurement of the inherent variation in the process, so that, when a result falls outside the limit, this indicates that it is unlikely that such a result could have occurred without there being a real change in the underlying situation. It follows that there is an infinite number of possible control limits, each one associated with a level of probability. Conventionally, the 1/40 and 1/1000 limits-the so-called 'warning' and 'action' limits-are usually used.

Control charts

Control charts, like any other control method, can be effective only if they are employed in the right place and if the correct action is taken on the results received. Unfortunately, such problems are more difficult to solve than the basic theory is to learn.

An unsuccessful application of the theory is likely to result in lack of confidence in control procedures in general, and to rebuild such confidence takes time. The first thing for the quality controller to do after mastering the theory is to discuss the control with the supervisory staff. Its application affects all of them and will only be successful if they understand what it is trying to achieve and if they are in agreement with its aims. At what process ought control charts to be installed ? This is closely linked with the question of where to institute control. If control is being instituted at the wrong point, the use of one particular method of control, i.e., the control chart, will be of no avail. The correct point is determined by a knowledge of textile machinery and processing rather than by statistics. For instance, consider the case of count control in spinning. Over the past few years, there has been a tendency for attention to be moved from the ringframe back to earlier processes.

The argument is heard that nothing can be done once the roving is in the ringframe creel, for a pinion change is as likely to make things worse as it is to improve them. Irrespective of the validity of this particular argument, it is clear that, at the outset, management must decide where it thinks the appropriate control points are. A decision on where to control is an indispensable prerequisite for deciding what action should be taken if the chart shows results out of control.

It we assume that the control charts have been implemented and results plotted, what should be done if a result falls outside the action limit ? The textbooks are usually vague and talk of an assignable cause being at work and indicating that appropriate action should be taken. The methods used and action must depend on the particular assignable cause. It follows that the next step in control-chart implementation is to consider what are the factors that cause results to fall outside the limits.

First, there are machine faults. After the control points have been determined, the next step is to eradicate machine defects and between machines variation. Owing to inadequate instrumentation or knowledge, it will often be impossible to do this completely. In many cases, there are no explicit performance standards, and the problem is reduced to getting all the machines to a similar level as a basis for over-all improvement. This again is the technologist's field, certain statistical methods being employed to assist in evaluating the effects of his efforts. The reduction of machine differences until a group of machines can be regarded as homogeneous leads to the question of the unit of control. This is yet another decision that has to be made in any control-chart application.

For instance, if several frames are mechanically similar and are being fed by one supply frame, it is often possible and economic to use one chart and change the frames where necessary en bloc. While the method of supply, which determines whether group control can be instituted, is under discussion, it is worth noting that failure to control the average values of machines in one process intend to cause excessive variation in machines at the subsequent process and that this cannot by eradicated by adjusting these latter machines. This is one of the reasons why the emphasis on control is increasingly on the earlier processes. It also demonstrates that control, to be effective, should be integrated.

Secondly, it may be that the result has fallen outside the limit because of an incorrect machine setting. Indeed, most of the emphasis usually centres on this cause. In many instances, as has already been illustrated, machine adjustment should be taken into account. Where adjustment is costly or troublesome, action limits should be chosen to ensure that unnecessary changes are made very infrequently. Again, most machines can be adjusted only by a discrete amount. No useful purpose is to be served by setting limits at ± 0.5 per cent if the minimum change is one tooth on a 50s pinion.

Another factor in adjustment in general is the type of variation to be controlled. In many textile processes, the reduction of short-term variation may lead to an increase in long-term variation. The control-chart design must take this into account. If the interest is mainly in long-term variation, it is better theoretically to make adjustments on the trend shown by several readings.

Unfortunately, this may necessitate a fairly complicated set of action rules, which the operative may find difficult to follow. In the end, management has to choose between what is theoretically best and what is practically possible.

Finally, mention must be made of the assumption that the results plotted on the charts are independent. In certain textile cases, this is not true, since cyclical forces are at work. Failure to correct these at the previous processes makes it difficult to decide what adjustments to make at the present one. To adjust downwards when the trend is downward may lead to over-correction and, with the normal limited sampling possible, it is often difficult to establish the particular phase of the cycle.

On the other hand, to include this cyclical fluctuation as part of the natural spread of the process would mean including part of the variation that the control system has been set up to remove. These fluctuations are not always constant, and many have not been satisfactorily explained. They provide an example of where the statistical model fails to describe adequately the situation under which control is being attempted.

The inevitable variability in textile processes implies the use of certain statistical methods as a necessary condition of the effective control of these processes. The control chart is one of the simpler methods available, and it has proved particularly useful in establishing realistic tolerances and enabling systematic machine adjustment, etc., to be established. It has the further advantage of being reasonably easy to interpret and can be sufficiently well understood by those who may well find certain other statistical methods and concepts beyond their understanding. Whether the control chart is successful or not depends on where and how it is introduced. The problems found in implementing such a control procedure are representative of those in introducing statistical methods in general. The problems are not normally of a statistical nature; rather does their solution involve an initimate knowledge of textile processing and of production conditions in the mill concerned. It follows that, in selecting a person to be responsible for statistical control procedures, it is usually better to employ a technologist with a grounding in statistics than to use a statistician who is not fully familiar with textile processes.

Impact of change

Whatever the importance of quality control in the textile industry has been up to the present, there is no doubt that the changes currently taking place will increase its importance in the future. Other chapters have shown that almost every section of the industry is undergoing a structural, managerial, or technological revolution. These revolutions will, in turn, markedly affect the quality position.

The actual level of production quality is not determined solely by control procedures or a certain managerial approach. More systematic control will help management to obtain the maximum out of the machines, materials, and operatives. Even so, much depends on the resources over which control is being instituted, whether this control is satisfactory or not. In all three groups, important changes are taking place. Although there are evident interrelationships, it is convenient here to consider these changes in two groups.

Materials

The dominant factor here is the growing importance of man-made fibres. Although their impact has probably been greatest on the cotton system, there is now no section that is not affected, influenced, or dominated by the products of the fibre producers. The influence is not restricted to the products of these firms because, in certain cases, they have sought, for a multitude of reasons, to exert direct financial influence and control in several sections. This subject is more appropriately dealt with in another chapter, but it is mentioned here to emphasize the fact that the influence of man-made fibres on the textile industry is often found in the most acute and direct form.

Two general points need making with regard to the fibres themselves. First, whereas variations in a particular natural fibre can be regarded as being of degree only, variations in man-made fibres often relate to the molecular structure itself. Secondly, and more important, the main properties of such fibres, and consequently of the resultant yam or fabric, are controllable to a greater extent than is the case with natural fibres. For example, the fineness of the fibre can be adjusted by changing the extrusion process. Again, a fibre producer can counterbalance the reduction in yarn strength resulting from coarsening the fibre by simultaneously increasing the staple length.

Quite apart from the additional properties that man-made fibres bring, the methods of manufacture are such that they can more easily be made to conform with the requirements of a particular end-use. The introduction of man-made fibres has had a fundamental impact in this case. With the multiplicity of properties found in fibres available at various prices, it is possible to blend together different fibres to produce a yarn tailor-made for a particular purpose, even where there is no one fibre available with all the desired qualities. Again, where an expensive fibre is needed to give a particular property, it is sometimes possible to reduce the total cost by blending with a cheaper fibre and still retain enough of the key property to enable the final product to conform with the specification.

It is suggested not that blending of natural fibres of different growths has not taken place but that the blending did not change the fundamental character of the final product, which always had the essential properties of cotton, wool, etc. Thus, on the material side, the increasing possibilities of fibre engineering has had a fundamental impact on end-use suitability. In the sense that quality control commences with the design of the product to meet the requirements of the ultimate customer, the growing importance of man-made fibres has brought about fundamental changes in the very basis of the subject matter.

Machines and operatives

There is no doubt that since 1945, and particularly since 1950, there has been a very rapid technological advance in almost all the processes associated with textile manufacture. To a certain extent, these advances have occurred as pre-war projects have in more recent years been successfully completed. The main driving force, however, has come from the marked changes in the labour situation found in the textile industries in many countries. The direction of the advance has reflected this influence very closely.

In many cases, the most important item in the final cost of a fabric or yam is that of raw materials. Individual companies, however, have little control over this item except in its selection. The position has deteriorated with the increase of governmental policies in the supply country, which has further reduced the influence of the purchaser. Attention has been increasingly directed towards the second most important factor of cost, that of labour. Even here, in a modern organized textile industry, the individual firm has little possibility of influencing the general level of wages, and its best way of influencing labour costs lies in the reduction of the total number of labour hours necessary to produce a certain product. Thus, even if the labour situation has remained unchanged, this has been a reasonable line of approach for firms seeking to improve their position.

In fact, of course, the whole labour position has been marketly changed by the war, and this has further encouraged firms to base their future policies on reducing labour content. Labour-saving developments have followed three main lines in textile processing. In the first place, there has been a reduction in the number of processes; secondly, there has been a trend towards fewer machines at each remaining process ; and, finally, there has been a reduction in the work demanded in tending each machine.

It is not necessary here to study the technical details associated with each of these lines of development. Not only have the improvements made it possible to produce yarn or fabric with fewer people and fewer machines, but they have also raised the level of production quality. It is this aspect that is considered here. In modernized mills, the scale of the operative problem is much reduced. Since the labour cost now constitutes a much smaller proportion of total cost, it is feasible and economic to offer higher rewards and to select the best of the labour market. This reduced demand is not restricted to direct operatives for there is also a reduction in the number of cleaners, oilers, etc., required, this group of jobs being a function of the machine-hours used rather than of the number of yards or pounds produced. With a reduced labour force, not only are the training problems fewer but the supervisory problems are also much reduced.

With regard to certain quality characteristics, the introduction of new machinery and ancillary equipment automatically brings about a quality improvement. It should not be assumed, however, that quality problems will automatically be solved with modernization. Although modernization aids quality, the relationship is rather a complex one.

Without high product quality, modernization is impossible. The two are closely linked; one is dependent upon the other. This will readily be appreciated when the type of modernization that is taking place is considered. The saving in labour arises largely from the use of fewer processes and machines. It follows that the degree of control needed at each process is correspondingly greater. Similarly, with fewer machines running at higher speeds, the level of maintenance has to be raised and the speed with which the machines' defects are revealed increased. Even with fewer machines, the number of operatives has been more than correspondingly reduced.

It follows that each operative is tending more spindles, more looms, etc. In view of this, the running conditions must be very closely standardized, a slight deviation from standard upsetting the whole work-load situation. This need for control is not limited to operatives and production machines. The running of air-conditioning plant, the condition of the floors, and the state of the many ancillary machines are all of great importance. These points provide a clear answer to many queries raised regarding the importance of quality control. For any textile company to remain competitive, it is necessary to modernize and re-equip in order to reduce the labour hours per pound or per yard of product manufactured. Such a reduction will only be achieved if there is a systematic, precise, and effective control of each process.

14

Plant Maintenance

The evolution of the textile industry has brought about big changes in the function of plant-engineering. The early development of the textile industry was achieved by the ingenuity and inventiveness of engineers and mechanics, engineers as such have not played a dominant part in the production side of the industry. Enlightened management is realizing, however, that expensive precision machinery needs the services of competent engineers and technicians.

Scope of the plant-engineering function

The responsibilities of the plant-engineering department may be considered in two parts, as follows.

Primary functions are those of a truly engineering nature, such as plant and building maintenance and the provision of services.

Secondary functions are those that have fallen to the engineer's lot by custom or, as is often the case, that do not fit conveniently into the established pattern of production, sales, and administration.

The plant-engineering department may be responsible for some or all of the functions in the following schedule.

Primary functions

A. maintenance of plant, machinery, and equipment;

B. maintenance of buildings, property, roads, waterways, etc.;

C. maintenance and servicing of road transport and of internal materials-handling vehicles;

D. provision and maintenance of services such as compressed air, steam for process and space-heating, effluent and waste disposal, air-conditioning, hot-water supplies;

E. provision and maintenance of utilities such as electricity, gas, and water;

F. operation and maintenance of private power plant.

Secondary Functions

G. plant protection, safety and security, fire precautions;

H. administration of insurance;

I. cost control and budgeting of engineering services;

J. stores procurement and storekeeping;

K. execution of plant-development programmes.

Organisation and administration

The size and organization of the plant-engineering department in any textile production unit depends on several factors, as follows:

i. the size of the unit;

ii. the diversity of its products and processes;

iii. geographical considerations; are all the processes concentrated in one place or are they split up into small widely separated units ?

iv. the structure of company organization; is production administration centralized or dispersed ?

v. the technical standard of the unit.

Many combinations of the above factors exist in practice in the industry, and it is therefore necessary to generalize by considering typical organizations.

In small self-contained units, it is common to find a chief engineer, of foreman grade, responsible to the works manager for the operation and maintenance of works services. He has charge of several tradesmen, including mechanics, electricians, and builders, together with boiler firemen and greasers. He will himself take an active part in directing and executing maintenance work.

In such a unit, it is also common to find that the chief engineer has little or no responsibility for the maintenance and repair of production machinery. This is handled by the heads of production departments, who may have machine mechanics in their charge. Such an organization can work splendidly in a small unit under the direction of a competent works manager, and many successful enterprises have begun in this way. As growth of the unit occurs, however, it is not sufficient merely to expand the existing organization, as has often happened. It is necessary to change the organization to utilize the advantages of increased size, and to meet the problems that arise. So far as the plant-engineering function is concerned, a larger production unit necessitates the employment of more personnel, and hence the need for delegation of responsibility.

The advantage, however, is that the unit is able to afford more highly trained personnel and specialist technicians, and is also able to relieve production departments of many matters of an engineering nature, which they had hitherto handled themselves.

Personnel

The numbers of tradesmen employed on plant maintenance and works services vary widely, even between firms of a simzilar size engaged on similar processes. Much depends on the desired maintenance standards and the efficiency with which the work is organized and carried out. With a properly staffed engineering department, it will be found that it is fully, and usefully, employed under normal running conditions.

The load is rarely steady, since a progressive enterprise is always in a state of development. Short-term peak loads can be met by the judicious use of overtime and by a reallocation of work, but prolonged overloads must be met either by an increase in personnel or by the use of outside contract.

The latter course has the advantage that it avoids an insidious growth of engineering staff, and, furthermore, makes available resources of men and equipment that it would be uneconomical to possess permanently.

Although instrument mechanics and electronic engineers are usual for this work to be done by the makers of the equipment or by specialist firms. This type of equipment is becoming widely used, so that a large production unit may well find it profitable to employ its own personnel, in order to reduce downtime, and to undertake planned maintenance.

Workshop facilities

In the past, the majority of textile production units possessed extensive workshop facilities, indeed some had foundries and pattern shops and made their own machines. Workshops still exist but on a much reduced scale, since it is generally more economical to buy spares from the machine-makers and to use the small engineering jobbing shops that abound in an industrialized area. The emphasis, nowadays, is on proper stores control and an efficient procurement policy.

This also means keeping in touch with sources of supply and with the many developments in factory equipment.

Maintenance systems

The aim of any maintenance system is to preserve the capital equipment so that it is available for full and effective use by the organization. Since the objective of the organization is to make a profit, the problem is best considered in monetary terms. In an under-maintained plant, the cost of production will be high owing to small availability of plant and low output relative to the capital employed.

As more maintenance is carried out on such a plant, the cost of maintenance will rise, but initially it will be more than offset by the reduced production costs that follow. There is, however, an economic limit to this process, because ultimately a further increase in maintenance will have little effect on production costs.

Classification of maintenance

Maintenance systems may be divided into two categories:

A. breakdown maintenance; and

B. planned maintenance.

Breakdown maintenance

In this system, attention is given to the plant only when it breaks down. It finds favour because the direct cost of maintenance is low. The maintenance-department overheads are kept at a minimum because the system requires very little paperwork or planning.

The plant will become run down and increasingly prone to failure. Coincidence of breakdown will stretch the resources of the maintenance department, and machine downtime will increase. Inevitably, maintenance costs will rise to meet the deteriorating situation, with no commensurate saving in production costs. The true cost of a breakdown is often much greater than is apparent. In the closely integrated production sequences that exist in the textile industry, the consequences of failure can be felt throughout the whole manufacturing process and may go far as to influence production schedules, with resultant customer dissatisfaction. The trend in the textile industry towards automation and high-production machines aggravates this situation, pure breakdown-maintenance system is just not acceptable for this type of plant. A system of planned maintenance is essential.

Planned maintenance

The general concept of planned maintenance is that service is given to plant and machinery on a planned basis, sufficient to keep it in a condition to meet normal operating requirements. In this category fine divisions are sometimes recognized, such as *preventive maintenance* and *Scheduled maintenance*, but, since these really define the extent to which planned maintenance (PM) is applied, it is not useful to consider them further in this text.

A properly applied PM system is capable of taking maintenance into the zone of least total cost, and some of the benefits that accrue are listed in Table 1.

Table 1

Benefits of PM	Result
Increased machine availability, owing to fewer breakdowns	Improved production efficiency, better delivery timing, and maintenance of goodwill
Better machine performance owing to correct timing and adjustment	Fewer rejects, improved product quality, and longer machine life
Fewer major repairs due to consequential of breakdowns	Better utilization of damage maintenance labour force and saving in overtime

Reduction in need for stand-by equipment plant	A saving in capital outlay on
Better spare-parts control	A saving in stores-holding
Attention drawn to common cause of failure	Improvement in design and reduction in breakdown frequency

The idea of planned maintenance is not new and has been practised throughout industry in one form or another since factories began. The reliability of the old mill engines and drives depended I directly on servicing by the engineer, and on his skilled anticipation of potential trouble, coupled with appropriate remedial action. Likewise, on production machinery, it is commonplace for a thorough cleaning and check to be made of all important parts and their settings at prescribed intervals. It is not so common, however, for PM principles to be applied to the whole field of plant maintenance, and it is more usual to find that the bulk of the maintenance-department activity is directed towards breakdown repairs.

The application of PM must be on a systematic basis. Furthermore, it cannot be done on the cheap, and a halfhearted attempt will be doomed to failure. Initially, there is a rise in total maintenance cost owing to the additional clerical stiff and paperwork necessary, and also because invariably it is found that much work has to be done on plant and machinery as a result of the first inspections. As the work done on the plant takes effect, the cost of breakdown maintenance begins to fall, and, because the general condition of the plant is being improved to an acceptable level, so the expenditure on the PM element of cost may be reduced. Thus the total maintenance cost will reduce to a figure that often levels off below that obtained initially.

The benefits, however, are felt very soon, because the reduction in breakdowns brings returns on the production side, as was indicated previously.

Practical application of planned maintenance

The following notes are based on a *PM* system, installed by Urwick Orr & Partners Ltd., the consultants, which is in successful operation in a spinning and manufacturing unit. It serves to illustrate the basic principles that may be applied to any production unit, but it is emphasized that the detail may be varied and adapted to suit individual circumstances.

Initial specifications

If one considers any item of plant, it is possible to list all the points that require attention to keep it in good order. The list could be expanded to show the frequency of this attention, what should be done with regard to each item, and what tools would be needed. Finally, the list could indicate who should carry out the required attention.For the item of plant under consideration, one may thus prepare a collection of instruction sheets, or specifications, each directing the tradesman on the work required to be done when he is sent out on what, for convenience, will be referred to as a 'PM tour'.

The manual issued with a new motor car is a good example of a PM schedule. It specifies what work should be done on each part of the car and how often it is required.

The hard work in a PM system is involved not in operating it, but in preparing the initial specifications. Until all the makers of industrial plant emulate the motor-vehicle manufacturers, the specifications have to be prepared with local resources.

Although a competent man can easily prepare the

specifications for a particular item of plant, the variety in even a small factory is formidable and probably deters many from establishing a PM system. The best method is to put the task into the hands of a good consultant, which thus allows the regular engineering staff to perform their normal duties. It is sufficient initially to set any reasonable arbitrary time interval between PM tours. After two or three tours, it becomes clear whether or not this frequency is adequate.

The classification of the jobs by trade and grade of labour deserves careful thought in order to make the best use of available resources. Semiskilled work can be collected into tours, skilled tradesmen thus being relieved of such jobs.

The system in action

Specifications as described above are prepared for every item of plant encompassed by the scheme. Several copies of each are systematically filed, and for this purpose a reference-numbering system is desirable. A typical *PM* specification for a tour to be carried out, at four-monthly intervals, by an electrician on the electrical parts of 200 automatic looms. In this case, the sheet is handed to the electrician at the appropriate time together with a shed plan and report sheet. He does the work specified on it, but, if he comes across an extensive job, e.g., the rewiring of a loom, he notes it in the report sheet, so that special action may be taken later without interrupting his *PM* tour.

On completion of the tour, the specification sheet and completed report sheet are returned to the office. The former is filed to be used again, and the latter is used for further action, as described below.

Planning the programme

It will be appreciated that the heart of this PM system

lies in the specification file. It becomes a routine matter to issue the tours at the proper time. Normal work-planning methods, such as visual wall charts, can be used for operating the timetable.

The future programme can be planned to prevent undesirable coincidence of tours and to make the best use of available labour resources in the light of the overall maintenance commitment. The programme must fit in with production commitments, too, and it is implicit in any well-run maintenance system that there is full and complete collaboration with the production departments.

Feedback and follow-up

The information that comes back from a PM tour is important. Any extensive repairs noted in the report sheet are tackled. It is possible that there will be several of a similar nature. Considering them together aids planning and helps stores procurement. The stores used in the course of the tour, together with defective materials recovered, can often help in the elimination of trouble spots.

A further aspect of following up a PM tour is a review of the tour itself. If few faults have been found, it may be prudent to reduce the frequency of the tour. Sometimes it is found that part of the tour should be done more often than the remainder. In such a case, the tour is split, and two new specification sheets are prepared, the original being scrapped.

Any change in production conditions, such as addition of a night shift, should be borne in mind, so that tour frequencies may be adjusted accordingly. The instructions on the tour can be modified. It is a mistake to try to put too much in the specification sheets in the beginning, especially if the work is being done by skilled men. Experience on the plant may, however, warrant the addition of special instructions.

Limitations

If it is borne in mind that the economic objective of any maintenance scheme is to incur the least total cost to the organization, it is clear that only in special cases is it worth while aiming for complete elimination of breakdown. Such special cases are where a breakdown may lead to safety hazards or to serious risk of fire or explosion. These risks are, in fact, largely covered by statutory requirements in law.

There are other breakdown risks that do not hazard life or property but may have serious consequences in the production unit. In this category may be included the security of the main power supply and other important services.

The total cost of a breakdown could run into hundreds of pounds per minute. Such breakdowns are worth preventing. At the other end of the scale, there are breakdowns which, if they occur, have nuisance value only. They have small effect upon production and cost little to put right. It is not desirable to include such items of equipment in a PM scheme.

Design for maintenance

When maintenance is tackled on a planned basis by a system such as has been described, the work of the tradesman acquires an element of repetition. He knows what has to be done, and can go through the routine swiftly and without mistakes. The technique of repairing by exchange of assembly has much to commend it and has been widely adopted in the armed forces. To be effective, the equipment should be designed to enable complete assemblies to be removed and replaced quickly and simply.

If a fault is found that is not easily rectified on the spot, the assembly is removed and a good one substituted. The defective assembly is then overhauled under proper conditions on a bench or fixture, where spare parts, test instruments, gauges, etc., are at hand.

This technique has the following advantages:

A. The production machine is shut down only while the fault is diagnosed and the assembly exchanged. There is no time lost while intricate repairs are undertaken.

B. Specialist labour is used to the best advantage, because simple training only is necessary to exchange assemblies.

C. Better conditions of cleanliness, etc., can be provided outside the production area.

There is much room for improvement in the design of textile machinery in this respect, but the following are just a few examples of cases where the facility already exists.

A. 'P lug-in' electrical components, such as motor starters, relays, and control panels, are fitted to many modern textile machines. In some cases, simple modifications can permit their use with advantage.

B. The Unifil winder can be removed from a loom, complete, by production personnel, and a good one substituted. The mechanic can then carry out repairs on a test rig on his own bench.

C. In the Sulzer weaving machine, the entire picking mechanism and other assemblies can be detached for specialist attention.

D. On many winding frames, a complete winder head can be exchanged quickly.

Electrical faults

The diagnosis of electrical faults on complex control gear

can sometimes be difficult and long. Such equipment by its very nature is rarely spared willingly from the production line, so that a systematic approach to fault-finding is important.

Apart from the obvious need, that of training selected personnel properly in this work, it is often possible to modify the circuits themselves to make the job easier. For example, key test points in a control system can be wired to a common test panel.

The use of shorting plugs, disconnecting links, etc., in this panel, together with that of conventional electrical test instruments, will usually track down a fault very quickly and avoid the tedious job of breaking joints in the main wiring system.

A machine that never breaks down has not yet been designed. It is to be hoped, therefore, that, as production plant becomes more complex and indicate, the designers will keep the maintenance problem in mind and make the plant engineer's job easier.

Lubrication

Proper lubrication is vital to the efficient operation of all mechanical plant. As such, it deserves careful organization and planning and should not be regarded as a lowly task to be given to the least intelligent workman.

Organization

Responsibility generally depends on the frequency with which lubrication is required and on the complexity of the task. Thus a machine operator may carry out simple daily lubrication, but much of the remainder would be done by a production-department man, specifically appointed for the job.

The lubrication of more complex items, such as lineshafting, motors, hydraulic systems, gearboxes, etc., is often an engineering-department responsibility. Whatever organization is selected, it should ensure that every lubrication task is adequately covered: that the personnel, time, frequency, and manner of the job have been assigned correctly.

Planned lubrication

Ideally, lubrication should be an integral part of planned maintenance and should, therefore, be included in the PM scheme. Consequently, the frequency and method will be reviewed in order to give the most economical coverage and to highlight the trouble spots for technical investigation.

Selection of lubricants

The technology of lubrication has made great progress in recent years. Lubricants are available to perform almost any duty. Selection and application are matters for an expert, and one is justified in having the services of reputable oil companies, which willingly carry out surveys and provide technical advice.

The number of lubricants in a factory can grow with every additional item of plant installed. Such growth should be resisted, since too many lubricants lead to confusion and to increased costs. Expert appraisal results in the recommendation of a small range to cover all needs.

Storage

A small piece of grit can ruin a precision lead to the shutdown of an expensive machine. Cleanliness is therefore storage of oil and grease and in all the utensils and equipment.

Stores procurement

There are many storekeeping methods in the textile industry, which range from a series of store cupboards in the charge of departmental heads to large central stores with complete stock-control systems operated by a skilled purchasing manager.

It is not intended to discuss the relative merits of the various storekeeping methods, but, since the plant engineer is usually involved with all of them, some comment is appropriate.

The objective of stores procurement is to have material and equipment available when it is wanted. This is achieved either by using the supplier's resources or by holding a stores stock. The choice depends on economic and time factors.

The holding of stocks ties up money that could otherwise be earning interest or be usefully employed in the business. Furthermore, stores occupy floor space, require time and paperwork in their accounting, and need to be well preserved.

On the other hand, the delivery from the suppliers may be protracted so that stores are not available when required, and, in addition, it is often possible by bulk buying to obtain discounts that offset the storage costs.

The establishment of economic stockholding is a function of good stores management, but technical considerations influence the variety and quantity of stocks of spare parts that have to be carried.

Stock variety

Every new machine that is installed in a factory creates a potential increase in the variety of spare parts required for maintenance. The use of imported machines aggravates the problem because they introduce fresh standards, and such items as screw threads, shaft sizes, etc., may be completely different from those already in the existing plant. One way to reduce variety is to introduce standardization and make every part held in stores serve as many items of plant as possible. The following are examples of some of the ways in which this can be done.

Electric motors

Although most modern British motors are made to British Standard dimensions, there are advantages in keeping the number of makes to a minimum. There are also many types and sizes of electric motor. With a little forethought, a range can usually be selected that will cover most duties. There is no harm in the odd machine's being equipped with a slightly oversize motor so that it is covered by the existing holding of spares.

Electrical-distribution equipment

The use of standard fuseboards, isolators, switchgear, contactors, etc., can save on the variety of spares to be held. The standards adopted should be specified on all new work. Here again, slightly oversize equipment may be acceptable rather than an additional spares holding.

V-belts and pulleys

This commonly used drive comes in all sizes. Where a choice is possible, it is worth selecting sizes that are similar to existing ones. For pulleys, the use of the tapered-bush fixing permits a pulley to fit several shaft sizes simply by changing the bush. This device also has the advantage of making the fitting and removal of pulleys very much easier.

Continental equipment

There is a welcome move towards the adoption of international standards, so that the procurement of spares for Continental equipment is becoming less of a problem. Where only an odd machine is involved, it may pay to carry out minor conversions, such as the alteration of electronic control circuits to accept British valves, and changing indicator lights to British Standards.

Stock quantities

The number of spares to be held in stock is determined by their rate of usage and by the promptness with which they can be delivered by the supplier. Any action that reduces the rate of usage win permit a reduction in stockholding. Where there is a high value of turnover in particular items, a technical investigation may be profitable. The choice of stock levels is influenced by the accuracy with which future usage is forecast.

A planned-maintenance system helps to keep stock levels down, because the planning of stores requirements is an integral part of this. Furthermore, when stores are purchased for a PM tour only a minimum time elapses before they are used.

The control of internal services: steam generation and utilisation

From a management standpoint, the objective is to provide an adequate supply of steam of the right quality, when and where it is wanted, at the least cost. This aspect is best considered in two parts:

A. generation of steam; boiler-house practice; and

B. distribution and use of steam.

Generation of steam

Before a boiler plant can be controlled effectively, it must be made to work efficiently. This is primarily a technical problem. Technologically, the control and administration of steam services are a broad and complex subject into which it is not proposed to delve too deeply. In seeking to improve the performance of any given plant, it will be found that there is an economic limit to the efficiency that is worth achieving. A point comes when it is better to consider replacing the plant with a modern one rather than spending money on the old.

Since the performance of the boiler plant is ultimately to be judged on its running Costs, it is valuable to note the principal elements of the cost of steam:

capital charges, interest, and depreciation
floor-space charges, rent, rates, etc.
insurance
running costs, mainly dependent on the amount of steam generated, namely:
fuel and handling
make-up water and feedwater treatment
ash disposal, ignition gas, etc.
electricity for ancillary equipment
maintenance, repairs, and statutory inspections
labour and overheads for boiler attendance.

It is convenient to express all the above costs in terms of pence per 1000 lb. of steam generated.

Labour

The number of man-hours to be devoted to boiler-h depends on the type of plant. A hand-fired boiler, for example, demands virtually full-time attendance throughout the steaming period, whereas a modern, fully automatic plant requires only occasional attention. In the latter case, therefore-, the boiler attendant can be employed profitably on other work in the factory when his time is not devoted to attending to the boiler.

Labour requirement is an important factor in evaluating new boiler plants. Indeed, comparison of various plants can be made only on the basis of *total* costs, coupled with an assessment of intangibles, such as space requirements, availability of fuel, etc. Labour cost is not very flexible' and, provided that efficient work schedules are established, little can be done in the way of control other than to ensure that the work is done properly.

Fuel

Except in very small plants, the cost of fuel is the biggest element in the running costs, and should therefore be controlled carefully.

Two factors are important:

i. the price of the fuel as delivered to the boiler house;

ii. the proportion of heat content of the fuel that can be made available in the steam, i.e., thermal efficiency.

Price of fuel

Steam can be raised from fuel of many kinds, ranging from sawdust to atomic energy. Two that are in common use will be considered, namely, coal and fuel oil.

Coal

Being a naturally occurring mineral, coal is a very variable product, depending on its source and after-treatment. It is classified in accordance with its combustion characteristics, and graded according to the size of the pieces in the load, e.g., singles, peas, etc. The pit-head price of coal depends on the characteristics of the fuel, such as its calorific value, caking properties, ash content, etc., and also on the grading required.

The price of similar coals varies also from one coalfield to another. Since a consumer is interested in the price of coal as it lies in his own bunkers, his choice is usually restricted to local coalfields in order to keep down haulage cost. The boiler plant is generally designed to bum local coal efficiently. Even so, there is a broad enough selection to warrant careful consideration of the choice, both of quality and of grade.

Actual trials in the plant concerned are the ultimate test, and in this connexion it will be found that the National Coal Board and reputable coal merchants will advise and assist willingly. The price structure of coal is now much more stable, and there is no longer either the need (or the opportunity) to negotiate prices by exploiting competition between one supplier and another. There remains, however, plenty of room for careful buying on terms acceptable to both consumer and supplier.

The prices of specific coals are adjusted automatically from time to time in line with quality variation as determined by pithead analysis.

Fuel oil

The structure of fuel-oil prices is much less complex than that for coal. The basic price depends on two factors:

A. the grade of fuel oil; and

B. the location of the consumer.

(A) Grade of fuel oil. Fuel oil is graded according to its viscosity in Redwood No. I seconds at 1000 F. Three grades are in common use for steam boilers, as indicated in Table 11.2. Nominal viscosity (sec.) Light 220 Medium 950 Heavy 3500 Table 2 .Gross calorific value is about 18,000-19,000 B.t.u./lb. for these grades. Light fuel oil is the most expensive but only simple combustion equipment is needed to bum it. Heavy fuel oil is the cheapest of those quoted above, but it requires specially designed equipment and careful pre-heating for efficient combustion, Heavy fuel oil is attractive where fuel consumption is high and the plant is under competent

Table 2

Nominal viscocity (sec)	
Light	220
Medium	950
Heavy	3500

supervision. *(B) Location of the consumer.* The price of fuel oil depends on the distance between the consumer and the principal oil-supply ports. The country is divided into zones on this basis, the three important ones being Inner Zone, nearest the ports, Outer Zone, the next, and General Zone, the rest. Basic oil prices are lowest in the Inner Zone.

All the important suppliers of fuel oil conform to the principles of the price structure. Nevertheless, there is keen competition between them, and it is possible to negotiate rebates on the current basic price, depending on the terms on which supplies are taken.

Thermal efficiency

A fuel that is acceptable in respect of price, quality, and availability having been selected, it remains to ensure that it is burnt efficiently. This means simply that the maximum weight of steam should be obtained from each pound of fuel burnt.

One way to keep a check on this is to measure the weight of steam delivered to the factory over a period of time and compare it with the fuel consumption in the same period. Any departure from 'normal' is soon noted, and corrective action can be taken. For the purpose of this check, fuel may be measured in the case of coal by weigh-ticket record, coupled with an estimate of bunker stock, and in the case of fuel oil by meter.

Steam can be measured directly by an integrating meter, or, alternatively, by metering the feedwater, provided that allowance is made for water loss by blowdown, etc. The figures obtained, while not suitable for accurate boiler testing, are sufficient to indicate when something is going wrong.

A boiler-house log book is useful. If properly kept, it can form a running record of plant performance and history that is most helpful in 'troubleshooting' and in planning maintenance requirements.

Boiler-house instruments

Fuel can be used efficiently only if the conditions under which it is consumed are carefully controlled. To achieve this, the values of certain factors must be known, and to measure them certain detecting instruments are necessary. If the instruments are permanently attached to the boiler plant, the fireman adjusts the combustion conditions so that they give optimum readings.

An alternative, but not so reliable, method is to use portable instruments to calibrate the plant for best performance under all load conditions. This alternative course is suitable for fully automatic equipment where correct combustion control is built into the mechanism.

The most important factor in good combustion of fuel is that the correct amount of air is supplied to the furnace. If too little is supplied, there is incomplete combustion, and heat is lost up the chimney in the form of unburnt gases. If too much is supplied, the excess air carries away heat up the chimney.

The $C0_2$ indicator (or recorder) coupled with a thermometer in the chimney base gives the information enabling the correct conditions to be obtained. Other instruments also desirable are:

A. feedwater and/or steam meters as described previously;

B. thermometers before and after the economizer to check economizer performance; and

C. draught gauges to measure airflow at various points in the flues.

Certain instruments, such as water-level gauges and

steam-pressure gauges, are required by law. As a result of the Clean Air Act, a smoke alarm or smoke-density-recording equipment is often fitted.

Maintenance

Good maintenance on a planned basis is particularly important on boiler plants because deterioration is quietly continuous and invariably results in a fall-off in performance: dust accumulates in the flues; cracks appear in brickwork and settings; air leaks into the flues; dampers warp and begin to fit badly; lagging breaks loose and permits heat loss; steam joints and glands begin to leak; and so on.

Performance records can indicate a need for maintenance, but there is no substitute for regular and critical inspection followed by appropriate attention.

Boiler-plant development

Boilers come in all kinds and in all sizes and bum many sorts of fuel. New techniques and designs are constantly being developed so that anything here written on the technical merits of various boilers would soon become outdated.

A man wishing to develop a boiler plant is faced with two questions:

A. should he renovate the old one; or

B. should he get rid of it and start afresh?

The answer lies in a critical analysis of the technical facts coupled with an appraisal of the *total* costs of each course of action.

Technical factors include assessment of the following.

A. The condition of the existing plant, and the length of its remaining life.

B. Whether it is big enough for its duty. If it is too big (as is often the case where boilers once supplied engines), can the plant be modified effectively by, say, running on one furnace instead of on two ?

C. Whether the plant can be made to comply with the requirements of the Clean Air Act.

D. What future running costs are likely to be in relation to the initial expenditure.

Modern boilers, operating at efficiencies of over 80 per cent and requiring negligible supervision, achieve running costs that are difficult to beat by renovating very old equipment. It is well worth considering the use of N.I.F.E.S. (National Industrial Fuel Efficiency Service) when boiler-plant and steam-service developments are under investigation.

Although the resident engineer is probably capable of weighing up the problem and making sound recommendations, N.I.F.E.S. can relieve him of much time-consuming test work. Furthermore, the N.I.F.E.S. engineers can bring their nationwide experience to bear on each problem.

Distribution and use of steam

To deliver the steam to the point where it will be used and to apply it efficiently is a technical problem that needs to be solved in accordance with best practice. It is the problem of management to control and use it effectively. To solve this management problem on the most effective use of the steam, it is necessary first to measure the usage and then to interpret the results obtained.

Ideally, steam meters should be fitted in all important steam feeds, so that consumption, for various sections of the plant, can be recorded. The information, can then be compared with the expected performance of each section and any deviations investigated.

In the textile industry, steam has three uses:

A. power

B. processing

C. space-heating.

Power

Although there are some very efficient steam-power plants still in use in the industry, they are being displaced by electric drives. It is likely that only in rare circumstances would private power plants be installed nowadays. The control of such plant is a specialist function and space does not permit our pursuing this further.

Processing

When it leaves the boiler house, each pound of steam contains an amount of heat energy, depending on its pressure, temperature, and dryness. This heat energy must do as much work as possible. In any process, it is usually possible to calculate the amount of heat energy required for each operation, whether it is heating liquids or evaporating water in a drying process. The weight of steam required to provide this energy can then be determined.

The ratio of actual usage to this theoretical usage is a measure of the efficiency of steam utilization. For practical steam records, it is usually more convenient to relate consumption to the weight of product processed. Such information has value in process-costing as well as in technical control.

Heat units are indestructible; energy is conserved in one form or another and it is sometimes possible to account for nearly all the units that are put into a process. Such knowledge is a useful guide to process improvement, for any expedient that reduces the wastage of heat units or permits them to be reused will improve the utilization efficiency.

The following are a few examples of typical losses in processing installations.

i. Unlagged pipes and vessels lose heat units to the surrounding air.

ii. Open-topped vessels: heat escapes from the surface of hot liquids; vessels should always be closed or covered.

iii. Underloaded plant: equipment that is larger than necessary for the weight of product in the process is very wasteful of heat.

iv. Hot liquids put down the drain carry away heat units that could be used in a heat exchanger to pre-heat liquids in another part of the process. This is an example of where heat units can be used more than once.

v. Steam pressure too high: if liquids are heated by direct injection of steam at too high a pressure, the steam bubbles to the surface without doing any work.

vi. There may be leaks in the system caused by, say, ill-fitting valves. Steam at a pressure of 100 lb./in.^{2} will escape at the rate of 56 lb./hr. through a 1/8-in.-diameter hole!

Steam for space-heating

Although there are many systems used for warming factories, steam is very commonly used. The following remarks on aspects of the control of space-heating by steam apply, broadly, to most other media. The object of space-heating is to provide proper working conditions for the operatives, and in certain circumstances for the process itself.

To maintain a constant temperature in a given room, it is necessary to supply sufficient heat units to balance exactly those that escape through walls, roofs, doors, ventilation fans, etc.

The heat units are supplied from the power and lighting load in the room, from personnel, from sunshine, etc., and the balance from the heating system. In short, the heat loss from a room determines the amount of heat that has to be supplied in order to maintain the temperature.

The heat loss varies with outside temperature and there is a close correlation between the fuel consumption for space-heating and the outside temperature. Records based on this fact are helpful in controlling space-heating costs. It follows, therefore, that economies in space-heating can be achieved by tackling the causes of heat loss. Some of these are as follows.

Inside temperature too high. It is estimated that a rise of 1°F in temperature will increase fuel bills by about 5 per cent. Thermostatic control solves this problem somewhat by ensuring that heat supplies are turned off automatically when the desired temperature is reached.

Poorly insulated buildings. Good thermal insulation is the exception rather than the rule. The traditional north-light single-storey shed is particularly bad. The use of modern insulation materials and double glazing can be economically sound with present-day heating costs. The Thermal Insulation (Industrial Buildings) Act, 1957, lays down minimum standards for the insulation of new heated buildings. An insulated building is not only easier to heat in winter, but is easier to keep cool in summer.

Uncontrolled ventilation and excessive air changes. Air escaping from a room carries heat with it. Ventilation should be controlled to give healthy and agreeable conditions inside; more than this is wasteful. In some processes, such as those that take place in the blowrooms of spinning mills, the opening machinery causes excessive ventilation. These places are difficult to keep warm, but it is sometimes possible to obtain air from other processes, where a large power load may require the dissipation of heat.

Control of services from public utilities

The principal utilities that serve the textile industry are electricity, water, gas, and effluent disposal. These utilities are usually metered to the consumer and charged for in accordance with a standard tariff, which varies in respect of the locality.

In managing services supplied by public utilities, three principles are important:

A. choosing the most favourable tariff terms to give least total cost of the service;

B. organizing the application of the service so that it is used efficiently; and

C. measuring, and then controlling, the service so that it is not wasted.

Electricity supply, being a major utility, has been selected to show how these principles are applied.

Electricity suppliers

Tariffs

Supplies to manufacturing and process units are usually charged for on industrial tariffs, which are now virtually standard throughout the country. Although there are differences in detail between the tariffs of one electricity board and those of another, they are based on a common principle.

In an industrial tariff, the charge for electricity is made up of the following parts.

Maximum demand. This charge is based on the peak load taken by the consumer in the accounting period. The MD meter usually records twice the maximum number of units consumed in a half-hour period. This element of the charge is designed to cover the costs incurred by the supplier in providing equipment and generating capacity capable of meeting the peak load.

Units charge. This is a direct charge for the kilowatt-hours recorded on the meters in the accounting period. The rate of charge per unit is scaled down as load factor increases. This is described below.

Fuel variation. This is a small charge based on each unit consumed depending on the cost of fuel used by the generating authority. The fuel charge is declared monthly and varies throughout the year.

Penalties. These are levied in certain circumstances, the more important being in respect of power factor (described below) and minimum payment. If the average power factor during the accounting period falls below a specified value, a charge is made.

Accounting period

There are two principal groups of industrial tariff-monthly and annual. In each group, there are various scales of charges according to the manner in which the supply is delivered, e.g., whether at high or medium voltage; whether the consumer owns the transformers or not. In a monthly tariff, every month is independent for accounting purposes. The meters are read monthly, and the maximum-demand meters are reset to zero.

With an annual tariff, however, the consumption pattern for the whole year up to March 31st is considered when the charge is calculated, although interim accounts based on provisional figures are presented monthly. The scales of charges on an annual tariff are substantially less than those of the monthly tariff, and there are other facilities that can be beneficial to the consumer.

Choice of tariff

In the control of electricity costs, the choice of the most suitable tariff is of prime importance. In this connexion, it is the author's experience that the area electricity boards cooperate in advising their consumers in the selection of the best method.

Monthly versus annual tariff

The charge for maximum demand on an annual tariff is over 15 per cent less than on the monthly one, but (subject to the restricted-period concession) it is based on the highest demand established during the whole accounting year. Thus, if the actual demand of the factory varies considerably from month to month owing to, say, seasonal business, the monthly tariff could be the better choice. On the other hand, a maximum demand that is virtually constant throughout the year indicates the use of an annual tariff.

In choosing an annual tariff, the year ahead should be considered. Any major increase or decrease of load in the year may nullify the advantages of this tariff. The annual tariff has certain features not applicable to other tariffs, as follows.

Restricted period

It is conceded at present that the highest maximum demand recorded in the four winter months from November to February inclusive, with the addition of only one-tenth of the excess recorded in any other month, shall be the chargeable MD for the year. Thus, if a factory registered a demand of 1200 kW in April and only 1000 kW maximum in the restricted period, the chargeable demand would be 1020 kW for the year.

Night-metered units

A fairly recent innovation is the facility for obtaining a rebate (0- 11 d./ unit by the North Western Electricity Board (N.W.E.B.) for electricity consumed between 11 p.m. and 7 a.m. The consumer must pay for installation of the meters, but on shift work the arrangement can be profitable.

The cost of electricity

Load factor can be deduced from the load characteristics of the factory. To achieve a load factor of 100 per cent, the factory would have to run continuously, night and day, with a fixed load equal to the maximum demand. In practice, the working hours of the factory influence the highest load factor that can be obtained, and even this is tempered by the steadiness of the load.

The loads in spinning and weaving tend to be very steady, and good performances can be recorded against the figures in the table. There is a close relation between load factor and cost per unit. From the curves it will be seen that a low load factor is expensive. A change from day-work to double-shift working can cut electricity costs by about 26 per cent. It is of note that in the scale of running charges a reduction in charge per unit occurs at 20 per cent load factor and a further reduction at 60 per cent.

Table 3

		Load factor %	
		Full month	normal year
Day-work	42½ hr./week	26	23.7

Double-shift	72½ hr./week	44.3	41.9
Three-shift	112½ hr./week	68.4	62.88

Power factor

When inductive loads such as electric motors are connected to an alternating-current supply, they cause a phase displacement, so that peak voltage and current do not occur at the same time. The effect is that a current, known as wattless current, which does not do any useful work, flows in the cables and wiring. Nevertheless, the cables have to be big enough to carry it, and power is consumed in pushing the current through the resistance of the cables.

The techniques of power-factor correction may be found by reference to electrical textbooks. A common method is to install capacitors, as near to the power-using equipment as practicable, so that the load on the factory-distribution system is eased. If the capacitors are connected at the supply point, however, this benefit is lost.

Reducing the electricity bill

Mention has been made of the proper choice of tariff to obtain the best terms for the supply, and of the effect of load factor on unit cost. Any action that raises the load factor, such as increasing working hours, will make supplies more economical. A reduction in maximum demand for the same unit consumption will also raise the load factor.

A critical analysis of the load pattern obtained by connecting a graphic recorder at the supply point can often indicate where the problem should be tackled. If the trace is steady and increases only as the lighting load comes on, there is little prospect of improvement, but, if it is irregular, the aim is to find the cause of the peaks and to eliminate them. It may be found necessary to stagger the operation of heavy electric loads, which are used intermittently, or to restrict the use of large pumps, etc., to times when the normal demand is low. A wide field is opened up when one considers the savings that can be made by using electricity more efficiently. In the majority of textile processes, only a minute fraction of the power supplied is actually required to manipulate the product. The remainder is wasted in friction in the mechanical parts of the machines and in losses in the system.

The following is a very short list of some common causes of power wastage:

stiff and poorly lubricated machines;

use of lineshafts instead of direct drives;

low power factors on internal distribution;

leakage of compressed air and use of excessive pressures;

poor thermal insulation of electrically heated spaces and hot-water installations; and

misuse of lighting: photoelectric control of lighting is being adopted, but it should be remembered that it only saves electricity at the running and fuel cost per unit, and will not normally affect the demand charge.

15

Textile Research Association

Cotton textile research association

Ahmedabad Textile Industry's Research Association (ATIRA), Bombay Textile Research Association (BTRA), South India Textile Research Association (SITRA) Coimbatore and Northern India Textile Research Association (NITRA) Ghaziabad are registered under the Societies Registration Act, 1860 (XXI of 1860).

The main objective of these institutions is to carry out research and render consultancy services to industry on various aspects of textile technology with a view to reducing the cost and improving the quality and durability of fabrics, reducing pollution, conserving energy and utilising waste, adopting new technology and improving the technology in the decentralised handloorn sector. A large number of projects of considerable importance were undertaken and the studies made by these Associations have helped to improve the efficiency and productivity of the textile industry.

The Research Associations have carried out original and innovative work in several fields of textiles. In addition to result oriented, short-term projects in the field of management in the textile industry, the research associations are also currently engaged in other specific projects such as measures for design development to modern twin jigger system for enhanced flexibility, quality, economy and ecology in batching dyeing;

development of indigenous online instrumentation for checking effluents parameters, objective measurement of structural parameters of unconventional yarns and their relationship with yarn properties; improving the skills of operatives for better performance of spinning mills; design development of indigenous low cost rotor for rotor spinning machine; study on work culture in high and low productivity in textile mills; studies on techno-economics of airjet spinning technology; development of two for one twisting spindles suitable for silk throwing, etc. Besides, useful R&D work is also being done on jute diversified products with Government of India - UNDP Funds.

Silk & art silk mill's research association, Mumbai (SAAMIRS)

The Silk & Art Silk Mills Research Association (SASMIRA), Mumbai is a Textile Research Association located at Mumbai. SASMIRAs principal activities include research and development, provision of technical services, testing and training facilities in the field of silk and art silk.

The main activities undertaken by SASMIRA during the year 1968-99 are outlined below:

SASMIRA being an Association of the powerloom sector, the projects undertaken by SASMIRA are aimed primarily at benefiting this sector. With increasing globalisation of markets, the powerloom sector needs to meet international competition, and SASMIRA's R&D efforts are directed towards this objective. SASMIRA traditionally has also been contributing towards self sufficiency in the area of national security through indigenisation and development of textile stores for Defence forces.

During the financial year 1998-99, SASMIRA has

started working on a Project entitled "Design and Development of a Light Fastness Tester with Features for Testing Samples under different conditions of Temperature and Humidity" sponsored by Department of Science & Technology, (DST), Government of India. During the year SASMIRA received 3 industry sponsored projects from (i) Gratex Wall Paper Ltd., (ii) Jaysynth Dyechem Ltd., (iii) Indian Oil Corporation Ltd. (IOC).

SASMIRA's technical cell renders technical support to the decentralised sector by helping them carry out tests and by giving advice aimed at solving working problems. SASMIRAs laboratories are also recognised by various Government Deptts and are being regularly utilised for their testing needs. Technical services, which is one of the important services offered by SASMIRA to assist industries to solve their problems arising during fabric production, is availed of substantially by the industry.

SASMIRA organises short-term training courses from time to time on various technological topics. The courses are designed to meet the requirements of the industry. Apart from regular courses, it has been decided to conduct tailor-courses according to the requirements of the Corporate Training sector. SASMIRA also operates two powerloom service centres at Bhiwandi.

Man-made textile research association, Surat (MANTRA)

MANTRA is one of the Textile Research Associations catering to the multifarious needs of the textile and allied industry at large. Activities of MANTRA are primarily aimed at planned and healthy growth of the decentralised textile industry. Activities undertaken by MANTRA during 199899 are outlined below:

MANTRA carried out a large number of projects approved by the Government and also sponsored by the industry. MANTRA intends to take up projects of R&D

and technical consultation in all areas related to quality and productivity improvement with emphasis on process and quality control, process and machinery development and the development of the value added products.

MANTRA's Testing and Technical Services division is being gradually strengthened for the past couple of years, where besides routine testing, technical services relating to trouble shooting assignments, trial run of industry's required samples etc. are also undertaken. To expedite the test reports, the procedure for preparation of reports and billing in this testing division has now been fully computerised.

In order to meet the scope of environmental pollution control and treatment services in the year 1997-98, MANTRA has established an Environmental Affairs Group. MANTRA is now Gujarat Pollution Control Board recognised Environmental Auditor to undertake Environmental Auditing of the industries as per Gujarat Pollution Control Boards' norms.

MANTRA has acquired a High Performance Thin Layer Chromatography (HPTLC) system. This system will be useful for analysis of organic compounds especially the amines and other dye intermediates, dyestuff, pentacholorophenol and pesticides.

Indian jute industries research association, Calcutta (IJIRA) R&D activities

Jute fiibre

1. Upgradation of jute Fibre by Enzyme Treatment has been completed and implemented in 22 jute mills. The enzyme production plant is producing enzyme and it is being distributed to the industry for their commercial trials. IJIRA has earned Rs. 7 lakhs during the year from this consultancy.

2. Project trials of JRC 321 have been completed with (i) conventional jute spinning system; (ii) fine yarn ring spinning system, (iii) blends; (iv) DREF and (v) Wrap spinning technology. The quality and productivity of yarn from this jute fibre has improved. Farmers have been advised for large-scale cultivation of this jute fibre -JRC 321.

3. Steam explosion technology for jute - Pilot mill trials at IAF, Germany and spinning trials in India with conventional jute spinning, fine yarn ring spinning, blended yam spinning in cotton system, open-end spinning trials have been completed. All these trials have shown promising results in producing very fine yarn and blends with cotton, acrylic and polyester, etc. The quality and productivity of yam has also improved considerably. The project was sponsored by the Ministry of Textiles, Government of India and Rs. 29 lakhs was sanctioned for this purpose from the Special jute Development Fund. Fabrication of the pilot mill equipment has been completed and installed in NJMC Unit Kinnison at Calcutta. In Phase II commercial trials will be conducted.

4. RBO (Rice Bran Oil) Technology for production of food grade jute bags. In order to meet the expanding global market of food grade jute bags IJIRA has developed a new batching oil as an eco-friendly fibre lubricant based on Rice Bran Oil (non-edible, grade 11) for processing of jute and allied fibres, which is totally safe for producing jute bags coming in contact with food. In other words RBO Technology is a market driven eco-friendly process technology.

Salient features of RBO technology

— Meets the International specification for food grade jute bags.

— Developed by IJIRA and patent applied in twelve countries.

— Technology has been validated from a recognised German Laboratory also.

— Eco-friendly process technology for jute and allied fibre processing.

— For catering to eco-sensitive and health sensitive overseas buyers.

— Currently RBO processed jute bags are being supplied for packing odour sensitive food products such as cocoa, coffee, hazelnuts and other food products.

— No dearth of raw material in the country, only 3.0% of current production of Rice Bran Oil of the country will meet total requirement of jute industry.

— Has the potentiality to substitute mineral oil with biodegradable vegetable oil for the entire industry.

— IJIRA has transferred this technology to 15 jute mills. IJIRA has earned Rs. 4.55 lakhs as consultancy charges so far.

Spinning & weaving

Under Transfer of Technology, various technologies for increasing spinning and weaving productivity, coupled with HRD programmes have been completed in 5 mills. They have increased the efficiency from 5 - 15% and 6 more mills are registered for transfer of this technology in their units. IJIRA has earned Rs. 4 lakhs through this consultancy during the year.

Jute machinery development

Fine yarn jute spinning technology using imported Mackie & Schlumberger make of machines has been successfully completed in Kinnison and Champdany Ind.

Ltd. respectively. They are able to produce yarns with 100% jute up to 4 lbs. This technology is now advocated for other organised jute mills and decentralised sector. For this purpose under UNDP Jute Machinery project, machineries are being developed for organised as well as decentralised jute mills. The following machineries will be ready by March, 1999:

Jute Ring Frame

Carding Machine

Intersecting Gill Drawing

Open Screw Gill Drawing

Improved Spreader Machine for high productivity

Activities under decentralised sector for transfer of technology

Training of entrepreneurs from tiny, small scale units and NGOs are being done for mini jute spinning, handloom weaving, bleaching, dyeing and finishing and handicrafts sector.

Jute geotextiles

During the period IJIRA helped two member mills to develop treated Jute Geotextiles for river bank protection and supplied the materials to the respective divisions under Irrigation & Waterways Directorate, Government of West Bengal. The materials were treated in a bitumen treatment plant under the supervision of IJIRA and sent to the destinations for protection of river banks at Pirgung, Maldah and Jalangi, Murshidabad.

IJIRA & Central Soil and Water Conservation Research & Training Institute (ICAR), Dehradun are transferring the technology of mines spoil stabilisation applying Jute Geotextiles in Himachal Pradesh through training and demonstration for small miners in the region. For the purpose the required jute Geotextile has been developed in collaboration with a member mill and despatched to the destination. The material has been installed in a site and in the other sites, it is in progress.

A repeat order of treated Jute Geotextile was received from Kandla Port Trust, Gujarat for construction of road on soft marine soil. The material was developed and treated in a jute mill under the supervision of IJIRA and sent to the destination. The inquiries received from BHEL, Tiruchirapalli and Border Roads Organisation, Delhi for Jute Geotextiles for construction of roads have been addressed, supplying all information. In the meantime the problems faced by a member mill while constructing a road and a shed on filled soil in the mill premises was attended to with the help of an expert from the Civil Engineering Department, Jadavpur University.

In addition IJIRA has developed another entrepreneur for treatment of geo-jute fabrics with rot resistant chemicals and bitumen and treated three types of fabrics. The fabrics are being tested in IJIRA laboratories.

At the request of JMDC, IJIRA developed specified jute sleeves in collaboration with a member mill and supplied the material to the Govt. of Arunachal Pradesh for trial. IJIRA also helped NCJD for developing jute sleeves for horticultural applications by Central Himalayan Rural Action Group, Nainital, a NGO working in Kumaon range.

Documents were supplied to NCJD for application of jute Geotextiles in Northeast India through North East Region Council and Darjeeling Gorkha Hill Council.

Documentation: Publication of a brochure on application jute Geotextiles for construction and repair of roads.

Wool research association, Thane, (WRA)

Wool Research Association was established and registered under the Societies Registration Act, 1860 in October, 1963. A group of members representing various woollen industries came forward to establish the Research and Development laboratory for the benefit of the woollen industry.

WRA is at present organised under five departments namely Physical Test House, Chemical Testing Laboratory, Eco-Testing Laboratory, Pilot Plant for Spinning and Weaving, Computer Aided Designing and Knitting, Colour Matching. WRA is offering the services for 100% wool and also for all types of woollen blends.

Sponsored projects

Completed Projects (In the stage of Technology Transfers)

(i) To develop the software package for training in weaving technology.

(ii) Development of designs for carpets and dhurries, for training and service to the small and medium scale carpet sector.

(iii) Value added utilisation of coarser varieties of Indian wool.

(iv) To make the natural dyeing of wool eco-friendly with viable test methods for labelling.

(v) To investigate the factors affecting eco-friendly processing of wool and its blends at various stages.

(vi) Modification of existing reactive dyes and application techniques for use in woollen industry.

On-going projects

(i) Computer Aided Embroidery Designing using WRA's CAD system and EMI-14B single head embroidery machine.

(ii) Development of economic friction spun multicomponent yarn for high tech (Industrial Fabrics) textiles.

(iii) To develop software for prediction of worsted yarn characteristics and optimizing various parameters of raw material input.

(iv) Development of Instrumental Analytical techniques/ methods for separation and identification of isomeric mixtures with special reference to eco-testing.

(v) To establish the standard test method and standards for woollen products for fibre to fabric.

Recently sanctioned projects July, 1998)

The following projects were sanctioned by Ministry of Textiles and were started from July, 1998.

(i) Development of different types of knitwear, outerwear, pullovers, knitted shawls from Repco Spun self twist yam by using wool and other fibres in suitable blends.

(ii) To develop cotton core and wrapped woollen yams on woollen spinning system and study its suitability for products like dress materials, furnishing and knitwear.

(iii) Development of innovative yams and fabrics using elastomers (lycra, natural rubber, nylon) blended with wool, cotton, acrylic and designing comfortable and fashion oriented garments.

(iv) Role of enzymes in wool processing.

(v) Isolation and identification of the most potent insecticides from their group of isomers and their use towards moth proofing.

Financial results

1993-94	1994-95	1995-96	1996-97	1997-98	1998-99 upto	1998-99 upto Nov '98	Mar '99
Sale Value	132.42	128.67	79.23	103.93	48.90	19.98	31.63
Cost of Sales	395.27	392.85	418.08	453.03	438.49	276.45	407.43
Operating loss	262.85	264.18	334.85	349.10	389.59	256.47	375.80
Other Income	21.13	20.66	21.67	20.88	17.55	26.49	40.77
Net Loss	241.72	243.52	313.18	328.22	372.04	229.98	335.03
Cash Loss	221.63	234.89	304.88	319.21	363.73	223.58	325.43
Cash loss	34.00	35.00	35.00	35.00	10.00	-	-

(Till Date 1998)

Machinery and equipments procured

(i) High Performance Thin Layer Chromatograph System and CAMAG AMD-2 Gradient Chamber with standard spares and accessories for HPTLC under upgradation/setting up Eco-Testing Laboratory at Wool Research Association, Thane.

(ii) Toyoda Expert Computerised Embroidery System Model 850 under the Project Titled "Computer Aided Embroidery Designing using WRA's CAD system and EMI-14B single head embroidery machine."

Transfer of technology and research utilisation

Terminal report Evaluation meeting of UNDP project

Recently, the Wool Research Association has completed the UNDP Project titled "R&D Programme for development of bi/multicomponent yarn from wool, jute and other fibres by using Friction Spinning Technology for Carpet, Dhurry, Blanket, Knitwear and Furnishing" and the terminal evaluation meeting and the project presentation was performed by WRA on 23rd April, 1998 among the Expert Committee members of UNDP Mission at New Delhi.

Jute-tex'98 (August to December, 1998)

Keeping in view the successful completion of the above project under UNDP-GOI (Jute), the four seminars at different locations in India were held and the technology developed and the skill obtained under the above said UNDP Project was transferred to the entrepreneurs. The seminars were:

Jute-tex'98 - value added jute diversified products

1. Government Polytechnic, Nagpur 12th August, 1998.
2. Government Polytechnic, Sholapur 11th September, 1998.

3. Guru Nanak Dev University, Amritsar 28th October, 1998

4.. University of Agriculture Sciences, Dharw on 8th December, 1998.

Workshop

A workshop was conducted under the project tided "Value Addition of Coarser Varieties of Indian Wool" which was completed in March, 1998. To transfer the R & D findings and the developments to the shepherd community of Karnataka region, it was organised at University of Agricultural Sciences, Dharwar on 9th December, 1998.

Special training programme/orientation programme (by WRA/ for WRA).

WRA has provided special training under the Orientation Programme to two technical persons from Pashulok, Uttar Pradesh and 2 technical persons from Central Wool Development Board, Jodhpur from 9th November to 14th November, 1998 for establishment of Industrial Service Centres.

The staff (designers) of WRA were deputed at Capital Automation Co. Ltd., New Delhi from 14th to 18th December, 1998 for training on Computer Aided Designing.

Similarly, they visited M/s Raymond Woollen Mills Ltd., Chindward, Nagpur from 28th December 1998 to Ist January 1999 for trials to be performed for plush designs with Capital Automation Vega Software and detailed discussion on Electronic Jacquard and Plush designs.

Educational activities

During the academic year 1998-99 WRA has started the following special training courses:

1. Computer Aided Textile Designing.
2. Instrumental Chemical Analysis.
3. Textile Testing & Quality Control.

The infrastructure for educational activities like classrooms, furniture, presentation aids, availability of experts and guest lecturers was developed and nearly 30 students benefited from the above courses.

16

SC/ST and Women Welfare in Textiles

Developmental commissioner for handicrafts

In the handicrafts sector about 32% of the outlay in respect of identified Central Sector Schemes is earmarked for the benefit of the Scheduled Caste, Scheduled Tribe and Women Artisans with an allocation of 15%, 75% and 10% respectively. The major schemes in which this allocation has been made are (i) training, (ii) design and technical development, (iii) marketing, (iv) exhibition and publicity, (v) survey and study, (vi) craft development centres, (vii) welfare and others schemes (viii) market development support, (ix) assistance to NEHHDC, (x) Museum, etc.

Out of the total persons trained in various crafts, nearly 24.5% belong to scheduled caste and 75% to scheduled tribe communities.

Welfare of women

In the handicrafts sector, women constitute a major segment of handicraft workers i.e. around 45% of the total workforce. Special attention is being paid to ensure that a large number of women artisans get benefit in all the development schemes such as training, marketing related programmes, national awards, exhibitions etc. being implemented by the office of the DC(HC), Voluntary organisations like Self Employed Women's Association. Ahmedabad, SRASHA, Calcutta, Mahila

Kalyan Samithi, Philibit, SHRUJAN Trust, Bhuj, etc. are being financially assisted to encourage women participation in various craft activities. Nearly 40% of artisans who have benefited under these schemes are women. During the year 1998-99, the total outlay for Special Component plan for Scheduled Caste, Tribal Sub-Plan and Sub-Plan for Women are as follows.

(Rs. in crores)

S.No.	Name of Scheme	Total outlay	TSP	SCP	WSp
1.	Training Schemes	26.72	2.66	5.32	3.07
2.	Design & Technical	5.56	0.33	0.66	0.38
3.	Marketing & Service Extn. Centres	3.76	0.25	0.50	0.50
4.	Exhibition & Publicity	2.14	0.22	0.44	0.12
5.	Museums	0.37	0.02	0.04	0.07
6.	Survey & Study	.1.00	0.11	0.22	0.02
7.	Craft Development Centres/CFCs	2.19	0.18	0.36	0.28
8.	Welfare & other Schemes	1.70	0.12	0.24	0.24
9.	Assistance to NEHHDC	0.75	0.03	0.04	0.10
10.	Assistance to Central State Corpn./Apex Coops. Societies for new sales outlets (Market Development)	6.30	0.22	0.44	0.72
11.	Export Promotion Regulation	0.35	-	-	-
12.	Capital head	3.81	-	-	-
13.	O/oD.C.(H)0.35	-	-	-	-

17

Information Technology

Ministry of Textiles has taken a major leap forward during the year 1998 in the application of Information Technology (IT) both by strengthening existing information infrastructure for management and creating Web based facility for providing online information on production, designs, markets and trade related developments in the areas of domestic and global textiles. National Informatics Centre (NIC) has been providing technical support in this task. Besides the Ministry has set up an Information Technology Task Force for recommending appropriate measures for induction of IT in textile sector to improve productivity and quality of products and servicing of buyers demands.

Computerisation and information infrastructure in the ministry

A Local Area Network (LAN) having 50 nodes has been established in the Ministry. This Net covers all officers and functional sections. Local Area Network is hooked up to Internet through a Radio Frequency Communication equipment. In the process, the facilities for E-mail and Internet browsing have also been provided.

With the benefit of the above infrastructure, it has been possible not only to maintain data bases but also retrieve data at various levels and in the shortest possible time. A data bank has already been created for storing data on various aspects of textile industry including data on production and prices. The database is being continuously updated and a monitoring system covering developments in textiles in both domestic and international fronts, has been put in place. The Computer Centre is also generating Monthly/Quarterly Reports on Textile Industry on the basis of above databases and these are being made available as a shared resource on LAN which are available to the clients for instant reference. These reports cover mostly all aspects of the industry like price, production, export, import with proper graphical representation. The system helps not only in day to day management but also in framing appropriate policy responses to changing environments in textiles.

A LAN has also been established with highspeed connectivity to Internet/NICNET through VSAT in the Office of the Textile Commissioner, Mumbai. This has facilitated on-line connection to the Ministry for day-to-day data updating and servicing other requirements.

A Local Area Network (LAN) is also being setup in the Office of the Development Commissioner (Handicrafts). Software packages for monitoring the progress of various schemes like Departmentally-run Training Scheme, Marketing Development Scheme, Financial Assistance to State Corporations/Apex Cooperative Societies, etc. are operational. Progress of Marketing and Service Centres is also being monitored. The Office has also planned to provide Pentium based machines as clients to the officers.

A LAN consisting of 7 clients has already been established in the Office of the Development Commissioner (Handlooms) and extended with the LAN of Ministry of Textiles. Internet/E-mail facilities are already available on LAN. Computerized monitoring systems for monitoring State-wise physical and financial performance of various schemes (10 in Nos.) operated by Office of D C (Handlooms) is operational. The system covers all major Plan/Non-Plan Schemes like Project Package Scheme, Integrated Handloom Development Scheme, Group Insurance Scheme, Handloom Development Centre Scheme, etc.

NICNET/ internet services for information exchange

in order to facilitate the data/mail transfer between Ministry and other organizations through Electronic Mail on day-to-day basis, NICNET/ Internet connectivity has also been established. Every officer in the Ministry has been allotted with an e-mail address for using electronic mail on the system. At present Ministry of Textiles, Office of Textile Commissioner, Mumbai, Office of Development Commissioner (Handlooms) and Office of Development Commissioner (Handicrafts) are already hooked on NICNET/Internet.

Some of the major Councils/Public Sector Undertakings under the Ministry like Apparel Export Promotion Council (AEPC), Synthetic & Rayon Textiles Export Promotion Council (SRTEPC), Handicrafts and Handlooms Export Corporation (HHEC), National Handloom Development Corporation (NHDC), Central Silk Board (CSB), National Institute of Fashion Technology (NIFT), Textiles Export Promotion Council (TEXPROCIL), Wool and Woollen Export Promotion Council (WWEPC), National Centre for Jute Diversification (NCJD) are hooked into internet and have E-mail addresses.

Home page on internet

A Home page for Ministry of Textiles has been designed and made available at the address http://www.nic.in/texmin on Internet. The Home page provides latest information on performance of various activities/schemes of the Ministry, Subordinate Offices, Attached Offices, Export Promotion Councils, Boards and maintain features for direct linkage to the web sites of various textile related organizations. This has enriched the information support significantly.

Economic research and market intelligence unit (ERMIU)

In a major development, the Ministry took the initiative for setting up of the ERMIU for ensuring that the textile industry in India is fully geared in terms of information requirements to face the challenges of growing international competition in the post MFA regime. The Hon'ble Minister of Textiles has formally inaugurated the ERMIU on 16th December, 1998 and the unit has become functional. This is the first time that a common data bank for textiles, which would also provide analysis, forecasts and trends, has been set up for the benefit of the industry and the Government.

The ERMIU (with main unit in Textile Commissioner's Office, Mumbai and Satellite Unit in the Ministry of Textiles, New Delhi and Textile Committee's Office, Mumbai) is designed to work as a nodal centre for collection and dissemination of information on production, designs and fashion as well as other market and trade related developments in the area of textiles. Such a move assumes added significance in view of the importance of textiles in the total export basket of the country. The ERMIU will be able to provide on-line information on the developments in the textiles sector to both foreign and domestic entrepreneurs and traders. Such information will be helpful to domestic manufacturers in planning production and marketing products.

ERMIU provides information related with textiles through Web enables applications to Government,

Industry and trade by organising data/information available at various organisations in India and abroad. ERMIU will conduct spot studies/surveys/census to study market intelligence and maintain a Data Bank of all such data.

ERMIU is equipped with an NT Server, Pentium Clients, Scanners and VSAT/RF for highspeed data communication. NIC provides its technical support to ERMIU. Web sites are set up on Internet for Mumbai and Delhi as http://ermiul.bom.nic.in and http://ub.nic.in/ermiudel respectively for disseminating the information.

Task force on I.T. for textiles

The Ministry has constituted a Task Force for suggesting measures for induction of I.T. in textiles sector for improving productivity and quality of production. While modernization and replacement of old and outdated machineries are necessary to enhance competitive strength of the industry, it is felt that a wholesale replacement and modernization may not be possible in one go. Therefore, retrofit automation by way of introducing micro electronic related innovations and other information technology products to textile units in the decentralized sector in particular, would be helpful for the growth of the sector. Moreover, there is an urgent need to introduce IT in manufacturing and design process as well as fashion intelligence and trade response. Accordingly, the Task Force has been asked to suggest measures for:

(a) appropriate use of micro processor base equipment, control systems and related technologies in different stages of manufacturing processes in textiles for production, planning, quality and cost control as well as sales and inventory management;

(b) utilization of computer integrated technology for

on-line development of designs and colour shades and facilitating quicker conversion of laboratory scale formulation to production scale operations;

(c) utilization of Internet/ISDN links and other media for presentation of textile products to select buyers and markets with a view to promote their sales; and

(d) application of electronic information gathering system for building global data base on all aspects of textiles sector.

The suggestions and recommendations of I .T. Task Force are likely to be available soon.